Deck Officer Study Guide

2015 - 2016 EDITION

Preparation for the United States Coast Guard
Merchant Marine License Examinations

VOLUME 4
RULES OF THE ROAD
INTERNATIONAL AND INLAND RULES

Edited by:

CAPTAIN JOSEPH S. MURPHY, II
Department of Marine Transportation
Massachusetts Maritime Academy

Academy Publishing Company
6 Munroe Parkway
Wareham, MA 02571

D1089144

ISBN 1-881349-00-4 (Volume 4)
ISBN 1-881349-02-0 (6 Volume Set)
Printed in the United States

TABLE OF CONTENTS

Rules of the Road - Volume 4

Preface... V
Rules of the Road Examination Specification... VIII
Deck License Examination Guidance XII
Rules of the Road Examination Preparation XII
Reading and Interpretation XIII
Protest Procedures XV
Acknowledgments... XVII

Navigation Rules & Regulations

Inland Navigation Rules:

PART A - GENERAL (RULES 1 - 3)
RULE 1 - Application 2
RULE 3 - Definitions.. 2

PART B - STEERING AND SAILING RULES (RULES 4 - 19)
SECTION/SUBPART 1 - CONDUCT OF VESSELS
IN ANY CONDITION OF VISIBILITY (RULES 4 - 10)
RULE 9 - Narrow Channels.. 2

SECTION/SUBPART 2 - CONDUCT OF VESSELS
IN SIGHT OF ONE ANOTHER (RULES 11 - 18)
RULE 13 - Overtaking.. 6
RULE 14 - Head-on Situations 6
RULE 15 - Crossing Situation 6

PART C - LIGHTS AND SHAPES (RULES 20 - 31)
RULE 21 - Definitions 7
RULE 24 - Towing and Pushing... 7
RULE 26 - Fishing Vessels.. 9
RULE 27 - Vessels Not Under Command/Restricted in Ability to Maneuver...... 9
RULE 30 - Vessels Anchored and Aground 10
RULE 31 - Seaplanes 11

PART D - SOUND AND LIGHT SIGNALS (RULES 32 - 37)
RULE 34 - Maneuvering and Warning Signals 11
RULE 35 - Sound Signals in Restricted Visibility.. 19

PART E - EXEMPTIONS (RULE 38 - ANNEXES 1 to 5)
ANNEX V - Pilot Rules 19

Navigation Rules & Regulations

Both International & Inland Navigation Rules:

PART A - GENERAL (RULES 1 - 3)
RULE 1 - Application 21
RULE 2 - Responsibility 21
RULE 3 - Definitions 21

PART B - STEERING AND SAILING RULES (RULES 4 - 19)
SECTION/SUBPART 1 - CONDUCT OF VESSELS
IN ANY CONDITION OF VISIBILITY (RULES 4 - 10)
RULE 5 - Look-out 25
RULE 6 - Safe Speed 25
RULE 7 - Risk of Collision 25
RULE 8 - Action to Avoid Collision 27
RULE 9 - Narrow Channels 28
RULE 10 - Traffic Separation Schemes 31

SECTION/SUBPART 2 - CONDUCT OF VESSELS
IN SIGHT OF ONE ANOTHER (RULES 11 - 18)
RULE 12 - Sailing Vessels 32
RULE 13 - Overtaking 33
RULE 14 - Head-on Situation 36
RULE 15 - Crossing Situation 37
RULE 17 - Action by the Stand-on Vessel 39
RULE 18 - Responsibilities Between Vessels 41

SECTION/SUBPART 3 - CONDUCT OF VESSELS
IN RESTRICTED VISIBILITY (RULE 19)
RULE 19 - Conduct in Restricted Visibility 44

PART C - LIGHTS AND SHAPES (RULES 20 - 31)
RULE 20 - Application 46
RULE 21 - Definitions 47
RULE 22 - Visibility of Lights 49
RULE 23 - Power-driven Vessels Underway 50
RULE 24 - Towing and Pushing 52
RULE 25 - Sailing Vessels Underway and Vessels Under Oars 59
RULE 26 - Fishing Vessels 62
RULE 27 - Vessels Not Under Command/Restricted in Ability to Maneuver 66
RULE 29 - Pilot Vessels 72
RULE 30 - Vessels Anchored and Vessels Aground 73

PART D - SOUND AND LIGHT SIGNALS (RULES 32 - 37)
RULE 32 - Definitions 75
RULE 33 - Equipment for Sound Signals 75
RULE 34 - Maneuvering and Warning Signals 76
RULE 35 - Sound Signals in Restricted Visibility 81
RULE 36 - Signals to Attract Attention 92
RULE 37 - Distress Signals 93

Navigation Rules & Regulations

Both International & Inland Navigation Rules:

PART E - EXEMPTIONS (RULE 38 - ANNEXES 1 to 5)
ANNEX II - Additional Signals for Fishing Vessels in Close Proximity 94

International Rules (72-COLREGS):

PART A - GENERAL (RULES 1 - 3)
RULE 1 - Applications... 95
RULE 3 - Definitions 95

PART B - STEERING AND SAILING RULES (RULES 4 - 19)
SECTION/SUBPART 1 - CONDUCT OF VESSELS
IN ANY CONDITION OF VISIBILITY (RULES 4 - 10)
RULE 9 - Narrow Channels 95

SECTION/SUBPART 2 - CONDUCT OF VESSELS
IN SIGHT OF ONE ANOTHER (RULES 11 - 18)
RULE 14 - Head-on Situation.. 97
RULE 15 - Crossing Situation 97
RULE 18 - Responsibilities Between Vessels... 97

SECTION/SUBPART 3 - CONDUCT OF VESSELS
IN RESTRICTED VISIBILITY (RULE 19)
RULE 19 - Conduct in Restricted Visibility 99

PART C - LIGHTS AND SHAPES (RULES 20 - 31)
RULE 23 - Power-driven Vessels Underway 99
RULE 24 - Towing and Pushing... 99
RULE 26 - Fishing Vessels 101
RULE 27 - Vessels Not Under Command/Restricted in Ability to Maneuver.............. 101
RULE 28 - Vessels Constrained by Their Draft.. 101

PART D - SOUND AND LIGHT SIGNALS (RULES 32 - 37)
RULE 33 - Equipment for Sound Signals.. 102
RULE 34 - Maneuvering and Warning Signals 102
RULE 35 - Sound Signals in Restricted Visibility... 106

RULES OF THE ROAD NOTES/DIAGRAMS//ILLUSTRATIONS
Rules of the Road Notes/Diagrams/Illustrations 108

U.S. Department of Transportation
United States Coast Guard

NAVIGATION RULES

INTERNATIONAL—INLAND

PREFACE

GOAL

The *Deck Officer Study Guide* was compiled to assist prospective deck license candidates enrolled in a structured curriculum or studying independently with their preparation for the following U. S. Coast Guard Merchant Marine license examinations and open-book renewal exercises:

License Examinations:

- Master   Oceans-Near Coastal-Inland-Great Lakes, Any Gross Tons
- Chief Mate   Oceans-Near Coastal-Inland-Great Lakes, Any Gross Tons
- Second Mate   Oceans-Near Coastal-Inland-Great Lakes, Any Gross Tons
- Third Mate/OICNW   Oceans-Near Coastal-Inland-Great Lakes, Any Gross Tons
- Master & Mate   Limited License, All Routes, All Tonnage Groups

Review & Renewal Exercises:

- Comprehensive Renewal Exercise, All Grades of License
- Rules of the Road Exercise, All Grades of License

Certification Examinations:

- Able Seaman/Lifeboatman, All Grades of Certification

PURPOSE

The U. S. Coast Guard posts the Merchant Marine examination question bank on the Internet which constitutes publication of the questions in the public domain. This information is made available to afford the public an opportunity to review and comment upon the questions' clarity and accuracy. The data base file contains the U. S. Coast Guard questions for all grades of license. The Merchant Marine examination bank is not an examination study guide. It is merely a question and answer file which divides the deck license questions up into five generic topic areas. The questions are not organized into specific categories and appear in random fashion.

The *Deck Officer Study Guide* eliminates the need for computer know-how and expensive computer equipment. Each volume of the *Deck Officer Study Guide* substantially reorganizes the sequence of the examination questions into clear-cut sections for each of the five deck disciplines. The objective of this effort is to provide you with quick access to definitive areas of required expertise in order to accelerate systematic study and stimulate cognitive learning. Each section of the *Deck Officer Study Guide* isolates the key concepts affording you an opportunity for a comprehensive self-testing program. This methodology defines your individual starting point for additional research and remedial skill development.

COMPREHENSIVENESS

The primary reference source consulted during the compilation of the *Deck Officer Study Guide* was the U. S. Coast Guard Merchant Marine question bank. The multiple choice questions in this publication are the actual questions which will appear on the current series of Merchant Marine license examination modules and renewal exercises. During the collation of this publication, more than 15,000 U. S. Coast Guard multiple choice questions, answers and associated references were analyzed and regrouped into specific examination subjects.

ACCURACY

For all questions requiring a mathematical or process solution, the correct answers have been determined by using the most commonly accepted method for solving such problems. A candidate using that method for solving the problem correctly should find an answer that corresponds exactly with his or her answer. A candidate using an alternate but valid method should choose the answer that is closest to his or her answer. Certain questions may contain a specific tolerance which is given in parentheses following the statement. The tolerance applies to that statement alone. There is never an intended or implied connection between any two questions in any part of this book nor on any section of the deck license examination. A concerted effort has been made to produce a study guide which is accurate and reflects current scholarship. This effort is especially difficult in many areas of marine science and technology because reference texts often provide conflicting opinions on individual issues. The aim of the *Deck Officer Study Guide* is to reflect on those differences and to consider alternative theories or interpretations. Ambiguities or inconsistencies are always brought to the immediate attention of the U. S. Coast Guard at the National Maritime Center (NMC-4B) in Arlington, VA. Your assistance and input is both solicited and vital to this effort because deference has been given to the U. S. Coast Guard's keyed answer in all cases throughout this publication.

TEXT ARRANGEMENT

The *Deck Officer Study Guide* is designed to be *"User Friendly"*. It provides quick access to definitive subject areas and/or key concepts. The body of the text is organized into the following seven distinct volumes:

- Volume 1   Deck General

- Volume 2   Navigation General

- Volume 3   Deck Safety

- Volume 4   Rules of the Road

- Volume 5   Navigation Problems Parts "A" & "B"

- Volume 6   Deck Examination Illustration Book (COMDTPUB P16721.6A)

- Volume 7   Lifeboatman (Lifeboatman Examination Only)

The seven volumes address the subject matter embodied in all sections of the current Merchant Marine license examination modules for all grades of deck license. The arrangement and content of each section was determined by utilizing the U. S. Coast Guard's examination specifications, as detailed in Table 46 CFR 10.910-2, *"License Codes"*.

The arrangement format for *Volume 4, Rules of the Road* presents each question with a sequential number which indicates both the volume number and a number unique to each question, next the U.S. Coast Guard database question number, followed by an appropriate Rule reference, the applicable system of Rules, a stem, which supplies needed information and poses the question, and four possible answers. The U. S. Coast Guard's keyed answer to each question in the *Volume 4, Rules of the Road* is indicated by the anchor symbol "⚓".

040343/RR00272   **RULE 9 (b)**

BOTH INTERNATIONAL & INLAND Two vessels are meeting as shown in a narrow channel. Vessel "A" is a sailing vessel. Vessel "B" is a power-driven vessel which can safely navigate only within the channel. Vessel "B" sounds the danger signal. Vessel "A" shall _____. See Illustration D037RR

    A. maintain course and speed

⚓ B. not impede the passage of vessel "B"

    C. sound one prolonged followed by two short blasts

    D. have the right of way

ILLUSTRATIONS

Some of the questions in this publication require the use of an illustration or diagram to answer the question correctly. All of the illustrations and diagrams were contained in COMDTPUB P16721.6A, *Merchant Marine Deck Examination Illustration Book, and January 1992 edition. Volume 6, Deck Examination Illustration Book* of the *Deck Officer Study Guide* is a reproduction of COMDTPUB P16721.6A. The latest illustrations and diagrams can be found on the NMC website. If a question requires the use of an illustration or diagram, it will be specifically stated in the lead-in sentence or stem of the question.

040343/RR00272   **RULE 9 (b)**

BOTH INTERNATIONAL & INLAND Two vessels are meeting as shown in a narrow channel. Vessel "A" is a sailing vessel. Vessel "B" is a power-driven vessel which can safely navigate only within the channel. Vessel "B" sounds the danger signal. Vessel "A" shall _____. See Illustration **D037RR**

    A. maintain course and speed

⚓ B. not impede the passage of vessel "B"

    C. sound one prolonged followed by two short blasts

    D. have the right of way

REFERENCES

Deck Examination Reference Texts have been cited whenever possible. Refer to and review the list of *Deck Examination Reference Texts* contained in *Volume 1, Deck General* of the *Deck Officer Study Guide*. **Preference has been given to the Examination Room Reference texts which are always preceded by an asterisk (*).** Use the examination room reference books as desk companions while studying and during self-testing exercises. Listed references may appear as an abbreviation or code. A table following the Preface in *Volume 1, Deck General of the Deck Officer Study Guide* lists the abbreviations and codes in alphabetical order and identifies the title of the reference. Some of the references listed are no longer available. As new questions are developed, they are drawn from current references. Over time, older references go out of print or are revised. If new reference material is published the U. S. Coast Guard reviews the questions in current use to ensure that they are still valid. The entire contents of any authorized Deck Examination Reference text may be used during all parts of the license examination with the exception of Rules of the Road during which NO reference material of any kind may be used.

MERCHANT MARINE EXAMINATION QUESTION STRUCTURE

All of the deck license examination modules are randomly generated. The examination questions do not follow in the same question sequence as those found in the *Deck Officer Study Guide*. Therefore, you must NEVER memorize lists of answers. This technique will not produce the desired results. The U. S. Coast Guard computer system is not programmed with an answer randomization capability but many of the questions in the test bank use identical question stems and/or similar answers with the answers rearranged in a different sequence; therefore, you must NEVER memorize answers by letter identity alone. New questions and updated examination modules will be generated by the U. S. Coast Guard in order to reflect changes in national and international regulations, shipboard procedures, or evolutionary changes in the marine industry. You must always be prepared to demonstrate your proficiency and knowledge of the subject matter rather than your mastery of the rote memorization of the questions themselves.

RULES OF THE ROAD EXAMINATION SPECIFICATIONS

Examination Modules   Passing Grade: (90%)

Oceans/Near Coastal, Any Gross Tons   **50 Questions**
- Inland Only   8-10 Questions
- Both International & Inland   32-34 Questions
- International Only   8-10 Questions

Near Coastal/Inland/Great Lakes, Limited Tonnage   **30 Questions***
- Inland Only   30 Questions
*   Both International & Inland   30 Questions

*   Any license issued with a route designator which includes waters governed by the 72-COLREGS must be administered with an International and Inland Rules of the Road examination.

EXAMINATION SUBJECTS

GENERAL
A.   Application
B.   National Maritime Law & Responsibility
C.   General Definitions

STEERING AND SAILING RULES
A.   Conduct of Vessels:
     In Any Condition of Visibility
     a.   Application
     b.   Look-out
     c.   Safe Speed
     d.   Risk of Collision
     e.   Action to Avoid Collision
     f.   Narrow Channels
     g.   Traffic Separation Schemes and Vessel Traffic Systems (VTS)
B.   Conduct of Vessels:
     In Sight of One Another
     a.   Application
     b.   Sailing Vessels
     c.   Overtaking
     d.   Head-on Situations
     e.   Crossing Situations
     f.   Give-Way Vessel
     g.   Stand-on Vessel
     h.   Responsibilities between Vessels
C.   Conduct of Vessels:
     In Restricted Visibility

LIGHTS AND SHAPES
A.   Application
B.   Definitions
C.   Visibility of Lights
D.   Lights & Day Shapes
     a.   Running Lights
     b.   Occupational Lights
     c.   Identity Signals
     d.   Shapes

SOUND & LIGHT SIGNALS
A.   Definitions
B.   Equipment
C.   Maneuvering Signals
D.   Warning Lights
E.   Sound Signals in Restricted Visibility
F.   Distress Signals

EXEMPTIONS

ANNEXES

PENALTY PROVISIONS

RULES OF THE ROAD

Module Number:	054XX
Module Description:	Upper level licenses, Oceans, Near Coastal
Number of Questions:	50 questions
Minimum Score:	90% (5 wrong)

SUBJECT	NUMBER OF QUESTIONS
PART A—GENERAL; Rules 1 to 3 Application, Responsibility, Definitions International Only; Inland Only; Both International & Inland	3
PART B—STEERING AND SAILING RULES; Rules 4 to 10 Section I—Conduct of Vessels in Any Condition of Visibility International Only; Inland Only; Both International & Inland	5
PART B—STEERING AND SAILING RULES; Rules 11 to 18 Section II—Conduct of Vessels in Sight of One Another International Only; Inland Only; Both International & Inland	7
PART B—STEERING AND SAILING RULES; Rule 19 Section III—Conduct of Vessels in Restricted Visibility International Only; Inland Only; Both International & Inland	7
PART C—LIGHTS AND SHAPES; Rules 20 to 22 Application & Definitions International Only; Inland Only; Both International & Inland	2
PART C—LIGHTS AND SHAPES; Rules 23 to 31 Vessel Task Lights & Dayshapes International Only; Inland Only; Both International & Inland	7
PART D—SOUND AND LIGHT SIGNALS; Rules 32 to 33 Definitions & Equipment for Sound Signals International Only; Inland Only; Both International & Inland	2
PART D—SOUND AND LIGHT SIGNALS; Rule 34 Maneuvering & Warning Signals International Only; Inland Only; Both International & Inland	7
PART D—SOUND AND LIGHT SIGNALS; Rule 35 Sound Signals in Restricted Visibility International Only; Inland Only; Both International & Inland	7
PART D—SOUND AND LIGHT SIGNALS; Rules 36 to 37 Signals to Attract Attention & Distress Signals International Only; Inland Only; Both International & Inland	1
PART E—EXEMPTIONS Exemptions; Annexes; Miscellaneous International Only; Inland Only; Both International & Inland	2

RULES OF THE ROAD

Module Number:	065XX
Module Description:	Lower level licenses, Great Lakes, Inland
Number of Questions:	30 questions
Minimum Score:	90% (3 wrong)

SUBJECT	NUMBER OF QUESTIONS
PART A—GENERAL; Rules 1 to 3 Application, Responsibility, Definitions International Only; Inland Only; Both International & Inland	2
PART B—STEERING AND SAILING RULES; Rules 4 to 10 Section I—Conduct of Vessels in Any Condition of Visibility International Only; Inland Only; Both International & Inland	3
PART B—STEERING AND SAILING RULES; Rules 11 to 18 Section II—Conduct of Vessels in Sight of One Another International Only; Inland Only; Both International & Inland	4
PART B—STEERING AND SAILING RULES; Rule 19 Section III—Conduct of Vessels in Restricted Visibility International Only; Inland Only; Both International & Inland	4
PART C—LIGHTS AND SHAPES; Rules 20 to 22 Application & Definitions International Only; Inland Only; Both International & Inland	1
PART C—LIGHTS AND SHAPES; Rules 23 to 31 Vessel Task Lights & Dayshapes International Only; Inland Only; Both International & Inland	4
PART D—SOUND AND LIGHT SIGNALS; Rules 32 to 33 Definitions & Equipment for Sound Signals International Only; Inland Only; Both International & Inland	1
PART D—SOUND AND LIGHT SIGNALS; Rule 34 Maneuvering & Warning Signals International Only; Inland Only; Both International & Inland	4
PART D—SOUND AND LIGHT SIGNALS; Rule 35 Sound Signals in Restricted Visibility International Only; Inland Only; Both International & Inland	4
PART D—SOUND AND LIGHT SIGNALS; Rules 36 to 37 Signals to Attract Attention & Distress Signals International Only; Inland Only; Both International & Inland	1
PART E—EXEMPTIONS Exemptions; Annexes; Miscellaneous International Only; Inland Only; Both International & Inland	2

RULES OF THE ROAD

Module Number:	066XX
Module Description:	Lower level licenses, Great Lakes, Inland
Number of Questions:	30 questions
Minimum Score:	90% (3 wrong)

SUBJECT	NUMBER OF QUESTIONS
PART A—GENERAL; Rules 1 to 3 Application, Responsibility, Definitions Inland Only	2
PART B—STEERING AND SAILING RULES; Rules 4 to 10 Section I—Conduct of Vessels in Any Condition of Visibility Inland Only	3
PART B—STEERING AND SAILING RULES; Rules 11 to 18 Section II—Conduct of Vessels in Sight of One Another Inland Only	4
PART B—STEERING AND SAILING RULES; Rule 19 Section III—Conduct of Vessels in Restricted Visibility Inland Only	4
PART C—LIGHTS AND SHAPES; Rules 20 to 22 Application & Definitions Inland Only	1
PART C—LIGHTS AND SHAPES; Rules 23 to 31 Vessel Task Lights & Dayshapes Inland Only	4
PART D—SOUND AND LIGHT SIGNALS; Rules 32 to 33 Definitions & Equipment for Sound Signals Inland Only	1
PART D—SOUND AND LIGHT SIGNALS; Rule 34 Maneuvering & Warning Signals Inland Only	4
PART D—SOUND AND LIGHT SIGNALS; Rule 35 Sound Signals in Restricted Visibility Inland Only	4
PART D—SOUND AND LIGHT SIGNALS; Rules 36 to 37 Signals to Attract Attention & Distress Signals Inland Only	1
PART E—EXEMPTIONS Exemptions; Annexes; Miscellaneous Inland Only	2

DECK LICENSE EXAMINATION GUIDANCE

The *Deck Officer Study Guide* provides excerpts from the *Guide for Administration of Merchant Marine Deck Examinations (Deck Guide)*, February 2002 with changes to Nov. 02 and a table of *Deck Examination Subjects*. The *Deck Guide* outlines the examination administration procedures, module rotation, and basic module structure for various grades of deck license. The U. S. Coast Guard Regional Examination Centers (RECs) are allowed some degree of latitude with regard to the administration of examinations. **You should personally confirm the module sequence, starting times and dates at the Regional Exam Center (REC) well in advance of your test day.**

The *Deck Examination Subjects Table* is designed to provide prospective license applicants with a detailed explanation of what subject areas may potentially appear in specific examination module. Be advised that, identical subject areas appear in different examination sections for various grades of license. Not every topic listed for a module will appear on every test, and different forms of a module can have different areas of emphasis. U. S. Coast Guard's examination specifications, as detailed in Table 46 CFR 10.910-2, *"License Codes"* contain the end caption:

"Any other subject considered necessary to establish the applicant's proficiency."

This catch-all statement has been rather liberally interpreted by the U. S. Coast Guard Merchant Marine Examination Branch to mean: *"No holds barred - Anything goes!"*

RULES OF THE ROAD EXAMINATION PREPARATION

The *Deck Officer Study Guide* organizes all of the U.S. Coast Guard's Rules of the Road questions into clear-cut sections, segregating every question rule-by-rule. The format is modeled after the Rules of the Road examination specifications which are based on the U. S. Department of Transportation, United States Coast Guard publication *Navigation Rules, International – Inland* (August 2014 Edition). The objective of this effort was to isolates the key concepts of each rule and to provide quick access to definitive areas of required expertise. I recommend that you read and carefully study the International and Inland parts of each rule. Study the rules one at a time, for example, read *Part A - General, Rule 1 - Application, International and Inland*. Then use the *Deck Officer Study Guide* to self-test your skills. Identify the questions which you got wrong. Note and record the rule references which are provided for each question contained in *Volume 4, Rules of the Road*. This method focuses on your individual weaknesses. It also clearly defines the starting point for additional research and remedial skill development. The most important step in your preparation is to review the material again and correct all of your mistakes. You must repeat this procedure, until you can consistently achieve above a 90% passing grade on all self-test examinations. This methodology will dramatically accelerate systematic study and stimulate cognitive learning because it incorporates both a comprehensive self-testing program and fundamental skill development based on your individual skill level.

REMEMBER, you must always be prepared to demonstrate your proficiency and knowledge of the subject matter rather than your mastery of rote memorization of the questions themselves.

BIBLIOGRAPHY

B1 U. S. Department of Transportation, United States Coast Guard. *Navigation Rules, International - Inland, COMDTINST M16672, August 2014 Edition*. Washington, DC: U.S. Government Printing Office, August 2014. **Available online at no cost: http://www.navcen.uscg.gov/pdf/navRules/CG_NAV_RULES_20140818.pdf**

B2 Block, R.A., *R.B.-169, Navigation Rules, revised ed. "K"*, Houma, LA: Marine Education Textbooks, 2008. (ISBN 1-933186-20-8).

B3 Cockcroft, A.N. and Lameijer, J.N.F., *A Guide to the Collision Avoidance Rules, 6th ed.*, Oxford, Heinemann Newnes, 2004. (ISBN 0750661798)

B4 Craig, H.H., *Farwell's Rules of the Nautical Road, 8th ed.*, Annapolis, MD, U.S. Naval Institute, 2004 (ISBN 1591140080)

B5 Farnsworth, B. A. and Young, L.C., *Nautical Rules of the Road, 3rd ed.*, Centreville, MD: Cornell Maritime Press, 1990. (ISBN 0-87033-408-5)

Reading & Interpretation

1.   Read the stem of the question.

a.   Get a feel for the gist of the question and what is actually being asked.

b.   Verify the applicable system of rules indicated in the lead-in statement or stem of each question before attempting to answer a particular question (i.e.) INLAND ONLY, BOTH INTERNATIONAL AND INLAND, or INTERNATIONAL ONLY. Upper level license Rules of the Road examinations are structured with approximately eight to ten (8-10) <u>INLAND ONLY</u>, eight to ten (8-10) <u>INTERNATIONAL ONLY</u> questions, and thirty-two to thirty-four (32-34) BOTH INTERNATIONAL AND INLAND questions for a total of fifty (50) questions. After 2012 most Rules modules contain 10-12 diagrams/illustrations. These predictions are only estimates based on past practice. Rules of the Road examination modules are no longer separated by governing rule systems. Therefore, in order to eliminate any possibility of confusion and to maximize your performance on the exam module, answer all of the INLAND ONLY questions first, then answer the INTERNATIONAL ONLY questions, and finally answer the BOTH INTERNATIONAL AND INLAND questions. This strategy will highlight the differences between the International and Inland Rules and help you define the legal tests framed by each rule.

2.   Re-read the stem of the question.

a.   Ascertain the applicable rule or rules addressed by the question.

b.   Locate the key word(s) (i.e. may, shall, vessel, power-driven, in sight of, restricted visibility, all, none, always, TRUE, FALSE, NOT, EXCEPT, etc.)

c.   Extract the pertinent information eliminating all the distracters and superfluous data.

3.   Picture the answer in your mind.

<u>Read what is written!</u> Never assume facts and/or information that are not specifically stipulated in the stem or answers to a particular question. If the stem and/or answers to the question do not describe a particular situation, it is <u>never intended or implied!</u> **Draw light displays, maneuvering situations, etc. to help you understand the situation posed by the question.** Be guided by the rules: *"Assumptions based on scanty information are dangerous and should be avoided".*

4.   Read all of the answers.

Read with an open mind especially if the answer that you are looking for is found. Do not base your answer on a preconceived notion of what you think the answer should be. Your answer to a particular question must be based solely on the information provided in the question. If you have to make an assumption to answer a particular question, you should write a protest or comment.

5.   Re-read all of the answers.

a.   Confirm again, the applicable rule or rules addressed by the question.

b.   Locate the key word(s).

c.   Extract the pertinent information eliminating all the distracters and superfluous data.

d.   Choose the correct answer. In some cases, more than one answer will appear to be correct. You must choose the <u>BEST</u> possible answer to the question. Your answer must meet all of the legal tests defined by the governing rule(s) in order to be correct. The answer must be correct in all situations of applicability, not just in some cases. Your answer will usually be the safest option described.

6. **Answer all of the questions.**

Begin by reading through the entire Rules of the Road examination module. Answer as many of the questions as you can on a piece of scratch paper. If you are not sure of the answer, skip the question. Your mind will be looking for the answer. The stem and/or answers to another question may trigger your response. Make notes on your scratch paper; identify the questions that you are not sure of. Take a little more time to re-read and think about the unanswered questions. Go back and make sure you answer any questions that were left blank. The number of questions left blank after the initial reading is a good indication of your performance outcome on the exam module. Although testing procedures may vary slightly at each Regional Examination Center (REC), it is common practice not to allow license candidates to mark in the test booklet itself. In order to eliminate any possibility of clerical errors, you should number and answer every question contained in the Rules of the Road examination module on a piece of scratch paper. Verify that the recorded answer is in fact your intended answer to the question and then transfer all of the answers to the U.S. Coast Guard answer sheet. Check to make sure that you have not made any clerical errors.

7. **Hand in your test booklet and answer sheet.**

Get up and leave the test room. <u>DO NOT GO BACK OVER THE TEST!</u> The temptation to change your answers will be greatest on the Rules of the Road examination module. <u>DO NOT</u> change your answers unless reasonable certainty exists. You must develop confidence in your short term memory.

8. **Answer Recapitulation**

ANSWER	TOTAL NUMBER OF QUESTIONS
Answer A	233 questions
Answer B	269 questions
Answer C	249 questions
Answer D	303 questions
TOTAL	1054 questions

Answer D   All of the above (46 questions) or Any of the above (3 questions)] correct 4.7% of the time.
Answer D   None of the above (20 questions) correct 1.9% of the time.

*   *The even distribution of answers eliminates the strategic guess as an effective option. When all else fails, if you are clueless, choose the longest answer.*

Protest Procedures

When a candidate has been informed of a failing grade and has failed the examination module by <u>no more than one question</u>, he or she will be given the opportunity to review each question for which he or she was not given credit. Immediately after their review and prior to departing the examination room following the review, he or she is to be given the opportunity to submit a protest on <u>no more than two missed questions</u>. The completed protest form(s), candidate answer sheet, and pertinent calculations are to be forwarded to the National Maritime Center for review. Following review of the protest, the REC will be informed as to the results of the candidate's protest and if necessary the final grade will be adjusted accordingly.

During the review, applicants may not change an answer previously marked on the answer sheet. To prevent alteration of an answer sheet, the incorrect answers will be highlighted or marked in ink. An applicant who alters a previously incorrect answer shall be treated as having cheated and barred from further testing for six months.

Protests are accepted under the following four conditions:
    a.   The form must be completed before the applicant leaves the examination room;
    b.   The candidate must have a failing grade on the module;
    c.   The comment must be about a question that was answered incorrectly; and
    d.   The question(s) commented about, if correct, would change the failing grade to a passing grade.

As a general rule, you must know the correct answer for a protest to be successful. You can usually identify the correct answer to the question by the process of elimination after the exam module has been corrected. The U.S. Coast Guard has a text, chapter and page reference for every question in the database. Most of the questions have been in the data bank for several years and therefore have been proofed by many license candidates. In almost every case the U.S. Coast Guard is correct.

You should write a protest/comment when:
    a.   no correct answer provided
    b.   more than one correct answer is found
    c.   the numerical spread between the answers provided is insufficient to determine the correct answer when the most commonly accepted method of solving such problems is utilized
    d.   the question is obviously defective
    e.   in order to explain your reasoning when the question is poorly worded, vague or ambiguous
    f.   when the reproductive quality of the test instrument or illustrations compromises your answer

ALWAYS ANSWER THE QUESTION WITH THE CORRECT ANSWER!

If you follow these simple guidelines, you can be effective with a protest:
    a.   Copy the entire question as stated in the examination booklet on the protest sheet.
    b.   Indicate your answer to the question. (My answer to Question No. 21 is D.)
    c.   **<u>You must attack the question.</u>** Explain the reason for your protest. State your assumptions, hypothesis, and the conclusion utilized to deduce your answer to the question. Provide your computations when they are required for the solution of the problem.
    d.   Cite your reference. You don't have to be too specific. For example: Rules of the Road, International Rules (72-COLREGS), Rule 35, if you are not sure.

The NMC reads what you have written. You want your protest to represent your professionalism and to be successful. This format will achieve both of these objectives. Protests/comments must be completed prior to leaving the examination room. Manage your time wisely. Write protests/comments after you have completed the examination module. Never engage in unwarranted personal or philosophical dissertations. When you encounter difficulty, don't fabricate gobbledygook, you're wasting everybody's time.

SAMPLE

COMMENT - PROTEST SHEET

_____ COMMENT   _____ PROTEST   (For Coast Guard use only)

APPLICANT'S NAME: _____ *Joseph S. Murphy, II* _____

MODULE NAME: _____ *Rules of the Road* _____

_____

MODULE NUMBER: _____ *05418-002* _____ QUESTION NUMBER: ___ *21* ___

If you believe there is something wrong with a question that prevents its being answered correctly, i.e., no correct answer or that you believe there is more than one correct answer shown, or the question is poorly worded, etc., please give all the details below. Include your reasons and all calculations for math problems such as: pump capacity, navigation, stability, or cargo. Provide what you believe to be the correct answer. Even if your comments will not affect your grade, they are considered very valuable and will be used to improve the quality of the questions used on future tests. If you fail this exam and submit your comments with your completed answer sheet for grading, each comment sheet for a question you did not receive credit will then become a protest for that question. Further, if you fail the examination module by <u>no more than one question</u>, you will be given the opportunity to review each question for which you were not given credit. Immediately after your review and without leaving the exam room following your review you may to submit a protest as indicated above on <u>no more than two missed questions</u> in addition to the comment sheets already submitted. If you are given the opportunity by the examiner to review your answer sheet after it has been graded and leave the exam room for **ANY REASON**, your protests will not be accepted.

Question No. 21

21.   BOTH INTERNATIONAL & INLAND *Fog signals for vessels NOT underway shall be sounded at intervals of not more than* _____.

    A.   15 minutes
    B.   5 minutes
    C.   2 minutes
    D.   1 minute

My answer to Question No. 21 is "D"

Rule 3 defines "underway" as a vessel, which is NOT at anchor, made fast to the shore, or aground. Vessels at anchor or aground sound prescribed fog signals at intervals of not more than one minute. Answer "D" is therefore correct in most situations. However, fishing vessels and vessels restricted in their ability to maneuver when carrying out their work at anchor sound the same signal when underway or when at anchor. In this case, the rules require a signal sounded at intervals of not more than 2 minutes consisting of three blasts in succession, namely one prolonged followed by two short blasts (Morse Code Letter "D" or the "Doing Signal")

Reference: Rule Int. 35 (g), 35 (h), Inland 35 (f), 35 (g).

Note: If you're not sure of the rule cite; indicate Rule 35 or simply the Inland & International Rules of the Road.

SIGNATURE _____ *Joseph S. Murphy, II* _____ DATE _____ *02/01/2002* _____

ACKNOWLEDGMENTS

A practical study guide of this scope and depth must acknowledge many debts - to other study guides of this and former generations, to maritime educators, marine scholars and subject matter experts who have worked so diligently to improve the educational standards and professional skills of the American Licensed Deck Officer.

The names of the scholars which follow have contributed primarily because of their commitment to the diffusion of knowledge. A preface is superfluous in respect of a work with such obvious purpose as this; but some acknowledgments are truly in order.

A collective acknowledgment of indebtedness is gratefully made; To my colleagues, one and all, from the Department of Marine Transportation at the Massachusetts Maritime Academy for their support, expertise and helpful suggestions made in informal conversations.

I am particularly grateful to:

Department of Marine Transportation, Massachusetts Maritime Academy
- CAPT. Linda Letourneau, Professor
- CAPT. Dave Mackey, Professor
- CAPT. Pat Modic, Professor
- CAPT. Jim Fitzpatrick, Associate Professor
- CAPT. John Belle, Associate Professor
- CAPT. Kerry Chicoine, Instructor

Department of Marine Transportation, Maine Maritime Academy
- CAPT. Sam Teel
- CAPT. Andy Chase
- CAPT. Ralph Pundt
- CAPT. Steve Tarrant
- CAPT. Sean Walsh

Department of Marine Transportation, California Maritime Academy
- CAPT. Tuuli Messer-Bookman

Department of Marine Transportation, New York Maritime College
- CAPT. Rick Smith
- CAPT. Jim McCoy

Department of Marine Transportation, Great Lakes Maritime College
- CAPT. Mike Surgalski

Department of Marine Transportation, U.S. Merchant Marine Academy
- CAPT. George Edenfield
- CAPT. Doug Hard
- CAPT. Brian Hall
- CAPT. Dan Hunt

for their continuing scholarship, valued counsel and years of dedication to Marine Science; and most of all, To my students at the Massachusetts Maritime Academy who have contributed ideas through their work and classroom discussions.

The opinions and guidance, herein, are my own, none of the mentioned contributors bears any responsibility for any of the material contained in this book.

CAPTAIN JOSEPH S. MURPHY, II
Department of Marine Transportation
Massachusetts Maritime Academy

Licensed Advancement Program Soft-**WARE** (**LAPWARE**) is the most complete license advancement program to help mariners study, prepare and test for the United States Coast Guard (USCG) Merchant Marine license examinations. LAPWARE was developed by Captain Joseph S. Murphy, II and Richard M. Plant.

The combined talents of Captain Murphy and Richard Plant in developing LAPWARE make this program second to none. LAPWARE allows users to study all of the deck license exam sections (Rules of the Road, Deck General, Navigation General, Deck Safety & Environmental Protection, and Navigation Problems). LAPWARE can be used by mariners for <u>ALL</u> grades of Merchant Marine license as well as by unlicensed mariners studying for their Lifeboatman and/or Able Bodied Seaman certification. Don't know what is on your exam; can't figure out how to do the problems; *LAPWARE does it for you!*

LAPWARE allows the user unlimited access via the Internet to all of the USCG database questions, with no review limits, grade or time locks at a very reasonable cost. Students can review questions selected by individual category as desired. The program will display the required diagrams and mathematical solutions for problems.

LAPWARE users can study anywhere they have access to the Internet. LAPWARE is especially beneficial to seagoing mariners, who can study at home on their own, eliminating extensive vacation time away from home, as well as, costly travel and lodging expenses. The authors recommend that students use LAPWARE in conjunction with a structured training program to develop the necessary knowledge base. LAPWARE is <u>NOT</u> designed to be a question and answer program similar to those used at many license prep schools where the candidate simply studies and memorizes the questions. As professionals, we want mariners to learn the skills necessary to competently serve as both <u>certified</u> and <u>qualified</u> merchant mariners or licensed deck officers.

No other license exam program on the market today even comes close to LAPWARE. We hope you enjoy using it and find it beneficial. Call all hands and help us pass the word about LAPWARE to your fellow mariners. Your feedback on our program would be greatly appreciated. You can contact us on the Internet at: lapware.org.

Rules of the Road

VOLUME 4

1

INLAND ONLY

2

BOTH INTERNATIONAL & INLAND

3

INTERNATIONAL ONLY

Academy Publishing Company

Deck Officer Study Guide

RULE 1 - APPLICATION

040001/RR00051   **RULE 1 (d); RULE 10;**
                                      RULE 6; RULE 34 (h)
INLAND ONLY Which statement is TRUE concerning the INLAND Navigation Rules?
A. They define moderate speed.
⚓ B. They list requirements for Traffic Separation Schemes.
C. They require communication by radiotelephone to reach a passing agreement.
D. All of the above

040002/RR00199   **RULE 1 (e);**
                                      Alternative Compliance
INLAND ONLY You are on a vessel that the Secretary has determined cannot comply with the spacing requirement for masthead lights. What is required in this situation?
A. The vessel must be altered to permit full compliance with the rules.
B. An all-round light should be substituted for the after masthead light and the stern light.
C. The vessel must carry only the lights that comply with the rules; the others may be omitted.
⚓ D. The vessel's lights must comply as closely as possible.

RULE 3 - DEFINITIONS

040003/RR00010   **RULE 3; RULE 28 [RESERVED]**
INLAND ONLY Which term is NOT defined in the INLAND Navigation Rules?
A. Restricted visibility
B. underway
⚓ C. Vessel constrained by her draft
D. Seaplane

040004/RR09119   **RULE 3 (o)**
INLAND ONLY The term "Great Lakes", as defined by the INLAND Rules of the Road, includes part of the

_____.
A. Calumet River
B. Chicago River
C. St. Lawrence River
⚓ D. All of the above

040005/RR09111   **RULE 3 (o)**
INLAND ONLY The term "Great Lakes", as defined by the INLAND Rules of the Road, does NOT include

_____.
A. portions of the Chicago River
B. portions of the Calumet River
⚓ C. the St. Lawrence River to Trois-Rivières
D. Saginaw Bay

040006/RR09132   **RULE 3 (q); RULE 3 (n)**
INLAND ONLY For the purpose of the INLAND Navigation Rules, the term "INLAND Waters" includes which of the following?
A. the Great Lakes in their entirety
B. U.S. waters out to three miles offshore
C. the St. Lawrence River to Anticosti Island
⚓ D. the Mississippi River System

040007/RR00016   **RULE 3 (q); RULE 3 (o)**
INLAND ONLY For the purpose of the INLAND Navigation Rules, the term "INLAND Waters" includes which of the following?
⚓ A. the Great Lakes on the United States side of the boundary
B. any lakes within state boundaries
C. the coastline of the United States out tone mile offshore
D. the waters surrounding any islands of the U.S.

RULE 9 - NARROW CHANNELS

IF THE STEM OF A QUESTION CONTAINS THE DESCRIPTIVE QUALIFIER "NARROW CHANNEL", THEN THE QUESTION SHOULD BE ANSWERED PURSUANT TO THE PROVISIONS OF RULE 9, INTERNATIONAL AND/OR INLAND AS APPLICABLE.

040008/RR00270   **RULE 9 (a) (i), (ii); RULE 34 (h)**
INLAND ONLY Two power-driven vessels are meeting in a narrow channel as shown in illustration D037RR below. Which of the following statements is TRUE? See DIAGRAM D037RR
A. Whistle signals must be exchanged in all situations when passing within one half mile of each other.
B. If agreement is reached by radiotelephone whistle signals must still be exchanged.
⚓ C. If agreement is reached by radiotelephone whistle signals are optional.
D. None of the above

040009/RR09133 **RULE 9 (a) (ii);**
RULE 14 (a); RULE 34 (a) (i)
INLAND ONLY A power-driven vessel proceeding downstream in a narrow channel on the Western Rivers sights another power-driven vessel moving upstream. Which vessel has the right-of-way?
- A. The vessel sounding the first whistle signal
- B. The vessel moving downstream with a following current
- C. The vessel located more towards the channel centerline
- D. The vessel moving upstream against the current

040010/RR00081 **RULE 9 (a) (ii)**
INLAND ONLY When two power-driven vessels are meeting on the Great Lakes, Western Rivers, or waters specified by the Secretary, where there is a current, which vessel shall sound the first passing signal?
- A. Either vessel
- B. The vessel that is towing regardless of the current
- C. The vessel going upstream stemming the current
- D. The vessel downbound with a following current

040011/RR00133 **RULE 9 (a) (ii)**
INLAND ONLY A power-driven vessel operating in a narrow channel with a following current on the Great Lakes or Western Rivers is meeting an upbound vessel. Which statement is TRUE?
- A. The downbound vessel must propose the manner and place of passage.
- B. The downbound vessel has the right-of-way.
- C. The downbound vessel must initiate the required maneuvering signals.
- D. All of the above

040012/RR09118 **RULE 9 (a) (ii)**
INLAND ONLY A power-driven vessel operating in a narrow channel with a following current on the Great Lakes or Western Rivers is meeting an upbound vessel. Which statement is TRUE?
- A. The upbound vessel must initiate the required maneuvering signals.
- B. The downbound vessel has the right-of-way
- C. The upbound vessel must propose the manner of passing.
- D. All of the above.

040013/RR00019 **RULE 9 (a) (ii)**
INLAND ONLY A power-driven vessel operating in a narrow channel with a following current on the Great Lakes or Western Rivers is meeting an upbound vessel. Which statement is TRUE?
- A. The upbound vessel must initiate the required maneuvering signals.
- B. The upbound vessel must propose the manner of passing.
- C. The downbound vessel has the right-of-way.
- D. All of the above

040014/RR00004 **RULE 9 (a) (ii)**
INLAND ONLY A power-driven vessel proceeding downstream in a narrow channel on the Western Rivers sights another power-driven vessel moving upstream. Which vessel has the right-of-way?
- A. The vessel moving upstream against the current
- B. The vessel sounding the first whistle signal
- C. The vessel located more towards the channel centerline
- D. The vessel moving downstream with a following current

040015/RR09121 **RULE 9 (a) (ii)**
INLAND ONLY Which is TRUE of a power-driven vessel, bound downstream, when meeting an upbound vessel on the Western Rivers?
- A. She shall initiate maneuvering signals.
- B. She has the right-of-way.
- C. She shall propose the manner of passage.
- D. All of the above

040016/RR00134 **RULE 9 (a) (ii)**
INLAND ONLY Which is TRUE of a vessel downbound with a following current when meeting an upbound vessel on the Western Rivers?
- A. She does not have the right-of-way, since the other vessel is not crossing the river.
- B. She must wait for a whistle signal from the upbound vessel.
- C. Neither vessel has the right-of-way.
- D. She has the right-of-way only if she is power-driven.

040017/RR09135 **RULE 9 (a) (ii)**
INLAND ONLY Which statement is TRUE of a power-driven vessel proceeding downbound with the current, when meeting an upbound vessel on the Western Rivers?
- A. She shall not impede the upbound vessel.
- B. She shall propose the manner of passage.
- C. She shall pass on the port side of the other.
- D. All of the above.

040018/RR09136 **RULE 9 (a) (ii)**
INLAND ONLY You are on a power-driven vessel proceeding down a channel, with the current, on a river on the Great Lakes System. If you meet another power-driven vessel who is upbound, what is your responsibility?
- A. waiting for the other vessel to signal her intentions, and then answering promptly
- B. proposing a safe way to pass
- C. backing down to get out of the way of the other vessel
- D. All of the above

040019/RR00401
RULE 9 (a) (ii);
RULE 14 (a); RULE 34 (a) (i)
INLAND ONLY Two power-driven vessels are meeting in a narrow channel on the Great lakes as shown in illustration D029RR below. Vessel "A" is downbound with a following current. Vessel "B" should do which of the following? See DIAGRAM D029RR
A. initiate the maneuvering signals
B. have the right-of-way
⚓ C. take action to permit safe passage
D. None of the above

040020/RR00269
RULE 9 (a) (ii);
RULE 14 (a); RULE 34 (a) (i)
INLAND ONLY Two power-driven vessels are meeting in a narrow channel on the Great Lakes as shown in illustration D037RR below. Vessel "A" is downbound with a following current. Vessel "A" shall do which of the following? See DIAGRAM D037RR
A. have the right-of-way
B. initiate the maneuvering signals
C. propose the manner of passage
⚓ D. All of the above

040021/RR00266
RULE 9 (a) (ii);
RULE 14 (a); RULE 34 (a) (i)
INLAND ONLY Two power-driven vessels are meeting in a narrow channel on the Great Lakes as shown in illustration D037RR below. Vessel "A" is downbound with a following current. Vessel "B" shall do which of the following? See DIAGRAM D037RR
A. initiate the maneuvering signals
B. propose the manner of passage
C. have the right-of-way
⚓ D. None of the above

040022/RR09137
RULE 9 (c)
INLAND ONLY A 150-meter vessel is proceeding down the course of a narrow channel in the Great Lakes System. A 60-meter vessel is starting to cross the channel. Which statement is TRUE?
A. The vessel in the channel must slow to her steerageway.
⚓ B. If the smaller vessel is engaged in fishing, he shall not impede the passage of the other vessel.
C. The larger vessel is considered to be a vessel restricted in her ability to maneuver.
D. The crossing vessel has the right-of-way.

040023/RR09134
RULE 9 (d)
INLAND ONLY A power-driven vessel crossing a river on the Western Rivers has the right-of-way over which vessel?
A. all vessels ascending and descending the river
B. vessels ascending the river
C. vessels descending the river
⚓ D. None of the above

*** COMMENT ***

RULE 9 (d) INLAND INDICATES THAT THE USE OF THE DANGER SIGNAL IS MANDATORY (SHALL). SEE RULE 9 (d) INLAND.

040024/RR09120
RULE 9 (d); RULE 34 (d)
INLAND ONLY You are navigating in a narrow channel and must remain in the channel for safe operation. Another vessel is crossing the channel ahead of you from your starboard and you doubt whether your vessel will pass safely. Which statement is TRUE?
⚓ A. You must sound the danger signal.
B. You must sound one short blast of the whistle and turn to starboard.
C. You must stop your vessel, since the other vessel is the stand-on.
D. You must stop your engines and you may sound the danger signal.

*** COMMENT ***

RULE 9 (d) INLAND INDICATES THAT THE USE OF THE DANGER SIGNAL IS MANDATORY (SHALL). SEE RULE 9 (d) INLAND.

040025/RR00001
RULE 9 (d); RULE 34 (d)
INLAND ONLY You are navigating in a narrow channel and must remain in the channel for safe operation. Another vessel is crossing the channel ahead of you from your starboard and you doubt whether your vessel will pass safely. Which statement is TRUE?
A. You must stop your engines and you may sound the danger signal.
⚓ B. You must sound the danger signal.
C. You must sound one short blast of the whistle and turn to starboard.
D. You must stop your vessel, since the other vessel is the stand-on.

RULE 9 (d) INLAND INDICATES THAT THE USE OF THE DANGER SIGNAL IS MANDATORY (SHALL). SEE RULE 9 (d) INLAND.

040026/RR00037   **RULE 9 (d); RULE 34 (d)**
INLAND ONLY You are operating a vessel through a narrow channel and your vessel must stay within the channel to be navigated safely. Another vessel is crossing your course from starboard to port, and you are in doubt as to her intentions. Which of the following actions should you take?
⚓ A.   must sound the danger signal
B.   should sound one short blast to show that you are holding course and speed
C.   are required to back down
D.   may sound the danger signal

*** COMMENT ***

RULE 9 (d) INLAND INDICATES THAT THE USE OF THE DANGER SIGNAL IS MANDATORY (SHALL). SEE RULE 9 (d) INLAND.

040027/RR09117   **RULE 9 (d); RULE 34 (d)**
INLAND ONLY Your vessel is proceeding down a channel, and can safely navigate only within the channel. Another vessel is crossing your bow from port to starboard, and you are in doubt as to her intentions. Which statement is TRUE?
A.   You should sound one prolonged and two short blasts.
⚓ B.   The sounding of the danger signal is mandatory.
C.   You should sound two short blasts.
D.   The sounding of the danger signal is optional.

*** COMMENT ***

RULE 9 (d) INLAND INDICATES THAT THE USE OF THE DANGER SIGNAL IS MANDATORY (SHALL). SEE RULE 9 (d) INLAND.

040028/RR00056   **RULE 9 (d); RULE 34 (d)**
INLAND ONLY Your vessel must remain in a narrow channel for safe operation. Another vessel is crossing the channel from your starboard. You do not think she will pass safely. You MUST take which action?
A.   sound one short blast of the whistle, and turn to starboard
B.   stop your vessel, since the other vessel has the right-of-way
⚓ C.   sound the danger signal
D.   stop your engines, and you may sound the danger signal

RULE 9 (d) INLAND INDICATES THAT THE USE OF THE DANGER SIGNAL IS MANDATORY (SHALL). SEE RULE 9 (d) INLAND.

040029/RR00020   **RULE 9 (d); RULE 34 (d)**
INLAND ONLY Your vessel is proceeding down a channel, and can safely navigate only within the channel. Another vessel is crossing your bow from port to starboard, and you are in doubt as to her intentions. Which statement is TRUE?
A.   You should sound one prolonged and two short blasts.
B.   You should sound two short blasts.
⚓ C.   The sounding of the danger signal is mandatory.
D.   The sounding of the danger signal is optional.

040030/RR00003   **RULE 9 (e) (i); RULE 34 (c), (d)**
INLAND ONLY In a narrow channel, you are underway on power-driven vessel "A" and desire to overtake power-driven vessel "B". After you sound two short blasts on your whistle, vessel "B" sounds five short and rapid blasts on the whistle. What action should you take?
A.   slow or stop and expect radical maneuvers from "B"
⚓ B.   hold your relative position, and then sound another signal after the situation has stabilized
C.   answer the five short blast signal then stop your vessel until the other vessel initiates a signal
D.   pass with caution on the port side of vessel "B"

040031/RR00009   **RULE 9 (g)**
INLAND ONLY Which statement is TRUE concerning narrow channels?
⚓ A.   You should avoid anchoring in a narrow channel.
B.   You should keep to that side of the channel which is on your port side.
C.   A vessel having a following current will propose the manner of passage in any case where two vessels are meeting.
D.   All of the above

<table>
<tr><td>

PART B STEERING & SAILING RULES
SECTION SUBPART II
CONDUCT OF VESSELS
IN SIGHT OF ONE ANOTHER

</td></tr>
</table>

RULE 13 - OVERTAKING

040032/RR09139   **RULE 13 (a)**
INLAND ONLY You are on vessel "A", and vessel "B" desires to overtake you on your starboard side as shown in illustration D031RR below. After the vessels have exchanged one blast signals what action should you take? See DIAGRAM D031RR
A. alter course to the right to give vessel "B" more sea room
⚓ B. hold course and speed
C. slow your vessel until vessel "B" has passed
D. alter course to the left to give vessel "B" more sea room

040033/RR00053   **RULE 13 (a)**
INLAND ONLY You are on power-driven vessel "A" and power-driven vessel "B" desires to overtake you on the starboard side as shown in illustration D038RR below. After the vessels have exchanged one blast signals what action should you take? See DIAGRAM D038RR
A. slow your vessel until vessel "B" has passed
B. alter course to the left
C. alter course to the left or right to give vessel "B" more sea room
⚓ D. hold course and speed

040034/RR09138   **RULE 13 (b)**
INLAND ONLY You are approaching a vessel displaying the lights as shown in illustration D075RR below. What type of situation is this? See DIAGRAM D075RR
A. crossing situation
B. special circumstance situation
⚓ C. overtaking situation
D. meeting head-on situation

RULE 14 - HEAD-ON SITUATION

040035/RR00012   **RULE 14 (a); RULE 34 (a) (i), (h)**
INLAND ONLY Your power-driven vessel is meeting another vessel head-on. To comply with the steering and sailing rules what action should you take?
A. sound one prolonged and two short blasts
⚓ B. exchange one short blast
C. exchange two short blasts
D. sound the danger signal

040036/RR09115   **RULE 14 (d); RULE 9 (a) (ii)**
INLAND ONLY When two power-driven vessels are meeting on the Great Lakes, Western Rivers, or waters specified by the Secretary, where there is a current, which vessel shall sound the first passing signal?
A. The vessel that is towing regardless of the current
B. Either vessel
⚓ C. The vessel downbound with a following current
D. The vessel going upstream stemming the current

040037/RR00071   **RULE 14 (d); RULE 9 (a) (ii)**
INLAND ONLY Which is TRUE of a power-driven vessel, bound downstream, when meeting an upbound vessel on the Western Rivers?
A. She shall initiate maneuvering signals.
B. She shall propose the manner of passage.
C. She has the right-of-way.
⚓ D. All of the above

040038/RR09128   **RULE 14 (d); RULE 9 (a) (ii)**
INLAND ONLY Which is TRUE of a vessel downbound with a following current when meeting an upbound vessel on the Western Rivers?
A. She does not have the right-of-way, since the other vessel is not crossing the river.
⚓ B. She has the right-of-way only if she is power-driven.
C. She must wait for a whistle signal from the upbound vessel.
D. Neither vessel has the right-of-way.

040039/RR00132   **RULE 14 (d); RULE 9 (a) (ii)**
INLAND ONLY Which statement is TRUE of a power-driven vessel proceeding downbound with the current, when meeting an upbound vessel on the Western Rivers?
A. She shall not impede the upbound vessel.
B. She shall pass on the port side of the other.
⚓ C. She shall propose the manner of passage.
D. All of the above

RULE 15 - CROSSING SITUATION

040040/RR09140   **RULE 15 (b); RULE 9 (d)**
INLAND ONLY Your vessel is crossing a river on the Great Lakes System. A power-driven vessel is ascending the river, crossing your course from port to starboard. Which statement is TRUE?
A. Your vessel has the right-of-way, but you are directed not to impede the other vessel.
⚓ B. The vessel ascending the river has the right-of-way.
C. The other vessel must hold as necessary to allow you to pass.
D. You are required to propose the manner of passage.

040041/RR00085   **RULE 15 (b)**
INLAND ONLY A power-driven vessel crossing a river on the Great Lakes or Western Rivers, must keep out of the way of which of the following power-driven vessels?
A. ascending the river without a tow
B. ascending the river with a tow
C. descending the river with a tow
⚓ D. All of the above

040042/RR00017   **RULE 15 (b)**
INLAND ONLY A power-driven vessel crossing on the Western Rivers has the right-of-way over which vessels?
A. vessels descending the river
B. vessels ascending the river
C. all vessels ascending and descending the river
⚓ D. None of the above

040043/RR00084   **RULE 15 (b); RULE 9 (d)**
INLAND ONLY You are in charge of a power-driven vessel crossing on the Western Rivers. You must keep out of the way of which vessel?
A. sail vessel ascending the river
B. sail vessel descending the river
C. power-driven vessel ascending the river
⚓ D. All of the above

PART C LIGHTS AND SHAPES

RULE 21 - DEFINITIONS

040044/RR04029   **RULE 21 (a), RULE 23 (d) (iii)**
INLAND ONLY The masthead light may be located at other than the fore and aft centerline on which power-driven vessel?
⚓ A. less than 12 meters in length
B. engaged in fishing
C. which has separate sidelights carried on the outboard extremes of the vessel's breadth
D. less than 20 meters in length

040045/RR00115   **RULE 21 (g)**
INLAND ONLY What is true of a "special flashing light"?
A. It is optional below the Baton Rouge Highway Bridge.
⚓ B. It may show through an arc of not less than 180°.
C. It flashes at the rate of 120 flashes per minute.
D. All of the above

040046/RR00117   **RULE 21 (g)**
INLAND ONLY Which is a characteristic of a "special flashing light"?
⚓ A. It must show through an arc of not less than 180° nor more than 225°.
B. It is required for all vessels being pushed ahead as part of a composite unit.
C. It must be of the same character and construction as the masthead light.
D. All of the above

040047/RR00068   **RULE 21 (g)**
INLAND ONLY Which is CORRECT regarding a "special flashing light"?
A. It must not show through an arc of more than 225°.
B. It must be yellow in color.
C. It must be placed as far forward as possible.
⚓ D. All of the above

RULE 23 - POWER-DRIVEN VESSELS UNDERWAY

040048/RR09125   **RULE 23 (e)**
INLAND ONLY Which statement is TRUE concerning lighting requirements for Great Lakes vessels?
⚓ A. An all-round white light may be carried in lieu of the second masthead light and stern light.
B. Sidelights for vessels over 50 meters are required to have only a two-mile range of visibility.
C. The showing of a forward masthead light is optional for vessels under 150 meters.
D. Great Lakes vessels are exempted from the requirement to show yellow towing lights.

RULE 24 - TOWING AND PUSHING

040049/RR00253   **RULE 24 (c) (i) - (ii), (f) (i)**
INLAND ONLY Vessels "A" and "B" are meeting on a river as shown in illustration D041RR below and will pass 1/4 mile apart. Which light(s) on the tug & barge will you see, if you are on vessel "A"? See DIAGRAM D041RR
A. a special flashing light
B. green sidelights
C. two white masthead lights in a vertical line
⚓ D. All of the above

040050/RR00083   **RULE 24 (c) (iii)**
INLAND ONLY If your tug is pushing a barge ahead at night and it is not a composite unit, which light(s) should show aft on your vessel?
A. A white stern light
⚓ B. Two towing lights
C. two red lights
D. A towing light over the stern light

040051/RR00080   **RULE 24 (c) (iii)**
INLAND ONLY While underway at night, you see two yellow lights displayed in a vertical line. What do the lights indicate to you?
A. vessel broken down
B. vessel fishing
C. opening in a pipeline
⚓ D. vessel pushing ahead

040052/RR00190   **RULE 24 (c) (iii)**
INLAND ONLY At night, you see the lights shown in illustration D075RR below. These lights are shown by what type of vessel? See DIAGRAM D075RR
A. barge being pushed ahead
B. barge being towed astern
C. tug towing a barge astern
⚓ D. tug pushing a barge ahead

040053/RR00055   **RULE 24 (c) (iii)**
INLAND ONLY What do the lights shown in illustration D075RR below represent? See DIAGRAM D075RR
A. vessel being towed astern
B. vessel underway and dredging
⚓ C. vessel pushing ahead
D. pipeline

040054/RR00072   **RULE 24 (c) (iii); RULE 13 (b)**
INLAND ONLY You are approaching a vessel displaying the lights as shown in illustration D075RR below. What type of situation is this? See DIAGRAM D075RR
A. meeting head-on situation
⚓ B. overtaking situation
C. crossing situation
D. special circumstance situation

040055/RR00044   **RULE 24 (f) (i)**
INLAND ONLY What lights are required for a barge being pushed ahead, not being part of a composite unit?
⚓ A. Sidelights and a special flashing light
B. Sidelights and a stern light
C. Sidelights, a towing light, and a stern light
D. Sidelights, a special flashing light, and a stern light

040056/RR09113   **RULE 24 (f) (i)**
INLAND ONLY What lights will a single vessel being towed alongside show?
A. only the outboard sidelight and a stern light
B. sidelights and a stern light
⚓ C. a special flashing light, sidelights, and a stern light
D. one all-round white light

040057/RR09142   **RULE 24 (f) (i)**
INLAND ONLY When is a vessel required to exhibit a special flashing light?
A. when at anchor in a fairway
⚓ B. when being pushed ahead
C. when towed astern
D. All of the above

040058/RR00018   **RULE 24 (f) (i)**
INLAND ONLY Which lights are required for a barge, not part of a composite unit, being pushed ahead?
⚓ A. Sidelights and a special flashing light
B. Sidelights, a towing light, and a stern light
C. Sidelights, a special flashing light, and a stern light
D. Sidelights and a stern light

040059/RR09114   **RULE 24 (f) (i)**
INLAND ONLY Vessels "A" and "B" are meeting on a river as shown in illustration D041RR below and will pass 1/4 mile apart. Which is one of the lights on vessel "B" that you will see if you are on vessel "A"?
A. yellow towing light
B. red sidelight
⚓ C. special flashing light
D. All of the above

040060/RR00254   **RULE 24 (f) (i)**
INLAND ONLY Vessels "A" and "B" are meeting on a river as shown in illustration D041RR below and will pass 1/4 mile apart. Which is one of the lights on vessel "B" that you will see if you are on vessel "A"? See DIAGRAM D041RR
A. red sidelight
⚓ B. special flashing light
C. yellow towing light
D. All of the above

040061/RR02076   **RULE 24 (f) (ii)**
INLAND ONLY Which lights are required for a single barge being towed alongside?
A. Sidelights and a stern light
B. Sidelights, a towing light, and a stern light
⚓ C. Sidelights, a special flashing light, and a stern light
D. Sidelights and a special flashing light

040062/RR00383
RULE 24 (f) (ii), (c) (i);
RULE 23 (c) (ii)
INLAND ONLY You are meeting "head on" a tug towing a barge alongside about a mile away. In addition to the white masthead lights which other lights do you see on the tug and tow combined?
- A. One green and one red sidelight and a special flashing light
- B. One green and one red sidelight on the outside of the unit
- C. The green and red sidelights marking each vessel and a special flashing light
- D. Only the green and red sidelights marking each vessel

040063/RR00039 **RULE 24 (g) (i) - (v); RULE 36**
INLAND ONLY Which indicates the presence of a partly submerged object being towed?
- A. A diamond shape on the towed object
- B. An all-round light at each end of the towed object
- C. A searchlight beamed from the towing vessel in the direction of the tow
- D. All of the above

040064/RR00200 **RULE 24 (g) (iv)**
INLAND ONLY What must a partially submerged object towed by a vessel show during the day?
- A. black ball only when the length of the tow exceeds 200 meters in length
- B. diamond shape regardless of length of the tow
- C. black ball
- D. diamond shape only when the length of the tow exceeds 200 meters in length

040065/RR00119 **RULE 24 (g) (v); RULE 36**
INLAND ONLY What MAY be used to indicate the presence of a partly submerged object being towed?
- A. The beam of a search light from the towing vessel shown in the direction of the tow
- B. A black cone, apex upward
- C. Two all-round yellow lights at each end of the tow
- D. All of the above

040066/RR00099 **RULE 24 (i) (i) - (ii)**
INLAND ONLY A power-driven vessel when pushing ahead or towing alongside on the Western Rivers (above the Huey P. Long Bridge on the Mississippi River at mile 106.1) shall exhibit which of the following configurations?
- A. sidelights and two towing lights
- B. one masthead light, sidelights, and stern light
- C. two masthead lights, sidelights, and stern light
- D. two masthead lights, sidelights, and two towing lights

RULE 26 - FISHING VESSELS

040067/RR04502
RULE 26 (f) (ii) (1) (A),
33 CFR 83.26; ANNEX II
INLAND ONLY Vessels engaged in fishing may show the additional signals as described in RULE 26 when they are in which of the following situations?
- A. trolling
- B. in close proximity to other vessels engaged in fishing
- C. fishing in a traffic separation zone
- D. in a narrow channel

040068/RR04730
RULE 26 (f) (ii) (1) (A),
33 CFR 83.26; ANNEX II
INLAND ONLY Which of the following signals may be exhibited by a vessel trawling in close proximity to other fishing vessels?
- A. A red light over a white light in a vertical line
- B. Two white lights in a vertical line
- C. Two fixed yellow lights in a vertical line
- D. All of the above

RULE 27 - VESSELS NOT UNDER COMMAND AND RESTRICTED IN ABILITY TO MANEUVER

*** COMMENT ***

WHEN OPERATING ON INLAND WATERS THE LEGAL TESTS FOR THE USE OF RAM LIGHTS ARE: 1. THE TOWING VESSEL NEED NOT BE POWER-DRIVEN, 2. THE TOWING VESSEL IS SEVERELY RESTRICTED WHEN TOWING ASTERN, PUSHING AHEAD OR ALONGSIDE. SEE RULE 27 (c), INLAND.

040069/RR00370 **RULE 27 (c)**
INLAND ONLY If a towing vessel and her tow are severely restricted in their ability to deviate from their course, lights in addition to the towing identification lights must be shown. These additional lights shall be shown if the tow is which of the following?
- A. towed alongside
- B. pushed ahead
- C. towed astern
- D. All of the above

040070/RR00103 **RULE 27 (d) (iv) (1), (2)**
INLAND ONLY Which light display would mark the opening in a pipeline where vessels could pass through?
- A. Three white lights in a vertical line on each side of the opening
- B. Two white lights in a vertical line on each side of the opening
- C. Three red lights in a vertical line on each side of the opening
- D. Two red lights in a vertical line on each side of the opening

040071/RR00273   **RULE 27 (d) (iv) (1), (2)**
INLAND ONLY While underway you sight the lights shown in illustration D081RR below with the yellow lights flashing, what action should you take? See DIAGRAM D081RR

A. stop until the red lights turn green
B. wait until the vessel ahead crosses your bow
C. proceed leaving all the lights on your starboard side
⚓ D. pass between the two sets of vertical red lights

040072/RR00282   **RULE 27 (d) (iv) (1), (2)**
INLAND ONLY While underway you sight the lights shown in illustration D081RR below with the yellow lights flashing. The lights displayed indicate which of the following? See DIAGRAM D081RR

A. vessel not under command
⚓ B. dredge pipeline
C. mine clearance vessel
D. vessel aground

040073/RR00277   **RULE 27 (d) (iv) (1), (2)**
INLAND ONLY While underway you sight the lights shown in illustration D081RR below with the yellow lights flashing. The lights displayed should have which of the following characteristics? See DIAGRAM D081RR

A. flashing at intervals of 120 flashes per minute
B. more than 50 meters apart
C. visible for at least one mile
⚓ D. visible at night and during periods of restricted visibility

040074/RR00311   **RULE 27 (d) (iv) (1), (2)**
INLAND ONLY Identify the operation indicated by the lights exhibited as shown in illustration D085RR below. See DIAGRAM D085RR

A. A submarine engaged in underway replenishment
B. Aircraft carrier engaged in the launching and recovery of aircraft
C. A vessel aground assisted by tugs
⚓ D. None of the above

040075/RR00312   **RULE 27 (d) (iv) (1), (2)**
INLAND ONLY You see the lights shown in illustration D085RR below while proceeding in a channel. What action should you take? See DIAGRAM D085RR

⚓ A. Slow down and pass between the two sets of double red lights.
B. Stop the vessel and await the red lights to change to green.
C. Proceed at full sea speed through the two sets of double red lights.
D. None of the above

040076/RR00313   **RULE 27 (d) (iv) (1), (2)**
INLAND ONLY You see the lights shown in illustration D085RR below while proceeding in a channel. Where should you pass? See DIAGRAM D085RR

⚓ A. A
B. B
C. C
D. D

RULE 30 - VESSELS ANCHORED AND VESSELS AGROUND

040077/RR00034   **RULE 30 (a) (i) - (ii), (g)**
INLAND ONLY A barge more than 50 meters long is required to show how many white anchor lights when anchored in a Secretary approved "special anchorage area"?

A. 3
B. 1
⚓ C. 2
D. None

040078/RR00063   **RULE 30 (g)**
INLAND ONLY Which of the following is TRUE for a vessel of less than 20 meters in length at anchor at night in a "special anchorage area designated by the Secretary"?

A. must show one white light
⚓ B. need not show any lights
C. must show two white lights
D. need show a light only on the approach of another vessel

040079/RR00114   **RULE 30 (h) (ii), (i)**
INLAND ONLY At night, what lights are required on barges moored in a group formation more than two barges wide?

⚓ A. Two unobstructed all-round white lights
B. Two unobstructed all-round red lights
C. All-round yellow lights placed at the corners of each barge in the group
D. Two yellow lights in a vertical line at the corner extremities of the group

040080/RR00064   **RULE 30 (h) (ii), (i)**
INLAND ONLY At night, which lights are required on barges moored in a group formation, more than two barges wide, and located where other vessels cannot navigate on both sides of the group?

A. Two red lights in a vertical line at the corner extremities of the group
⚓ B. Two unobstructed all-round white lights
C. Two unobstructed all-round yellow lights
D. All-round white lights placed at the corners of each barge in the group

040081/RR00104 **RULE 30 (h) (ii), (i)**
INLAND ONLY Which light(s) shall be shown at night on a moored barge which reduces the navigable width of any channel to less than 80 meters?
⚓ A. Two unobstructed all-round white lights
B. Two yellow lights in a vertical line at the stern
C. A red light placed on all four corners
D. A red light placed on the two corners farthest from the bank

040082/RR00029 **RULE 30 (h) (iii), (j)**
INLAND ONLY A fleet of moored barges extends into a navigable channel. What is the color of the lights on the barges?
A. Red
B. Amber
C. Yellow
⚓ D. White

040083/RR09110 **RULE 30 (k) (i)**
INLAND ONLY At night, a barge moored in a slip used primarily for mooring purposes shall exhibit which of the following?
A. a white light at each corner
B. a red light at the bow and stern
C. a flashing yellow light at each corner
⚓ D. no required lights

RULE 31 - SEAPLANES

040084/RR09141 **RULE 31**
INLAND ONLY Yellow lights are NOT used to identify which of the following?
⚓ A. a seaplane on the water
B. purse seiners
C. the heads of tows being pushed ahead by tugboats
D. a dredge pipeline on a trestle

040085/RR00013 **RULE 31**
INLAND ONLY Yellow lights are NOT used to identify which of the following?
A. the heads of tows being pushed ahead by tugboats
B. a dredge pipeline on a trestle
⚓ C. a seaplane on the water
D. purse seiners

PART D SOUND AND LIGHT SIGNALS

RULE 34 - MANEUVERING AND WARNING SIGNALS

*** COMMENT ***

THE MANEUVERING AND WARNING SIGNALS REQUIRED BY RULE 34 (a) ARE TO BE SOUNDED BY POWER-DRIVEN VESSELS ONLY WHEN INSIGHT OF ONE ANOTHER. THEY ARE SIGNALS OF INTENT. SEE RULE 34 (a) INLAND.

040086/RR00821 **RULE 34 (a), (h)**
INLAND ONLY One and two short blast signals must be sounded on INLAND waters when _____.
A. two power-driven vessels are crossing within half a mile of each other and NOT in sight of each other
B. two sailing vessels are in sight of one another and meeting at a distance of one quarter mile
⚓ C. two power-driven vessels are in sight of one another and are meeting at a distance of one half mile
D. two power-driven vessels are in sight of one another and will cross at a distance of one mile

040087/RR00261 **RULE 34 (a)**
INLAND ONLY While underway and in sight of another power-driven vessel forward of your beam, more than 0.5 mile away, you put your engines full speed astern. Which statement concerning whistle signals is TRUE?
A. You must sound three short blasts on the whistle.
⚓ B. You need not sound any whistle signals.
C. You must sound whistle signals only if the vessels are meeting.
D. You must sound one blast if backing to starboard.

040088/RR00226 **RULE 34 (a) (3)**
INLAND ONLY While underway and in sight of another vessel a mile ahead you put your engines on astern propulsion. Which statement concerning whistle signals is TRUE?
A. You must sound whistle signals only if the vessels are meeting.
B. You must sound one blast if backing to starboard.
⚓ C. You need not sound any whistle signals.
D. You must sound three short blasts on the whistle.

040089/RR00262 **RULE 34 (a), (h)**
INLAND ONLY When power-driven vessels are in sight of one another, passing signals shall be sounded when _____.
⚓ A. meeting or crossing within half a mile of each other
B. meeting or crossing at any distance
C. meeting within one mile of each other
D. crossing within one mile of each other

040090/RR00021   **RULE 34 (a) (i)**
INLAND ONLY The stand-on vessel in a crossing situation sounds one short blast of the whistle. This means that the vessel _____.
- A.   intends to leave the other on her port side
- B.   is changing course to port
- C.   is changing course to starboard
- D.   intends to hold course and speed

040091/RR00007   **RULE 34 (a) (i)**
INLAND ONLY When power-driven vessels are crossing, a signal of one short blast by either vessel means _____.
- A.   "I intend to leave you on my port side"
- B.   "I intend to change course to starboard"
- C.   "I intend to hold course and speed"
- D.   "I am altering course to starboard"

040092/RR00059   **RULE 34 (a) (i)**
INLAND ONLY When power-driven vessels are in a crossing situation, one short blast by either vessel would mean _____.
- A.   "I intend to change course to starboard"
- B.   "I request a departure from the rules"
- C.   "I intend to leave you on my port side"
- D.   "I intend to hold course and speed"

040093/RR00249   **RULE 34 (a) (i), (ii)**
INLAND ONLY You are on a power-driven vessel "I" as shown in illustration D036RR below. Vessel "II" is a power-driven vessel engaged in fishing that will pass within 1/2 a mile of your vessel. Which action should you take? See DIAGRAM D036RR
- A.   sound one short blast, reduce speed and turn to starboard.
- B.   Hold course and speed without giving a signal.
- C.   sound the danger signal and reduce speed.
- D.   sound one short blast and await response from the fishing vessel.

040094/RR00346   **RULE 34 (a) (i); RULE 15 (a)**
INLAND ONLY Two power-driven vessels are crossing within a half a mile of each other as shown in illustration D042RR below. Vessel "A" sounds one short blast on the whistle, what does this signal mean? See DIAGRAM D042RR
- A.   "I intend to leave you on my starboard side"
- B.   "I intend to leave you on my port side"
- C.   "I am altering my course to starboard"
- D.   None of the above

040095/RR00336   **RULE 34 (a) (i); RULE 15 (a)**
INLAND ONLY Two power-driven vessels are crossing within a half a mile of each other as shown in illustration D042RR below. Vessel "A" sounds one short blast on the whistle. What action should vessel "B" take? See DIAGRAM D042RR
- A.   alter course to the right or slowdown
- B.   sound the danger signal and slow to moderate speed
- C.   maintain course and speed without sounding any signals
- D.   sound one short blast and maintain course and speed

040096/RR00340   **RULE 34 (a) (i); RULE 15 (a)**
INLAND ONLY Two power-driven vessels are crossing within a half a mile of each other as shown in illustration D042RR below. Vessel "A" sounds one short blast on the whistle. What should Vessel "B" sound? See DIAGRAM D042RR
- A.   three short blasts
- B.   two short blasts
- C.   two prolonged blasts followed by two short blasts
- D.   one short blast

040097/RR00219   **RULE 34 (a) (i), (h)**
INLAND ONLY You are proceeding up a channel in Chesapeake Bay and are meeting an outbound vessel. There is no current. You MUST _____.
- A.   propose or answer one or two blast whistle signals given by the other vessel if passing within 1/2 mile
- B.   stop your vessel, letting the outbound vessel sound the signals for meeting and passing
- C.   keep to that side of the channel which is on your vessel's port side
- D.   give the outbound vessel the right-of-way

040098/RR00078   **RULE 34 (a) (i)**
INLAND ONLY Under the INLAND Navigation Rules, what is the meaning of a one short blast signal used when meeting another vessel?
- A.   "I intend to leave you on my starboard side."
- B.   "I am turning to port."
- C.   "I intend to leave you on my port side."
- D.   "I am turning to starboard."

040099/RR00095   **RULE 34 (a) (i)**
INLAND ONLY You are meeting another vessel in INLAND waters, and she sounds one short blast on the whistle. This means that she _____.
- A.   is changing course to port
- B.   desires to depart from the Rules
- C.   intends to leave you on her port side
- D.   is changing course to starboard

040100/RR09112   **RULE 34 (a) (i) (1), (a) (ii);**
RULE 9 (a) (ii)
INLAND ONLY You are proceeding against the current on a river in the Great Lakes System. You are meeting a downbound vessel. Both vessels are power-driven. The other vessel sounds one short blast. You must _____.

A. sound three short blasts
B. hold course and speed
C. change course to port
⚓ D. sound one short blast

040101/RR00088   **RULE 34 (a) (i); RULE 9 (a) (ii)**
INLAND ONLY Two power-driven vessels are meeting in the situation as shown in illustration D037RR below. What does one short blast by vessel "A" mean? See DIAGRAM D037RR

A. "I intend to pass on your starboard side"
B. "My intention is to hold course and speed"
⚓ C. "I intend to leave you on my port side"
D. "I am altering my course to starboard"

040102/RR00257   **RULE 34 (a) (i); RULE 9 (a) (ii)**
INLAND ONLY Two power-driven vessels are meeting in the situation as shown in illustration D037RR below. What does one short blast from either vessel mean? See DIAGRAM D037RR

A. "I am altering my course to starboard."
⚓ B. "I intend to leave you on my port side."
C. "I intend to hold course and speed."
D. "I intend to pass on your starboard side."

040103/RR00090   **RULE 34 (a) (i)**
INLAND ONLY Two vessels are in a starboard to starboard meeting situation and will pass well clear approximately 1/4 mile apart. Which action should each vessel take?

⚓ A. sound a two blast whistle signal and maintain course.
B. Maintain course and sound no signal.
C. sound a one blast whistle signal and turn to starboard.
D. sound a three blast whistle signal and turn to port.

040104/RR00015   **RULE 34 (a) (i)**
INLAND ONLY Under the INLAND Navigation Rules, what is the meaning of the two short blasts signal used when meeting another vessel?

A. "I am turning to starboard."
B. "I am turning to port."
⚓ C. "I intend to leave you on my starboard side."
D. "I intend to leave you on my port side."

040105/RR00070   **RULE 34 (a) (i) (2);**
RULE 34 (a) (ii); RULE 9 (a) (ii)
INLAND ONLY Two power-driven vessels, "A" and "B" , are meeting in a narrow channel as shown in illustration D029RR below. Which statement is TRUE concerning whistle signals between the vessels? See DIAGRAM D029RR

A. Vessel "A" should sound one short blast and vessel "B" should sound two short blasts.
B. Neither vessel should sound any signal as no course change is necessary.
C. Both vessels should sound one short blast.
⚓ D. Both vessels should sound two short blasts.

040106/RR00050   **RULE 34 (a) (i); RULE 9 (a) (ii)**
INLAND ONLY Vessels "A" and "B" are meeting on a river as shown in illustration D029RR below and will pass about 1/4 mile apart. Which statement is TRUE? See DIAGRAM D029RR

A. The vessels should exchange two blast whistle signals and pass port to port.
⚓ B. The vessels should exchange two blast whistle signals and pass starboard to starboard.
C. Both vessels should continue on course and pass without sounding any whistle signals.
D. The vessels should pass port to port and must sound whistle signals only if either vessel changes course.

040107/RR00268   **RULE 34 (a) (i)**
INLAND ONLY Two power-driven vessels are meeting in the situation as shown in illustration D037RR below and will pass within 1/2 mile of each other. What does two short blasts from either vessel mean? See DIAGRAM D037RR

A. "I intend to leave you on my port side."
⚓ B. "I intend to leave you on my starboard side."
C. "I am altering my course to port."
D. "I am altering my course to starboard."

040108/RR00251   **RULE 34 (a) (i); RULE 9 (a) (ii)**
INLAND ONLY power-driven vessels "A" and "B" are meeting on a river as shown in illustration D041RR below and will pass about 1/4 mile apart. Which action should the vessels take? See DIAGRAM D041RR

A. The vessels should continue on course and pass without sounding any whistle signals.
⚓ B. The vessels should exchange two blast whistle signals and pass starboard to starboard.
C. The vessels should exchange one blast whistle signals and pass starboard to starboard
D. The vessels should pass starboard to starboard and must sound whistle signals only if either vessel changes course.

040109/RR00077   **RULE 34 (a) (i); RULE 9 (a) (ii)**
INLAND ONLY Two power-driven vessels, "A" and "B", are meeting on a river as shown in illustration D041RR below and will pass about 1/4 mile apart. What action should the vessels take? See DIAGRAM D041RR

A.   The vessels should exchange one blast whistle signals and pass starboard to starboard.

B.   Both vessels should continue on course and pass without sounding any whistle signals.

C.   The vessels should pass starboard to starboard and must sound whistle signals only if either vessel changes course.

⚓ D.   The vessels should exchange two blast whistle signals and pass starboard to starboard.

040110/RR00250   **RULE 34 (a) (i), (ii)**
INLAND ONLY You are on a power-driven vessel "I" as shown in illustration D036RR below. Vessel "II" is a power-driven vessel engaged in fishing that will pass within 1/2 a mile of your vessel. You sound one short blast on the whistle. Vessel "II" does not sound any signal. Which action should you take? See DIAGRAM D036RR

A.   Sound two short blasts and change course to port.

B.   Sound one short blast, reduce speed and turn to starboard.

⚓ C.   Sound the danger signal and reduce speed.

D.   Hold course and speed without giving a signal.

040111/RR00023   **RULE 34 (a) (ii), (h)**
INLAND ONLY Passing signals shall be sounded on INLAND waters by _____ .

⚓ A.   a power-driven vessel when crossing less than half a mile ahead of another power-driven vessel

B.   all vessels upon sighting another vessel rounding a bend in the channel

C.   a towing vessel when meeting another towing vessel on a clear day with a 0.6 mile CPA (Closest Point of Approach)

D.   All of the above

040112/RR00098   **RULE 34 (a) (ii), (d); RULE 15**
INLAND ONLY You are aboard the stand-on vessel in a crossing situation. You sound a one blast whistle signal. The give-way vessel answers with a two blast whistle signal. You should sound the danger signal and take what action?

⚓ A.   take precautionary action until a safe passing agreement is made

B.   maneuver around the stern of the other vessel

C.   maintain course and speed as you are the stand-on vessel

D.   come around sharply to port

040113/RR00247   **RULE 34 (a) (ii)**
INLAND ONLY You are on power-driven vessel "I" and in sight of power-driven vessel "II" as shown in illustration D036RR below. Vessel "II" sounds one short blast. What action should you take if you agree? See DIAGRAM D036RR

A.   sound one short blast and slow down or turn to starboard

B.   hold course and speed and sound no signal

⚓ C.   sound one short blast and hold course and speed

D.   sound the danger signal and slow to moderate speed

040114/RR00052   **RULE 34 (a) (ii), (h)**
INLAND ONLY Whistle signals shall be exchanged by power-driven vessels in sight of one another when _____ .

A.   course changes are necessary to pass

B.   doubt exists as to which side the vessels will pass on

⚓ C.   they are passing within half a mile of each other

D.   passing agreements have been made by radio

040115/RR00129   **RULE 34 (a) (ii), (h)**
INLAND ONLY You are a power-driven vessel proceeding in a channel in INLAND waters and are meeting an outbound power-driven vessel. Your responsibilities include _____ .

A.   stopping your vessel and letting the outbound vessel initiate signals for passing

B.   giving the outbound vessel the right-of-way

C.   keeping to that side of the channel which is on your vessel's port side

⚓ D.   exchanging whistle signals if passing within half a mile

040116/RR00043   **RULE 34 (a) (ii), (d); RULE 14**
INLAND ONLY You are meeting another power-driven vessel head-on and sound one short blast as a passing signal. The other vessel answers with two short blasts. What should be your next action?

A.   Pass astern of the other vessel.

B.   Hold your course and speed.

C.   Pass on the other vessel's starboard side.

⚓ D.   sound the danger signal.

040117/RR00031   **RULE 34 (b) (i)**
INLAND ONLY At night, a light signal consisting of two flashes by a vessel indicates _____ .

A.   that the vessel is in distress

B.   an intention to leave another vessel to port

C.   an intention to communicate over radiotelephone

⚓ D.   an intention to leave another vessel to starboard

040118/RR00143   **RULE 34 (b) (iii)**
INLAND ONLY A light used to signal passing intentions must be an _____.
A. alternating white and yellow light
B. alternating red and yellow light
⚓ C. all-round white or yellow light
D. all-round white light only

040119/RR00087   **RULE 34 (b) (iii)**
INLAND ONLY Which statement is TRUE concerning the light used for maneuvering signals?
A. It must be an all-round light.
B. It must be synchronized with the whistle.
C. It may be white or yellow.
⚓ D. All of the above

040120/RR00727   **RULE 34 (c) (i)**
INLAND ONLY Maneuvering signals shall be sounded on INLAND waters by _____.
⚓ A. power-driven vessels overtaking and in sight of one another
B. all vessels meeting or crossing at a distance within half a mile of each other and not in sight of one another
C. all vessels when meeting, crossing, or overtaking and in sight of one another
D. power-driven vessels crossing at a distance within half a mile of each other and NOT in sight of one another

040121/RR00216   **RULE 34 (c) (i)**
INLAND ONLY Signals shall be sounded by a power-driven vessel intending to overtake _____.
A. any vessel when both are in sight of one another
⚓ B. another power-driven vessel when both power-driven vessels are in sight of one another
C. another power-driven vessel only when within half a mile of that power-driven vessel
D. any vessel when within half a mile of that vessel

040122/RR00094   **RULE 34 (c) (i) - (ii), (d)**
INLAND ONLY You are overtaking another power-driven vessel and sound a whistle signal indicating that you intend to pass the vessel along her starboard side. If the other vessel answers your signal with five short and rapid blasts, you should _____.
⚓ A. not overtake the other vessel until both vessels exchange the same passing signal
B. sound five short and rapid blasts and pass along her starboard side
C. pass the other vessel along her starboard side
D. not overtake the other vessel until she sounds another five short and rapid blast signal

040123/RR00008   **RULE 34 (c) (i)**
INLAND ONLY If you were coming up on another power-driven vessel from dead astern and desired to overtake on the other vessel's starboard side, which whistle signal would you sound?
A. two short blasts
⚓ B. One short blast
C. Two prolonged blasts followed by two short blasts
D. One prolonged blast

040124/RR00025   **RULE 34 (c) (i); RULE 9 (e) (i)**
INLAND ONLY In a narrow channel, a power-driven vessel desiring to overtake another power-driven vessel on the other vessel's starboard side will sound a whistle signal of _____.
A. two prolonged blasts followed by two short blasts
B. two short blasts
C. two prolonged blasts followed by one short blast
⚓ D. one short blast

040125/RR00101   **RULE 34 (c) (i); RULE 9 (e) (i)**
INLAND ONLY You are overtaking another power-driven vessel in a narrow channel. The other vessel will have to move to allow you to pass. You wish to overtake the other vessel on her starboard side. Your first whistle signal should be _____.
A. two short blasts
B. two prolonged blasts followed by one short blast
C. two prolonged blasts followed by two short blasts
⚓ D. one short blast

040126/RR00061   **RULE 34 (c) (i); RULE 9 (e) (i)**
INLAND ONLY Your power-driven vessel is overtaking another power-driven vessel in a narrow channel. You wish to overtake her on her starboard side. You should sound a whistle signal of _____.
A. one prolonged and one short blast
⚓ B. one short blast
C. at least five short blasts
D. two prolonged blasts followed by one short blast

040127/RR00107   **RULE 34 (c) (i)**
INLAND ONLY A power-driven vessel intends to overtake another power-driven vessel on the overtaken vessel's port side. What whistle signal should be sounded in order to state this intention?
A. 2 prolonged and 2 short blasts
B. 1 short blast
⚓ C. 2 short blasts
D. 1 prolonged and 1 short blast

040128/RR00065   **RULE 34 (c) (i)**

INLAND ONLY A power-driven vessel intends to overtake another power-driven vessel on the overtaken vessel's port side. Which whistle signal should be sounded in order to state this intention?

⚓ A. 2 short blasts
    B. 2 prolonged and 1 short blasts
    C. 1 short blast
    D. 2 prolonged and 2 short blasts

040129/RR00028   **RULE 34 (c) (i); RULE 9 (e) (i)**

INLAND ONLY A power-driven vessel overtaking another in a narrow channel, and wishing to pass on the other vessel's port side, would sound a whistle signal of _____.

    A. one short blast
    B. two prolonged blasts followed by two short blasts
    C. two prolonged blasts followed by one short blast
⚓ D. two short blasts

040130/RR00011   **RULE 34 (c) (i)**

INLAND ONLY When you are overtaking another power-driven vessel and desire to pass on her left or port hand, you should sound _____.

⚓ A. two short blasts
    B. two prolonged blasts followed by two short blasts
    C. one short blast
    D. one long blast

040131/RR00045   **RULE 34 (c) (i); RULE 9 (e) (i)**

INLAND ONLY You are overtaking another power-driven vessel in a narrow channel, and you wish to overtake on the other vessel's port side. You will sound a whistle signal of _____.

    A. two prolonged blasts followed by one short blast
    B. two prolonged blasts followed by two short blasts
⚓ C. two short blasts
    D. one short blast

040132/RR00108   **RULE 34 (c) (i); RULE 9 (e) (i)**

INLAND ONLY You are overtaking another power-driven vessel in a narrow channel. The other vessel will have to move to allow you to pass. You wish to overtake the other vessel and leave her on your starboard side. Your FIRST whistle signal should be _____.

    A. two prolonged blasts followed by one short blast
⚓ B. two short blasts
    C. one short blast
    D. two prolonged blasts followed by two short blasts

040133/RR00105   **RULE 34 (c) (i); RULE 9 (e) (i)**

INLAND ONLY You are overtaking another power-driven vessel in a narrow channel. The other vessel will have to move to allow you to pass. You wish to overtake the other vessel and leave her on your starboard side. Your first whistle signal should be _____.

    A. one short blast
    B. two prolonged blasts followed by two short blasts
    C. two prolonged blasts followed by one short blast
⚓ D. two short blasts

040134/RR00246   **RULE 34 (c) (i) - (ii); RULE 9 (e) (i)**

INLAND ONLY You are on power-driven vessel "A" in a narrow channel as shown in illustration D032RR below. power-driven vessel "B" sounds two short blasts. What signal should you sound if you are in agreement? See DIAGRAM D032RR

    A. not answer the whistle signals from vessel "B"
    B. sound two prolonged followed by two short blasts
⚓ C. sound two short blasts
    D. None of the above

040135/RR00106   **RULE 34 (c) (i) - (ii), (d)**

INLAND ONLY You are overtaking another power-driven vessel and sound a whistle signal indicating that you intend to pass the vessel along her starboard side. If the other vessel answers your signal with five short and rapid blasts, you should _____.

    A. sound five short and rapid blasts and pass along her starboard side
    B. pass the other vessel along her starboard side
    C. not overtake the other vessel until she sounds another five short and rapid blast signal
⚓ D. not overtake the other vessel until both vessels exchange the same passing signal

040136/RR00042   **RULE 34 (c) (ii)**

INLAND ONLY You are underway in a narrow channel, and are being overtaken by another power-driven vessel. The overtaking vessel sounds the signal indicating his intention to pass you on your starboard side. You signal your agreement by sounding _____.

⚓ A. one short blast
    B. two prolonged blasts
    C. one prolonged, one short, one prolonged, and one short blast in that order
    D. two prolonged followed by two short blasts

040137/RR00235   **RULE 34 (c) (ii)**
INLAND ONLY Vessel "A" is power-driven and overtaking power-driven vessel "B" as shown in illustration D017RR below and will pass without changing course. What signal should vessel "A" sound? See DIAGRAM D017RR
A. one short blast
⚓ B. two short blasts
C. no signal
D. one prolonged blast

040138/RR00096   **RULE 34 (e), (a)**
INLAND ONLY You are approaching a sharp bend in a river. You have sounded a prolonged blast and it has been answered by a vessel on the other side of the bend. Which statement is TRUE?
A. No further whistle signals are necessary.
⚓ B. If power-driven, both vessels must exchange passing signals when in sight and passing within one-half mile of each other.
C. Both vessels must immediately sound passing signals whether or not they are in sight of each other.
D. The vessel downriver must stop her engines and navigate with caution.

040139/RR00049   **RULE 34 (g)**
INLAND ONLY A power-driven vessel, when leaving a dock or berth, is required to sound _____.
A. no signal is required.
B. four short blasts
C. one long blast
⚓ D. one prolonged blast

040140/RR00150   **RULE 34 (g)**
INLAND ONLY A power-driven vessel, when leaving a dock or berth, must sound what signal?
A. No signal is required.
B. Three short blasts
C. A long blast
⚓ D. A prolonged blast

040141/RR00082   **RULE 34 (g)**
INLAND ONLY A vessel leaving a dock or berth must sound a prolonged blast of the whistle only if _____.
A. her engines are going astern
⚓ B. she is a power-driven vessel
C. other vessels can be seen approaching
D. visibility is restricted

040142/RR00002   **RULE 34 (g)**
INLAND ONLY What is the required whistle signal for a power-driven vessel leaving a dock or berth?
A. Two prolonged blasts
B. One short blast
⚓ C. One prolonged blast
D. Two short blasts

040143/RR00086   **RULE 34 (g)**
INLAND ONLY What is the whistle signal used to indicate a power-driven vessel leaving a dock?
A. No signal is necessary
B. Three short blasts
⚓ C. One prolonged blast
D. One short blast

040144/RR00093   **RULE 34 (g)**
INLAND ONLY While underway in a harbor you hear a vessel sound a prolonged blast. This signal indicates that this vessel _____.
⚓ A. is moving from a dock
B. is backing her engines
C. is at anchor
D. desires to overtake your vessel

040145/RR00014   **RULE 34 (g)**
INLAND ONLY You have made your vessel up to a tow and are moving from a pier out into the main channel. Your engines are turning ahead. What whistle signal should you sound?
A. Three long blasts
⚓ B. One prolonged blast
C. One prolonged and two short blasts
D. Five or more short rapid blasts

040146/RR00030   **RULE 34 (g), (a)**
INLAND ONLY Which signal must a power-driven vessel give, in addition to one prolonged blast, when backing out of a berth with another vessel in sight 0.5 nm away?
A. 1 blast
B. 2 short blasts
⚓ C. 3 short blasts
D. no additional signal

040147/RR00060   **RULE 34 (h); (a) (ii)**
INLAND ONLY Two power-driven vessels are meeting on a clear day and will pass less than half a mile apart. In this situation whistle signals _____.
A. must be exchanged
B. must be exchanged only if course changes are necessary by either vessel
C. may be exchanged
⚓ D. must be exchanged if passing agreements have not been made by radio

040148/RR00041   **RULE 34 (h)**
INLAND ONLY Two vessels in a crossing situation have reached agreement by radiotelephone as to the intentions of the other. In this situation, whistle signals are _____.
A. required when crossing within one mile
B. required
C. required if crossing within half a mile
⚓ D. not required, but may be sounded

040149/RR00097 **RULE 34 (h)**
INLAND ONLY Which statement is TRUE concerning a passing agreement made by radiotelephone?
- A. A vessel which has made such an agreement must also sound whistle signals.
- B. Such an agreement is prohibited by the Rules.
- ⚓ C. If agreement is reached by radiotelephone, whistle signals are optional.
- D. Whistle signals must still be exchanged when passing within half a mile of each other.

040150/RR00022 **RULE 34 (h), (a) (i)**
INLAND ONLY You are crossing the course of another vessel which is to your starboard. You have reached an agreement by radiotelephone to pass astern of the other vessel. You MUST _____.
- A. sound one short blast
- B. sound two short blasts
- C. change course to starboard
- ⚓ D. None of the above

040151/RR00032 **RULE 34 (h), (c) (i); RULE 9 (e) (i)**
INLAND ONLY You are overtaking a power-driven vessel in a narrow channel and wish to leave her on your starboard side. You may _____.
- A. proceed to overtake her without sounding whistle signals
- ⚓ B. attempt to contact her on the radiotelephone to arrange for the passage
- C. sound four short blasts
- D. All of the above

040152/RR00005 **RULE 34 (h), (c) (i); RULE 9 (e) (i)**
INLAND ONLY You are overtaking a power-driven vessel in a narrow channel and wish to leave her on your starboard side. You may _____.
- A. sound five short blasts
- ⚓ B. attempt to contact her on the radiotelephone to arrange for the passage
- C. proceed to overtake her without sounding whistle signals
- D. All of the above

040153/RR00073 **RULE 34 (h), (c) (i); RULE 9 (e) (i)**
INLAND ONLY You are overtaking another power-driven vessel in a narrow channel and wish to leave her on your starboard side. You may _____.
- A. sound four short blasts
- B. sound one short blast
- C. overtake her without sounding whistle signals
- ⚓ D. attempt to contact her on the radiotelephone to arrange for the passage

040154/RR00239 **RULE 34 (h)**
INLAND ONLY Vessels "A" and "B" are meeting on a river as shown in illustration D029RR below and will pass 1/4 mile apart. Which statement is TRUE? See DIAGRAM D029RR
- ⚓ A. The vessels may reach agreement by radiotelephone and sound no whistle signal.
- B. The vessels must exchange one blast whistle signals and pass starboard to starboard
- C. The vessels must exchange two blast whistle signals and pass port to port.
- D. Both vessels should continue on course and pass without sounding any whistle signals.

040155/RR00241 **RULE 34 (h)**
INLAND ONLY Vessels "A" and "B" are meeting on a river as shown in illustration D029RR below and will pass 1/4 mile apart. Which statement is TRUE? See DIAGRAM D029RR
- ⚓ A. If a passing agreement is reached by radiotelephone, whistle signals are optional, and the vessels should pass starboard to starboard as agreed.
- B. Whistle signals must be exchanged in all cases when passing within one half mile of each other.
- C. The vessels should pass port to port and must sound whistle signals only if either vessel changes course.
- D. The vessels should exchange two blast signals and pass port to port.

040156/RR00374 **RULE 34 (h)**
INLAND ONLY Vessels "A" and "B" are meeting on a river as shown in illustration D029RR below and will pass 1/4 mile apart. Which statement is TRUE? See DIAGRAM D029RR
- A. Whistle signals must be exchanged in all situations when passing within one half mile.
- B. The vessels should exchange two blast whistle signals and pass port to port.
- C. The vessels should pass port to port and must sound whistle signals only if either vessel changes course.
- ⚓ D. If a passing agreement is reached by radiotelephone whistle signals are optional.

040157/RR00258   **RULE 34 (h)**
INLAND ONLY Vessels "A" and "B" are meeting on a river as shown in illustration D041RR below and will pass 1/4 mile apart. Which statement is TRUE? See DIAGRAM D041RR
A. If a passing agreement is reached by radiotelephone whistle signals are still required.
B. Whistle signals must be exchanged in all situations when passing within one half mile.
C. If a passing agreement is reached by radiotelephone, whistle signals are optional.
D. None of the above

RULE 35 - SOUND SIGNALS IN RESTRICTED VISIBILITY

040158/RR00110   **RULE 35 (g), (l)**
INLAND ONLY Which statement is TRUE concerning the fog signal of a sailing vessel 25 meters in length, anchored in a "special anchorage area" approved by the Secretary?
A. The vessel shall sound three blasts on the whistle every 2 minutes.
B. The vessel shall sound one blast of the whistle every 2 minutes.
C. The vessel is not required to sound a fog signal.
D. The vessel shall ring a bell for 5 seconds every minute.

040159/RR00048   **RULE 35 (l) (i), (ii)**
INLAND ONLY Which statement is TRUE concerning the fog signal of a vessel 15 meters in length, anchored in a "special anchorage area" approved by the Secretary?
A. The vessel shall sound three blasts on the whistle every 2 minutes.
B. The vessel shall sound one blast of the foghorn every 2 minutes.
C. The vessel shall ring a bell for 5 seconds every minute.
D. The vessel is not required to sound a fog signal.

040160/RR00386   **RULE 35 (l) (ii)**
INLAND ONLY Which statement is TRUE concerning the fog signal of a barge 35 meters in length, anchored in a "special anchorage area" approved by the Secretary?
A. The vessel is not required to sound a fog signal.
B. The vessel shall sound three blasts on the whistle every 2 minutes.
C. The vessel shall sound one blast of the whistle every 2 minutes.
D. The vessel shall ring a bell for 5 seconds every minute.

040161/RR00385   **RULE 35 (l) (ii)**
INLAND ONLY Which statement is TRUE concerning the fog signal of a canal boat 25 meters in length, anchored in a "special anchorage area" approved by the Secretary?
A. The vessel is not required to sound a fog signal.
B. The vessel shall ring a bell for 5 seconds every minute.
C. The vessel shall sound three blasts on the whistle every 2 minutes.
D. The vessel shall sound one blast of the whistle every 2 minutes.

PART E ANNEXES

ANNEX V - PILOT RULES

040162/RR00047   **ANNEX V; 33 CFR 88.05 (a), (b)**
INLAND ONLY A flashing blue light is used to identify which of the following vessels?
A. law enforcement vessels
B. U.S. submarines
C. dredge pipelines on trestles
D. air-cushion vessels in the nondisplacement mode

040163/RR00100   **ANNEX V; 33 CFR 88.05 (a), (b)**
INLAND ONLY Which light(s) are permitted ONLY for law enforcement vessels?
A. a flashing blue light
B. an alternately flashing red and yellow light
C. two red lights in a vertical line
D. a flashing yellow light

040164/RR00006   **ANNEX V; 33 CFR 88.05 (a), (b)**
INLAND ONLY Which of the following is indicated by a vessel displaying a flashing blue light?
A. a law enforcement vessel
B. a vessel transferring dangerous cargo
C. a vessel engaged in a race
D. a work boat

040165/RR00026   **ANNEX V; 33 CFR 88.05 (a), (b)**
INLAND ONLY Which of the following may be displayed by a law enforcement boat?
A. flashing red light
B. flashing amber light
C. flashing blue light
D. blue flag

040166/RR00057   **ANNEX V; 33 CFR 88.05 (a), (b)**
INLAND ONLY While underway during the day you sight a small motorboat showing a flashing blue light. What does the blue light indicate?
A. law enforcement boat
B. boat involved in a race
C. Coast Guard Auxiliary Vessel on regatta patrol
D. rescue boat

040167/RR00352   ANNEX V; 33 CFR 88.07 (a), (b)
INLAND ONLY A commercial vessel engaged in public safety activities may display a(n) identity light(s). Which of the following is appropriate for these activities?
A. flashing yellow light
B. flashing blue light
⚓ C. alternately flashing red and yellow light
D. alternately flashing blue and red light

040168/RR00138   ANNEX V; 33 CFR 88.07 (a), (b)
INLAND ONLY A law enforcement vessel patrolling a marine regatta may exhibit a flashing blue light or which of the following alternates?
A. two amber lights in a horizontal line
B. a fixed green light over a red flashing light
⚓ C. an alternately flashing red and yellow light
D. a high intensity flashing white light (strobe)

040169/RR09144   ANNEX V; 33 CFR 88.07 (b);
33CRF 88.07 (a)
INLAND ONLY A vessel engaged in public safety activities may display an alternately flashing red and yellow light. This special light may be used by a vessel engaged in which of the following?
⚓ A. firefighting
B. submarine operations
C. law enforcement
D. river bank protection

040170/RR00142   ANNEX V; 33 CFR 88.07 (a), (b);
RULE 20 (b)
INLAND ONLY The special light for a vessel engaged in public safety activities must meet which of the following requirements?
A. be as far forward as possible
⚓ B. not interfere with the visibility of the navigation lights
C. not be visible more than 22 1/2 degrees abaft the beam
D. be on top of the mast or highest structure of the vessel

040171/RR00141   ANNEX V; 33 CFR 88.07 (a), (b);
RULE 15; RULE 17
INLAND ONLY You are the stand-on vessel in an overtaking situation. The other vessel is showing an alternately flashing red-and-yellow light. What action should you take?
A. Give-way
B. Heave to
⚓ C. Stand on
D. Alter course to assist

040172/RR00228   ANNEX V; 33 CFR 88.07 (a), (b)
INLAND ONLY A vessel engaged in public safety activities may display an alternately flashing red and yellow light. This special light may be used by a vessel engaged in which of the following?
A. river bank protection
B. law enforcement
⚓ C. patrolling a regatta
D. a pair of trawlers hauling nets

040173/RR09143   ANNEX V; 33 CFR 88.07 (b);
33CRF 88.07 (a)
INLAND ONLY A vessel engaged in public safety activities may display an alternately flashing red and yellow light. Which of the following vessels may exhibit this special light?
A. a vessel restricted in her ability to maneuver
B. a vessel engaged in river bank protection
⚓ C. a vessel engaged in search and rescue
D. a vessel not under command

040174/RR00163   ANNEX V; 33 CFR 88.07 (a), (b)
INLAND ONLY Which of the following may be displayed by a commercial vessel engaged in public safety activities?
A. flashing blue light
B. alternately flashing blue and red light
⚓ C. alternately flashing red and yellow light
D. flashing yellow light

040175/RR09145   ANNEX V; 33 CRF 88.07 (a)
INLAND ONLY You sight a vessel displaying an alternating red and yellow light. What does this light indicate?
A. a vessel restricted in its ability to maneuver
⚓ B. a vessel engaged in public safety activities
C. a law enforcement vessel
D. a vessel in distress

PART A GENERAL

RULE 1 - APPLICATION

040176/RR09102 **RULE 1 (e);**
RULE 23 (d) (iii) International; RULE 23 (d) Inland
BOTH INTERNATIONAL & INLAND The masthead light may be displaced from the centerline on which of the following vessels?
A. a power-driven vessel 12 meters in length
B. an air-cushion vessel in nondisplacement mode
⚓ C. a vessel of special construction
D. a vessel engaged in trolling

040177/RR04091 **RULE 1 Footnote**
BOTH INTERNATIONAL & INLAND An authorized light to assist in the identification of submarines operating on the surface is a(n) _____.
A. flashing sidelight
B. blue rotating light
⚓ C. intermittent flashing amber/yellow light
D. flashing white light

040178/RR04501 **RULE 1 Footnote**
BOTH INTERNATIONAL & INLAND For identification purposes at night, U.S. Navy submarines on the surface may display an intermittent flashing light of which color?
A. White
B. Blue
C. Red
⚓ D. Amber (yellow)

040179/RR04825 **RULE 1 Footnote**
BOTH INTERNATIONAL & INLAND What is a light signal authorized by the Secretary of the Navy as an additional navigational light for a ship of war?
A. Two yellow lights in a vertical line for a carrier launching aircraft
⚓ B. Intermittent flashing amber beacon for submarines
C. Green masthead and yardarm lights for a vessel engaged in mineclearing operations
D. Yellow flares indicating torpedo firing exercises

040180/RR04678 **RULE 1 Footnote**
BOTH INTERNATIONAL & INLAND Which is a light signal authorized by the Secretary of the Navy as an additional navigational light for a ship of war?
A. Green masthead and yardarm lights indicating mine clearance operations
⚓ B. Intermittent flashing amber (yellow) beacon for submarines
C. Yellow flares indicating torpedo firing exercises
D. Red-white-red lights in a vertical line for a carrier, launching aircraft

RULE 2 - RESPONSIBILITY

040181/RR04874 **RULE 2 (a)**
BOTH INTERNATIONAL & INLAND What would be a "special circumstance" under the Rules?
A. Vessel at anchor
B. Speed in fog
C. Two vessels meeting
⚓ D. More than two vessels crossing

040182/RR04543 **RULE 2 (a)**
BOTH INTERNATIONAL & INLAND Which situation would be a "special circumstance" under the Rules?
⚓ A. More than two vessels meeting
B. Speed in fog
C. Two vessels crossing
D. Vessel at anchor

040183/RR04090 **RULE 2 (b)**
BOTH INTERNATIONAL & INLAND According to the Navigation Rules, you may depart from the Rules when _____.
A. out of sight of land
⚓ B. you are in immediate danger
C. no vessels are in sight visually
D. no vessels are visible on radar

040184/RR04705 **RULE 2 (b)**
BOTH INTERNATIONAL & INLAND In complying with the Rules, of what must the mariner take due regard?
A. Radar information about nearby vessels
B. Limited backing power of his vessel
C. The occupation of the other vessel, if known
⚓ D. All of the above

RULE 3 - DEFINITIONS

040185/RR04579 **RULE 3 (a)**
BOTH INTERNATIONAL & INLAND As defined in the Rules, the term "vessel" includes _____.
A. seaplanes
B. nondisplacement craft
C. barges
⚓ D. All of the above

040186/RR04411 **RULE 3 (a)**
BOTH INTERNATIONAL & INLAND For the purpose of the Rules, except where otherwise required, the term _____.
A. "vessel restricted in her ability to maneuver" includes fishing vessels
B. "vessel engaged in fishing" includes a vessel fishing with trolling lines
⚓ C. "vessel" includes seaplanes
D. "seaplane" includes nondisplacement craft

040187/RR04024   **RULE 3 (a)**
BOTH INTERNATIONAL & INLAND The word "vessel", in the Rules, includes _____.
⚓ A. nondisplacement craft
B. a barge permanently affixed to the shore
C. a drilling unit attached to the Outer Continental Shelf
D. All of the above

040188/RR04835   **RULE 3 (a)**
BOTH INTERNATIONAL & INLAND The word "vessel", in the Rules, includes which of the following?
A. a drilling unit attached to the Outer Continental Shelf
B. a barge permanently affixed to the shore
⚓ C. wing in ground craft
D. All of the above

040189/RR04467   **RULE 3 (a)**
BOTH INTERNATIONAL & INLAND Under the Rules, the term "vessel" includes _____.
A. non-self-propelled raft
B. hovercrafts
C. seaplanes
⚓ D. All of the above

040190/RR04135   **RULE 3 (b)**
BOTH INTERNATIONAL & INLAND A vessel is being propelled both by sail and by engines. Under the Rules, the vessel is _____.
⚓ A. a power-driven vessel
B. a sail vessel
C. not covered under any category
D. a "special circumstance" vessel

040191/RR04532   **RULE 3 (b)**
BOTH INTERNATIONAL & INLAND The term "power-driven vessel" refers to any vessel _____.
A. traveling at a speed greater than that of the current
B. making way against the current
C. with propelling machinery onboard whether in use or not
⚓ D. with propelling machinery in use

040192/RR04831   **RULE 3 (b)**
BOTH INTERNATIONAL & INLAND Which craft is a "power-driven vessel" under the Rules of the Road?
A. A trawler on her way to the fishing grounds
B. An auxiliary sailing vessel, using her engine
C. A canoe propelled by a small outboard motor
⚓ D. All of the above

040193/RR04423   **RULE 3 (d)**
BOTH INTERNATIONAL & INLAND Which statement is TRUE concerning a "vessel engaged in fishing"?
A. The vessel sounds the same fog signal as a vessel underway, making no way.
⚓ B. The vessel may be using nets, lines, or trawls.
C. The vessel may be trolling.
D. The vessel shows 2 lights in a vertical line, white over red.

040194/RR04054   **RULE 3 (d)**
BOTH INTERNATIONAL & INLAND A vessel is "engaged in fishing" when _____.
⚓ A. she is using fishing apparatus which restricts her maneuverability
B. she has any fishing gear on board
C. her gear extends more than 100 meters from the vessel
D. she is using any type of gear, other than lines

040195/RR04314   **RULE 3 (d)**
BOTH INTERNATIONAL & INLAND In order for a vessel to be "engaged in fishing" she must be _____.
A. underway
B. using a seine of some type
⚓ C. using gear which restricts her maneuverability
D. using gear which extends more than 50 meters outboard

040196/RR04521   **RULE 3 (d)**
BOTH INTERNATIONAL & INLAND According to the Navigation Rules, all of the following are engaged in fishing EXCEPT a vessel _____.
⚓ A. trolling
B. setting nets
C. trawling
D. using a dredge net

040197/RR04030   **RULE 3 (f)**
BOTH INTERNATIONAL & INLAND The NAVIGATION RULES define a "vessel not under command" as a vessel which _____.
A. from the nature of her work is unable to keep out of the way of another vessel
B. is moored, aground or anchored in a fairway
C. by taking action contrary to the rules has created a special circumstance situation
⚓ D. through some exceptional circumstance is unable to maneuver as required by the rules

040198/RR04195   **RULE 3 (f)**
BOTH INTERNATIONAL & INLAND All of the following vessels are "restricted in their ability to maneuver" EXCEPT a vessel _____.
A. laying a pipeline
⚓ B. not under command
C. dredging
D. mineclearing

040199/RR04034   **RULE 3 (g)**
BOTH INTERNATIONAL & INLAND A vessel "restricted in her ability to maneuver" is one which _____.
A. through some exceptional circumstance is unable to maneuver as required by the rules
B. due to adverse weather conditions is unable to maneuver as required by the rules
C. has lost steering and is unable to maneuver
⚓ D. from the nature of her work is unable to maneuver as required by the rules

040200/RR04381   **RULE 3 (g)**
BOTH INTERNATIONAL & INLAND A vessel that is defined as "restricted in her ability to maneuver" is unable to keep out of the way of another vessel due to _____.
A. some exceptional circumstances
B. a danger of navigation
⚓ C. the nature of her work
D. her draft

040201/RR04836   **RULE 3 (g)**
BOTH INTERNATIONAL & INLAND By definition which vessel is unable to keep out of the way of another vessel?
A. Vessel towing
B. Sailing vessel
⚓ C. Vessel restricted in her ability to maneuver
D. Vessel engaged in fishing

040202/RR04670   **RULE 3 (g)**
BOTH INTERNATIONAL & INLAND What determines if a vessel is "restricted in her ability to maneuver"?
A. Whether or not all of the vessel's control equipment is in working order
⚓ B. Whether the nature of the vessel's work limits maneuverability required by the Rules
C. The vessel's draft in relation to the available depth of water
D. Whether or not the vessel is the give-way vessel in a meeting situation

040203/RR04181   **RULE 3 (g), (c)**
BOTH INTERNATIONAL & INLAND According to the Rules, which vessel is NOT "restricted in her ability to maneuver"?
⚓ A. A sailing vessel
B. A vessel servicing a navigation marker
C. A vessel mineclearing
D. A vessel dredging

040204/RR05150   **RULE 3 (g) (i); RULE 10 (k)**
BOTH INTERNATIONAL & INLAND There are two classes of vessels which do not have to comply with the rule regarding traffic separation schemes, to the extent necessary to carry out their work. One of those is a vessel _____.
A. engaged in fishing
B. towing another
C. on pilotage duty
⚓ D. servicing a navigational aid

040205/RR04715   **RULE 3 (g) (ii)**
BOTH INTERNATIONAL & INLAND What is a "vessel restricted in her ability to maneuver"?
A. A deep-draft vessel that can only navigate in a dredged channel
B. A vessel fishing with a bottom trawl that must remain on course
C. A large tanker that is being towed as a dead ship to dry dock
⚓ D. A vessel laying revetment mats to provide bank protection along a channel

040206/RR04153   **RULE 3 (g) (iii)**
BOTH INTERNATIONAL & INLAND A vessel transferring cargo while underway is classified by the Rules as a vessel _____.
⚓ A. restricted in her ability to maneuver
B. not under command
C. constrained by her draft
D. in special circumstances

040207/RR04433   **RULE 3 (g) (iii), (g) (i), (g) (iv), (b)**
BOTH INTERNATIONAL & INLAND Which vessel is NOT to be regarded as "restricted in her ability to maneuver"?
A. A vessel transferring provisions while underway
B. A vessel launching aircraft
⚓ C. A pushing vessel and a vessel being pushed when connected in a composite unit
D. A vessel servicing a navigation mark

040208/RR04366   **RULE 3 (g) (v)**
BOTH INTERNATIONAL & INLAND Which vessel is a "vessel restricted in her ability to maneuver" under the Rules?
  A. A vessel mineclearing
  B. A vessel engaged in fishing
  C. A vessel not under command
  D. A vessel at anchor

040209/RR04310   **RULE 3 (g) (v)**
BOTH INTERNATIONAL & INLAND Which vessel is to be regarded as a vessel "restricted in her ability to maneuver"?
  A. A vessel which has lost the use of her steering gear
  B. A vessel fishing with trawls
  C. A vessel with a draft of such depth that she cannot change her course
  D. A vessel engaged in mineclearing

040210/RR04538   **RULE 3 (g) (vi)**
BOTH INTERNATIONAL & INLAND What is a vessel "restricted in her ability to maneuver"?
  A. A vessel constrained by her draft
  B. A vessel underway in fog
  C. A vessel towing unable to deviate from her course
  D. A vessel not under command

040211/RR04842   **RULE 3 (i)**
BOTH INTERNATIONAL & INLAND Which vessel is "underway" according to the Rules?
  A. A vessel engaged in towing, not making way
  B. A pilot vessel at anchor
  C. A vessel made fast to a single point mooring buoy
  D. A vessel which has run aground

040212/RR04455   **RULE 3 (i)**
BOTH INTERNATIONAL & INLAND Which vessel is "underway" within the meaning of the Rules?
  A. A vessel tied tan offshore mooring buoy
  B. A vessel drifting with the engine stopped
  C. A vessel at anchor with the engine turning
  D. A vessel aground with the engine turning

040213/RR04844   **RULE 3 (j)**
BOTH INTERNATIONAL & INLAND What does the word "breadth" mean?
  A. Breadth at the uppermost continuous deck
  B. Molded breadth
  C. Breadth at the load waterline
  D. Greatest breadth

040214/RR04700   **RULE 3 (j)**
BOTH INTERNATIONAL & INLAND What does the word "length" refer to?
  A. Registered length
  B. Waterline length
  C. Length overall
  D. Length between the perpendiculars

040215/RR04845   **RULE 3 (j)**
BOTH INTERNATIONAL & INLAND Which of the following in illustration D086RR below represents the length of a vessel as defined by the Rules? See DIAGRAM D086RR
  A. A
  B. B
  C. C
  D. D

040216/RR04819   **RULE 3 (j)**
BOTH INTERNATIONAL & INLAND In illustration D087RR below, which represents the breadth as defined in the Rules? See DIAGRAM D087RR
  A. A
  B. B
  C. C
  D. D

040217/RR04832   **RULE 3 (k)**
BOTH INTERNATIONAL & INLAND A vessel is "in sight" of another vessel when she _____.
  A. can be observed visually from the other vessel
  B. can be observed by radar
  C. has determined that risk of collision exists
  D. is sounding a fog signal which can be heard on the other vessel

040218/RR04674   **RULE 3 (k)**
BOTH INTERNATIONAL & INLAND You are on watch in fog. Which vessel is "in sight"?
  A. A vessel that you can see from the bridge
  B. A vessel from which you can hear the fog signal
  C. A radar target of which you have determined the course and speed
  D. All of the above

040219/RR04088   **RULE 3 (l)**
BOTH INTERNATIONAL & INLAND The term "restricted visibility" as used in the Rules refers _____.
  A. to any condition where visibility is restricted
  B. only to fog
  C. to visibility where you cannot see shore
  D. only to visibility of less than one-half of a mile

PART B STEERING & SAILING RULES
SECTION SUBPART I
CONDUCT OF VESSELS
IN ANY CONDITION OF VISIBILITY

RULE 5 - LOOK-OUT

040220/RR04592 **RULE 5**
BOTH INTERNATIONAL & INLAND A proper look-out shall be maintained _____.
A. at night and during restricted visibility
B. only at night
C. only during restricted visibility
⚓ D. at all times

040221/RR04140 **RULE 5**
BOTH INTERNATIONAL & INLAND The rule regarding look-outs applies _____.
A. in restricted visibility
B. in heavy traffic
C. between dusk and dawn
⚓ D. All of the above

RULE 6 - SAFE SPEED

040222/RR04344 **RULE 6**
BOTH INTERNATIONAL & INLAND "safe speed" is defined as that speed where _____.
A. you are traveling slower than surrounding vessels
B. you can stop within your visibility range
⚓ C. you can take proper and effective action to avoid collision
D. no wake comes from your vessel

040223/RR04020 **RULE 6**
BOTH INTERNATIONAL & INLAND A vessel must proceed at a safe speed _____.
A. in congested waters
⚓ B. at all times
C. in restricted visibility
D. during darkness

040224/RR04622 **RULE 6**
BOTH INTERNATIONAL & INLAND The Navigation Rules state that a vessel shall be operated at a safe speed at all times so that she can be stopped within _____.
A. the distance of visibility
B. the distance that it would require for the propeller to go from full ahead to full astern
⚓ C. a distance appropriate to the existing circumstances and conditions
D. 1/2 the distance of visibility

040225/RR04058 **RULE 6 (a) (iii)**
BOTH INTERNATIONAL & INLAND Which factor is listed in the Rules as one which must be taken into account when determining safe speed?
A. The construction of the vessel
⚓ B. The maneuverability of the vessel
C. The experience of vessel personnel
D. All of the above must be taken into account.

040226/RR04609 **RULE 6 (a) (iv), (a) (vi), (a) (iii)**
BOTH INTERNATIONAL & INLAND In determining "safe speed", all of the following must be taken into account EXCEPT the _____.
A. draft of your vessel
⚓ B. maximum horsepower of your vessel
C. presence of background lights at night
D. maneuverability of your vessel

040227/RR04848 **RULE 6 (a) (v)**
BOTH INTERNATIONAL & INLAND The Rules state that certain factors are to be taken into account when determining safe speed. One of the factors is the _____.
A. maximum speed of your vessel
B. radio communications that are available
⚓ C. current
D. temperature

040228/RR04594 **RULE 6 (a) (v)**
BOTH INTERNATIONAL & INLAND The Rules state that certain factors are to be taken into account when determining safe speed. Those factors include _____.
A. aids to navigation that are available
B. maximum attainable speed of your vessel
⚓ C. state of wind, sea, and current, and the proximity of navigational hazards
D. temperature

040229/RR04847 **RULE 6 (b) (v)**
BOTH INTERNATIONAL & INLAND The rules require which factor to be taken into account when determining safe speed?
⚓ A. The location of vessels detected by radar
B. The experience of the vessel's crew
C. The construction of the vessel
D. All of the above

RULE 7 - RISK OF COLLISION

040230/RR04571 **RULE 7 (a)**
BOTH INTERNATIONAL & INLAND Risk of collision is considered to exist if _____.
A. a special circumstance situation is apparent
B. four vessels are nearby
C. a vessel has a steady bearing at a constant range
⚓ D. to here is any doubt that a risk of collision exists

040231/RR04861   RULE 7 (a); RULE 2 (a); RULE 5
BOTH INTERNATIONAL & INLAND When navigating in thick fog with the radar on, you should _____.

A. station the look-out in the wheelhouse to keep a continuous watch on the radar
B. secure the sounding of fog signals until a vessel closes within five miles
⚓ C. station a look-out as low down and far forward as possible
D. keep the radar on the shortest available range for early detection of approaching vessels

040232/RR04016   RULE 7 (a), (b)
BOTH INTERNATIONAL & INLAND Which statement is TRUE concerning a vessel equipped with operational radar?

A. The safe speed of such a vessel will likely be greater than that of vessels without radar.
B. The use of a radar excuses a vessel from the need of a look-out.
⚓ C. She must use this equipment to obtain early warning of risk of collision.
D. The radar equipment is only required to be used in restricted visibility.

040233/RR04379   RULE 7 (a), (b)
BOTH INTERNATIONAL & INLAND Which statement is TRUE concerning risk of collision?

A. Risk of collision exists if the vessels will pass within half a mile of each other.
B. Risk of collision never exists if the compass bearing of the other vessel is changing.
⚓ C. Proper use shall be made of radar equipment to determine risk of collision.
D. Risk of collision must be determined before any action can be taken by a vessel.

040234/RR04545   RULE 7 (a)
BOTH INTERNATIONAL & INLAND You are approaching another vessel and are not sure whether danger of collision exists. What must you assume?

⚓ A. to here is risk of collision
B. the other vessel is also in doubt
C. you are the give-way vessel
D. All of the above are correct.

040235/RR04862   RULE 7 (a); RULE 19 (e)
BOTH INTERNATIONAL & INLAND You are underway in thick fog. You have not determined if risk of collision exists. Which statement is TRUE?

A. The radar should always be kept on a short-range scale.
B. Fog signals are only required when a vessel is detected by radar.
⚓ C. Your speed must be reduced to bare steerageway.
D. A look-out is not required if the radar is on.

040236/RR04347   RULE 7 (b), (d) (i)
BOTH INTERNATIONAL & INLAND To determine if risk of collision exists, a vessel which is fitted with radar must use _____.

A. compass bearings
B. radar scanning
C. radar plotting
⚓ D. All of the above

040237/RR04322   RULE 7 (d) (i)
BOTH INTERNATIONAL & INLAND In which situation does a risk of collision exists?

A. A vessel is 22° abaft your port beam, range increasing, bearing is constant.
⚓ B. A vessel is on your starboard quarter, range decreasing, bearing is constant.
C. A vessel is 22° on your port bow, range increasing, bearing changing slightly to the right.
D. A vessel is broad on your starboard beam, range decreasing, bearing changing rapidly to the right.

040238/RR04301   RULE 7 (d) (i)
BOTH INTERNATIONAL & INLAND In which situation would risk of collision definitely exist?

A. A vessel is broad on your starboard beam, range decreasing, bearing changing rapidly to the right.
⚓ B. A vessel is on your starboard quarter, range decreasing, bearing is constant.
C. A vessel is 22 degrees on your port bow, range increasing, bearing changing slightly to the right.
D. A vessel is 22 degrees abaft your port beam, range increasing, bearing is constant.

040239/RR04478   RULE 7 (d) (i)
BOTH INTERNATIONAL & INLAND Risk of collision exists when an approaching vessel has a(n) _____.

A. decreasing bearing only
B. generally steady range and increasing bearing
C. increasing range and bearing
⚓ D. generally steady bearing and decreasing range

040240/RR04593   RULE 7 (d) (i) - (ii)
BOTH INTERNATIONAL & INLAND Risk of collision may be deemed to exist under which of the following situations?

A. if you observe both sidelights of a vessel ahead for an extended period of time
B. even when an appreciable bearing change is evident, particularly when approaching a vessel at close range
C. if the compass bearing of an approaching vessel does NOT appreciably change
⚓ D. All of the above

040241/RR04343   **RULE 7 (d) (i) - (ii)**
BOTH INTERNATIONAL & INLAND Risk of collision may exist _____.
A. if you observe both sidelights of a vessel ahead for an extended period of time
B. if the compass bearing of an approaching vessel does NOT appreciably change
C. even when an appreciable bearing change is evident, particularly when approaching a vessel at close range
D. All of the above

040242/RR04424   **RULE 7 (d) (i)**
BOTH INTERNATIONAL & INLAND The Rules state that risk of collision shall be deemed to exist _____.
A. if the bearing of an approaching vessel does not appreciably change
B. whenever a vessel crosses ahead of the intended track of another vessel
C. whenever two vessels approach from opposite directions
D. if one vessel approaches another so as to be overtaking

040243/RR04850   **RULE 7 (d) (i)**
BOTH INTERNATIONAL & INLAND The Rules state that risk of collision shall be deemed to exist _____.
A. if one vessel approaches another so as to be overtaking
B. if the bearing of an approaching vessel does not appreciably change
C. whenever a vessel crosses ahead of the intended track of another vessel
D. whenever two vessels are on opposite courses

040244/RR04435   **RULE 7 (d) (i), (b)**
BOTH INTERNATIONAL & INLAND Which procedure(s) shall be used to determine risk of collision?
A. Watching the compass bearing of an approaching vessel
B. Systematic observation of objects detected by radar
C. Long-range radar scanning
D. All of the above

040245/RR04279   **RULE 7 (d) (i)**
BOTH INTERNATIONAL & INLAND You are watching another vessel approach and her compass bearing is not changing. This means that _____.
A. a risk of collision exists
B. the other vessel is dead in the water
C. a special circumstances situation exists
D. you are the stand-on vessel

040246/RR04039   **RULE 7 (d) (i)**
BOTH INTERNATIONAL & INLAND You see another vessel approaching, and its compass bearing does not significantly change. This would indicate that _____.
A. you are the stand-on vessel
B. the other vessel is dead in the water
C. risk of collision exists
D. a special circumstances situation exists

040247/RR04526   **RULE 7 (d) (ii)**
BOTH INTERNATIONAL & INLAND Which statement is TRUE concerning risk of collision?
A. Risk of collision always exists when the compass bearing of an approaching vessel changes appreciably.
B. Risk of collision always exists when two vessels pass within one mile of each other.
C. The stand-on vessel must keep out of the way of the other vessel when risk of collision exists.
D. Risk of collision may exist when the compass bearing of an approaching vessel is changing appreciably.

RULE 8 - ACTION TO AVOID COLLISION

040248/RR04642   **RULE 8 (a); RULE 19 (d) (i)**
BOTH INTERNATIONAL & INLAND By radar alone, you detect a vessel ahead on a collision course, about 3 miles distant. Your radar plot shows this to be a meeting situation. You should _____.
A. turn to port
B. maintain course and speed and sound the danger signal
C. maintain course and speed and sound no signal
D. turn to starboard

040249/RR04497   **RULE 8 (a)**
BOTH INTERNATIONAL & INLAND What is a requirement for any action taken to avoid collision?
A. The action taken must include changing the speed of the vessel.
B. The action must be positive and made in ample time.
C. When in sight of another vessel, any action taken must be accompanied by sound signals.
D. All of the above

040250/RR04146   **RULE 8 (a)**
BOTH INTERNATIONAL & INLAND When taking action to avoid collision, you should _____.
A. not make any large speed changes
B. not make any large course changes
C. make sure the action is taken in enough time
D. All of the above

040251/RR04853   **RULE 8 (a), (b), (e);**
                                      RULE 15; RULE 34 (d)
BOTH INTERNATIONAL & INLAND You are approaching another vessel on crossing courses. She is about one mile distant and is on your starboard bow. You believe she will cross ahead of you but she sounds a whistle signal of five short blasts. You should _____.

A. answer the signal and hold course and speed
B. initiate a passing signal that will allow for a half mile clearance
⚓ C. make a large course change, and slow down if necessary
D. reduce speed slightly

040252/RR04075   **RULE 8 (a), (b), (e);**
                                      RULE 15; RULE 34 (d)
BOTH INTERNATIONAL & INLAND You are approaching another vessel. She is about one mile distant and is on your starboard bow. You believe she will cross ahead of you. She then sounds a whistle signal of five short blasts. You should _____.

⚓ A. make a large course change, and slow down if necessary
B. wait for another whistle signal from the other vessel
C. reduce speed slightly to make sure she will have room to pass
D. answer the signal and hold course and speed

040253/RR04400   **RULE 8 (c)**
BOTH INTERNATIONAL & INLAND When action to avoid a close-quarters situation is taken, a course change alone may be the most effective action provided that _____.
⚓ A. it is a large course change
B. the course change is to starboard
C. it is done in a succession of small course changes
D. it is NOT done too early

040254/RR04856   **RULE 8 (c)**
BOTH INTERNATIONAL & INLAND When in sight of another vessel and there is sufficient sea room, any action taken to avoid collision must _____.
⚓ A. not result in another close-quarters situation
B. be accompanied by sound signals
C. include a speed change
D. All of the above

040255/RR04581   **RULE 8 (e)**
BOTH INTERNATIONAL & INLAND A vessel shall slacken her speed, stop, or reverse her engines, if necessary, to _____.
A. be stopped in an appropriate distance
B. avoid collision
C. allow more time to assess the situation
⚓ D. All of the above

040256/RR04855   **RULE 8 (e)**
BOTH INTERNATIONAL & INLAND Under the Rules, any vessel may slacken her speed, stop, or reverse her engines to _____.
⚓ A. allow more time to assess the situation
B. attract the attention of another vessel
C. create a crossing situation
D. All of the above

RULE 9 - NARROW CHANNELS

IF THE STEM OF A QUESTION CONTAINS THE DESCRIPTIVE QUALIFIER "NARROW CHANNEL", THEN THE QUESTION SHOULD BE ANSWERED PURSUANT TO THE PROVISIONS OF RULE 9, INTERNATIONAL AND/OR INLAND AS APPLICABLE.

040257/RR04617   **RULE 9 (a) International;**
                                      RULE 9 (a) (i) Inland;
BOTH INTERNATIONAL & INLAND A vessel proceeding along a narrow channel shall _____.
A. not overtake any vessels within the channel
B. when nearing a bend in the channel, sound a long blast of the whistle
C. avoid crossing the channel at right angles
⚓ D. keep as near as safe and practicable to the limit of the channel on her starboard side

040258/RR04858   **RULE 9 (a) International;**
                                      RULE 9 (a) (i) Inland
BOTH INTERNATIONAL & INLAND When underway in a channel, you should if safe and practicable _____.
A. stay near the middle of the channel
B. keep to the starboard side of any vessels you meet
C. exchange whistle signals with any other vessels in the channel
⚓ D. keep to the side of the channel which lies to your starboard

040259/RR04095   **RULE 9 (a) International;**
                                      RULE 9 (a) (i) Inland
BOTH INTERNATIONAL & INLAND When underway in a channel, you should keep to the _____.

A. side of the channel that has the widest turns
B. port side of the channel
C. middle of the channel
⚓ D. starboard side of the channel

040260/RR04334   **RULE 9 (b)**

BOTH INTERNATIONAL & INLAND In narrow channels, vessels of less than what length shall not impede the safe passage of vessels which can navigate only inside that channel?

A. 50 meters
B. 100 meters
C. 65 meters
⚓ D. 20 meters

040261/RR04505   **RULE 9 (b)**

BOTH INTERNATIONAL & INLAND Vessels of less than what length may not impede the passage of other vessels which can safely navigate only within a narrow channel or fairway?

A. 10 meters
⚓ B. 20 meters
C. 30 meters
D. 40 meters

040262/RR04306   **RULE 9 (b)**

BOTH INTERNATIONAL & INLAND Which vessel is directed not to impede the passage of a vessel which can only navigate inside a narrow channel?

A. A vessel not under command
B. A vessel engaged in surveying
⚓ C. A vessel of less than 20 meters in length
D. All of the above

040263/RR04442   **RULE 9 (b)**

BOTH INTERNATIONAL & INLAND Which vessel shall not impede the passage of a vessel which can only navigate inside a narrow channel?

⚓ A. A vessel of less than 20 meters in length
B. A vessel not under command
C. A vessel engaged in surveying
D. All of the above

040264/RR04619   **RULE 9 (b) - (c)**

BOTH INTERNATIONAL & INLAND Which vessel is NOT to impede the passage of a vessel which can only navigate safely within a narrow channel?

A. Any sailing vessel
B. A vessel engaged in fishing
C. Any vessel less than 20 meters in length
⚓ D. All of the above

040265/RR04320   **RULE 9 (b)**

BOTH INTERNATIONAL & INLAND Which vessel shall NOT impede the passage of a vessel which can safely navigate only within a narrow channel or fairway?

A. A vessel dredging
⚓ B. A sailing vessel
C. A vessel servicing an aid to navigation
D. All of the above

040266/RR04864   **RULE 9 (b) - (c)**

BOTH INTERNATIONAL & INLAND Which vessel shall NOT impede the passage of a vessel which can safely navigate only within a narrow channel or fairway?

A. A vessel fishing
B. A vessel sailing
C. A vessel of less than 20 meters in length
⚓ D. All of the above

040267/RR00272   **RULE 9 (b)**

BOTH INTERNATIONAL & INLAND Two vessels are meeting in a narrow channel as shown in illustration D037RR below. Vessel "A" is a sailing vessel. Vessel "B" is a power-driven vessel which can safely navigate only within the channel. Vessel "B" sounds the danger signal. Vessel "A" shall take what action? See DIAGRAM D037RR

A. sound one prolonged followed by two short blasts
B. have the right-of-way
C. maintain course and speed
⚓ D. not impede the passage of vessel "B"

040268/RR04859   **RULE 9 (c)**

BOTH INTERNATIONAL & INLAND A sailing vessel is proceeding along a narrow channel and can safely navigate ONLY inside the channel. The sailing vessel approaches a vessel engaged in fishing in the narrow channel. Which statement is TRUE?

A. Each vessel should be displaying signals for a vessel constrained by her draft.
B. The vessels are required to exchange signals.
⚓ C. The fishing vessel is directed not to impede the passage of the sailing vessel.
D. Each vessel should move to the edge of the channel on her port side.

040269/RR04863   **RULE 9 (c)**

BOTH INTERNATIONAL & INLAND A sailing vessel is proceeding along a narrow channel and can safely navigate ONLY inside the channel. The sailing vessel approaches a vessel engaged in fishing. Which statement is TRUE?

A. Each vessel should move to the edge of the channel on her port side.
B. The fishing vessel must sound the danger signal.
C. Both vessels should be displaying the signal for a vessel restricted in her ability to maneuver.
⚓ D. The fishing vessel shall not impede the passage of the sailing vessel.

040270/RR04555   **RULE 9 (c)**
BOTH INTERNATIONAL & INLAND A sailing vessel is proceeding along a narrow channel and can safely navigate ONLY inside the channel. The sailing vessel approaches a vessel engaged in fishing. Which statement is TRUE?
A. Each vessel should be displaying signals for a vessel constrained by her draft.
B. Each vessel should move to the edge of the channel on her port side.
C. The sailing vessel must keep out of the way of the fishing vessel.
D. The fishing vessel is directed not to impede the passage of the sailing vessel.

040271/RR00242   **RULE 9 (c)**
BOTH INTERNATIONAL & INLAND You are on Vessel "A" engaged in fishing in a narrow channel as shown in illustration D037RR below. Vessel "B" is a tanker proceeding in the channel. Vessel "B" sounds five short and rapid blasts. What action should you take? See DIAGRAM D037RR
A. sound one prolonged followed by two short blasts
B. not answer the whistle signals from vessel "B"
C. not impede the passage of vessel "B"
D. maintain course and speed

040272/RR04857   **RULE 9 (d)**
BOTH INTERNATIONAL & INLAND A vessel approaching a narrow channel shall _____.
A. keep as close as possible to the edge of the channel on her port side
B. avoid crossing the channel if it impedes another vessel navigating in the channel
C. anchor only in the middle of the channel
D. not overtake any vessels within the channel

040273/RR04737   **RULE 9 (d)**
BOTH INTERNATIONAL & INLAND You are approaching a narrow channel. Another vessel in the channel can only be navigated safely in that channel. You should _____.
A. sound three short blasts, and take all way off your vessel
B. hold your course and speed if she is on your port bow
C. not cross the channel if you might impede the other vessel
D. sound two prolonged blasts followed by one short blast

040274/RR04036   **RULE 9 (d)**
BOTH INTERNATIONAL & INLAND You are preparing to cross a narrow channel. You see a vessel that can only be navigated safely within the channel. You should _____.
A. hold your course and speed
B. sound the danger signal
C. initiate an exchange of passing signals
D. not cross the channel if you might impede the other vessel

040275/RR04391   **RULE 9 (d), (b)**
BOTH INTERNATIONAL & INLAND You are crossing a narrow channel in a small motorboat. You sight a tankship off your port bow coming up the channel. Which statement is TRUE?
A. The tankship is the stand-on vessel because it is to port of your vessel.
B. You cannot impede the safe passage of the tankship.
C. You are the stand-on vessel because the tankship is to port.
D. The tankship is the stand-on vessel because it is the larger of the two vessels.

040276/RR04355   **RULE 9 (d), (b)**
BOTH INTERNATIONAL & INLAND You are crossing a narrow channel in an 18-meter tug when you sight a loaded tankship off your port bow coming up the channel. Which statement is correct?
A. The tankship is the stand-on vessel because it is in the channel.
B. The tankship is the stand-on vessel because it is the larger of the two vessels.
C. Neither vessel is the stand-on vessel because the tankship is crossing.
D. You cannot impede the safe passage of the tankship.

040277/RR04009   **RULE 9 (d), (b)**
BOTH INTERNATIONAL & INLAND Your 15-meter tug is underway and crossing a deep and narrow channel. A large container vessel is off your port bow on a steady bearing. Which statement is TRUE concerning this situation?
A. You are not to impede the safe passage of the container vessel in the channel.
B. The container vessel is the stand-on as it is the larger vessel.
C. You should maintain course and speed.
D. None of the above

040278/RR04219   **RULE 9 (d), (b)**
BOTH INTERNATIONAL & INLAND Your 15-meter vessel is crossing a narrow channel and a large cargo vessel to port is within the channel and crossing your course. You must _____.
⚓ A. not cross the channel if you might impede the other vessel
B. hold course and speed
C. sound the danger signal
D. initiate an exchange of passing signals

040279/RR04299   **RULE 9 (d), (b)**
BOTH INTERNATIONAL & INLAND You are crossing a narrow channel on your 15-meter vessel. A deeply loaded cargo vessel is proceeding down the channel as shown in illustration D040RR below. In this situation, which statement is correct? See DIAGRAM D040RR
A. You are the stand-on vessel because you are less than 65 feet in length.
⚓ B. You cannot impede the passage of the cargo vessel.
C. The RULE of Special Circumstances applies in this case.
D. The cargo vessel is the stand-on vessel because she is running with the current.

040280/RR00193   **RULE 9 (d)**
BOTH INTERNATIONAL & INLAND You are on vessel "B" and crossing a narrow channel. Vessel "A", who can only navigate within the channel, is on your port bow and crossing as shown in illustration D040RR below. Which action should you take? See DIAGRAM D040RR
⚓ A. Give way to the other vessel.
B. sound the danger signal.
C. Increase speed and cross his bow.
D. Maintain course and speed as the ship is on your port bow.

040281/RR00194   **RULE 9 (d); RULE 34 (d)**
BOTH INTERNATIONAL & INLAND You are on vessel "A" and proceeding down a narrow channel as shown in illustration D040RR below. You can only navigate within the channel and vessel "B" is crossing so as to involve risk of collision. Which action would be most prudent? See DIAGRAM D040RR
A. Back down and allow vessel "B" to cross ahead.
B. Maintain course and speed.
C. Alter course to starboard to give him more room.
⚓ D. sound the danger signal and take evasive action.

RULE 10 - TRAFFIC SEPARATION SCHEMES

040282/RR04240   **RULE 10; RULE 1 (d)**
BOTH INTERNATIONAL & INLAND Systems of inbound and outbound lanes to promote the safe flow of vessel traffic in certain areas around the world are known as _____.
A. restricted maneuverability channels
B. collision avoidance fairways
⚓ C. traffic separation schemes
D. merchant vessel reporting systems

040283/RR04465   **RULE 10; RULE 1 (d)**
BOTH INTERNATIONAL & INLAND Traffic separation schemes _____.
A. provide routing and scheduling procedures to reduce shipping delays
B. prohibit vessels carrying hazardous cargoes from entering waters that are environmentally sensitive
C. provide traffic patterns in congested areas, so that vessels can operate without having a separate lookout
⚓ D. provide inbound and outbound lanes to promote the safe flow of vessel traffic

040284/RR04256   **RULE 10; RULE 1 (d)**
BOTH INTERNATIONAL & INLAND Traffic separation schemes established by the International Maritime Organization _____.
A. provide vessel reporting systems to assist in search and rescue in the event of a vessel casualty
B. prohibit vessels carrying hazardous cargoes from entering waters that are environmentally sensitive
C. provide routing and vessel scheduling procedures to reduce shipping delays
⚓ D. provide inbound and outbound lanes to promote the safe flow of vessel traffic

040285/RR04577   **RULE 10; RULE 6; RULE 17**
BOTH INTERNATIONAL & INLAND Which statement about the Navigation Rules is TRUE?
A. The rules permit a stand-on vessel to take action prior to being in extremis.
B. The rules require vessels to comply with Traffic Separation Scheme regulations.
C. The rules use the term "safe speed."
⚓ D. All of the above are correct.

040286/RR05400   **RULE 10 (b) (i)**
BOTH INTERNATIONAL & INLAND A vessel using a traffic separation scheme shall NOT _____.
A. enter the separation zone
B. cross a traffic lane
C. engage in fishing the separation zone
⚓ D. proceed in an inappropriate traffic lane

040287/RR06570   **RULE 10 (b) (ii)**
BOTH INTERNATIONAL & INLAND A traffic separation zone is that part of a traffic separation scheme which _____.
A. is designated as an anchorage area
B. separates traffic proceeding in one direction from traffic proceeding in the opposite direction
C. is located between the scheme and the nearest land
D. contains all the traffic moving in the same direction

040288/RR05300   **RULE 10 (b) (ii)**
BOTH INTERNATIONAL & INLAND A traffic separation zone is that part of a traffic separation scheme which _____.
A. is designated as an anchorage area
B. is between the scheme and the nearest land
C. separates traffic proceeding in one direction from traffic proceeding in the opposite direction
D. contains all the traffic moving in one direction

040289/RR06550   **RULE 10 (b) (iii)**
BOTH INTERNATIONAL & INLAND In a traffic separation scheme, when joining a traffic lane from the side, a vessel shall do so _____.
A. only in case of an emergency or to engage in fishing within the zone
B. never
C. at as small an angle as possible
D. as nearly as practical at right angles to the general direction of traffic flow

040290/RR06540   **RULE 10 (e) (i), (h) (i), (c)**
BOTH INTERNATIONAL & INLAND A vessel may enter a traffic separation zone _____.
A. to cross the traffic separation scheme
B. in an emergency
C. to engage in fishing within the zone
D. All of the above

040291/RR05350   **RULE 10 (g)**
BOTH INTERNATIONAL & INLAND A vessel using a traffic separation scheme shall _____.
A. avoid anchoring in areas near the termination of the scheme
B. cross a traffic lane at as small an angle as possible
C. utilize the separation zone for navigating through the scheme if she is impeding other traffic due to her slower speed
D. only anchor in the separation zone

040292/RR04591   **RULE 10 (g)**
BOTH INTERNATIONAL & INLAND A vessel using a traffic separation scheme shall _____.
A. avoid anchoring in areas near the termination of the scheme
B. use the separation zone for navigating through the scheme if she is hindering other traffic due to her slower speed
C. only anchor in the separation zone
D. avoid crossing traffic lanes, but if obliged to do so, shall cross on as small an angle as is practical

040293/RR09122   **RULE 10 (j)**
BOTH INTERNATIONAL & INLAND A sailing vessel shall not impede the safe passage of a _____.
A. law enforcement vessel
B. pilot vessel enroute to a pilot station
C. power-driven vessel following a traffic lane
D. All of the above

040294/RR04063   **RULE 10 (l)**
BOTH INTERNATIONAL & INLAND There are two classes of vessels which, to the extent necessary to carry out their work, do not have to comply with the rule regarding traffic separation schemes. One of these is a vessel _____.
A. towing another
B. engaged in fishing in a traffic lane
C. engaged on pilotage duty
D. servicing a submarine cable

```
PART B STEERING & SAILING RULES
       SECTION SUBPART II
       CONDUCT OF VESSELS
     IN SIGHT OF ONE ANOTHER
```

RULE 12 - SAILING VESSELS

040295/RR04093   **RULE 12 (a) (i)**
BOTH INTERNATIONAL & INLAND Which statement is TRUE concerning two sailing vessels?
A. When both vessels have the wind on the same side, the vessel to leeward shall keep out of the way.
B. A sailing vessel with the wind forward of the beam on her port side shall keep out of the way of a sailing vessel with the wind forward of the beam on the starboard side.
C. A sail vessel with the wind abaft of the beam must keep out of the way of a vessel sailing into the wind.
D. None of the above

040296/RR09124   **RULE 12 (a) (i)**
BOTH INTERNATIONAL & INLAND You are on a sailing vessel with the wind on the starboard side and are approaching another sailing vessel that has the wind on the port side. Which action should you take?
⚓ A. Maintain course and speed.
B. Reduce sail and hold course.
C. Alter course away from the other vessel.
D. Any maneuver to avoid collision.

040297/RR09123   **RULE 12 (a) (i)**
BOTH INTERNATIONAL & INLAND You are under sail making 5 knots. The apparent wind is broad on the port beam at 10 knots. You see another sailing vessel dead ahead on a meeting course. What action is correct?
A. Both vessels must maneuver to avoid collision.
B. Only the other vessel must maneuver to avoid collision.
C. You are only required to maneuver if collision cannot be avoided by maneuver of the other vessel.
⚓ D. You must keep out of the way of the other vessel.

040298/RR04549   **RULE 12 (a) (i)**
BOTH INTERNATIONAL & INLAND Two sailing vessels are approaching each other as shown in illustration D003RR below. Which statement is correct? See DIAGRAM D003RR
⚓ A. Vessel "II" should stand on because she has the wind on her starboard side.
B. Vessel "I" should stand on because she has the wind on her port side.
C. Vessel "I" should stand on because she is close-hauled.
D. Neither vessel is the stand-on vessel because they are meeting head-on.

040299/RR04028   **RULE 12 (a) (ii)**
BOTH INTERNATIONAL & INLAND If two sailing vessels are running free with the wind on the same side, which one must keep clear of the other?
⚓ A. The one to windward
B. The one that sounds the first whistle signal
C. The one to leeward
D. The one with the wind closest abeam

040300/RR04866   **RULE 12 (a) (ii)**
BOTH INTERNATIONAL & INLAND If two sailing vessels are running free with the wind on the same side, which one must keep clear of the other?
A. The one with the wind closest astern
B. The one to leeward
⚓ C. The one to windward
D. The one with the wind closest abeam

040301/RR04536   **RULE 12 (a) (iii)**
BOTH INTERNATIONAL & INLAND If a sailing vessel with the wind on the port side sees a sailing vessel to windward and cannot tell whether the other vessel has the wind on the port or starboard side, she shall _____.
A. sound the danger signal
B. turn to port and come into the wind
C. hold course and speed
⚓ D. keep out of the way of the other vessel

RULE 13 - OVERTAKING

040302/RR09127   **RULE 13 (a)**
BOTH INTERNATIONAL & INLAND A sailing vessel must keep course and speed when _____.
A. to windward of another sailing vessel
⚓ B. being overtaken
C. to leeward of another sailing vessel
D. crossing a vessel engaged in fishing

040303/RR04550   **RULE 13 (a)**
BOTH INTERNATIONAL & INLAND Which statement concerning an overtaking situation is correct?
A. The overtaking vessel must maintain course and speed.
B. The overtaking vessel is the stand-on vessel.
C. Neither vessel is the stand-on vessel.
⚓ D. The overtaking vessel must keep out of the way of the other.

040304/RR04434   **RULE 13 (a)**
BOTH INTERNATIONAL & INLAND Which statement correctly applies to a situation where a sailing vessel is overtaking a power-driven vessel?
⚓ A. The sailing vessel must keep out of the way of the power-driven vessel.
B. The power-driven vessel must keep out of the way of the sailing vessel.
C. The vessel which has the other vessel to the right must keep out of the way.
D. A "special circumstance" situation exists.

040305/RR09126   **RULE 13 (a)**
BOTH INTERNATIONAL & INLAND You are under sail and overtaking a tug and tow. Which action is correct?
A. Both vessels are required to maneuver to avoid collision.
⚓ B. You must maneuver to avoid the tug and tow.
C. You must maneuver to avoid collision only if the tug is to leeward and the wind is on your port side.
D. The power-driven tug must maneuver to avoid collision.

040306/RR04105   **RULE 13 (a); RULE 12**
BOTH INTERNATIONAL & INLAND Which statement is TRUE concerning two sailing vessels approaching each other?
A. A sailing vessel overtaking another is the give-way vessel.
B. When each is on a different tack, the vessel on the starboard tack shall keep out of the way.
C. A sailing vessel seeing another to leeward on an undetermined tack shall hold her course.
D. All of the above

040307/RR04868   **RULE 13 (a); RULE 12**
BOTH INTERNATIONAL & INLAND Which statement is TRUE concerning two sailing vessels approaching each other?
A. The vessel making the most speed is the give-way vessel.
B. A sailing vessel overtaking another is the give-way vessel.
C. A sailing vessel seeing another to leeward on an undetermined tack shall hold her course.
D. All of the above

040308/RR04043   **RULE 13 (a); RULE 17**
BOTH INTERNATIONAL & INLAND You are the watch officer on a power-driven vessel and notice a large sailing vessel approaching from astern. You should _____.
A. slow down
B. sound one short blast and change course to starboard
C. hold your course and speed
D. sound two short blasts and change course to port

040309/RR04869   **RULE 13 (a); RULE 18 (a)**
BOTH INTERNATIONAL & INLAND Power-driven vessels must keep out of the way of sailing vessels except _____.
A. on the INLAND Waters of the United States
B. when the sailing vessel is overtaking
C. when they are making more speed than the power-driven vessel
D. in a crossing situation

040310/RR04525   **RULE 13 (a); RULE 18 (a)**
BOTH INTERNATIONAL & INLAND Sailing vessels are stand-on over power-driven vessels except _____.
A. on the INLAND waters of the U.S.
B. in a meeting situation
C. when they are the overtaking vessel
D. in a crossing situation

040311/RR04134   **RULE 13 (a)**
BOTH INTERNATIONAL & INLAND Vessel "A" is overtaking vessel "B" as shown in illustration D009RR below. Which vessel is the stand-on vessel? See DIAGRAM D009RR
A. Vessel "B"
B. Both vessels must keep clear of the other.
C. Neither vessel
D. Vessel "A"

040312/RR00231   **RULE 13 (a)**
BOTH INTERNATIONAL & INLAND Vessel "A" is overtaking vessel "B" as shown in illustration D017RR below. In this situation vessel "B" is which of the following? See DIAGRAM D017RR
A. stand-on vessel
B. give-way vessel
C. burdened vessel
D. None of the above

040313/RR00232   **RULE 13 (a)**
BOTH INTERNATIONAL & INLAND Vessel "A" is overtaking vessel "B" as shown in illustration D017RR below. Vessel "B" should do which of the following? See DIAGRAM D017RR
A. should hold her course and speed
B. should slow down until vessel "A" has passed
C. should change course to the right
D. may steer various courses and vessel "A" must keep clear

040314/RR04023   **RULE 13 (a), (b)**
BOTH INTERNATIONAL & INLAND A sailing vessel is overtaking a tug and tow as shown in illustration D043RR below. Which statement is CORRECT? See DIAGRAM D043RR
A. The tug is the stand-on vessel because it is towing.
B. The sailing vessel is the stand-on vessel because it is under sail.
C. The tug is the stand-on vessel because it is being overtaken.
D. The sailing vessel is the stand-on vessel because it is overtaking.

040315/RR04060   **RULE 13 (b)**
BOTH INTERNATIONAL & INLAND A vessel approaching your vessel from 235° relative is in what type of situation?
A. Passing
B. Overtaking
C. Meeting
D. Crossing

040316/RR04575 **RULE 13 (b)**
BOTH INTERNATIONAL & INLAND A vessel is overtaking when she can see which light(s) of a vessel ahead?
A. Only a sidelight of the vessel
B. One sidelight and a masthead light of the vessel
C. The masthead lights of the vessel
⚓ D. Only the stern light of the vessel

040317/RR04045 **RULE 13 (b)**
BOTH INTERNATIONAL & INLAND A vessel shall be deemed to be overtaking when she can see at night _____.
A. a sidelight and one masthead light of the vessel
⚓ B. only the stern light of the vessel
C. any lights except the masthead lights of the vessel
D. only a sidelight of the vessel

040318/RR04389 **RULE 13 (b)**
BOTH INTERNATIONAL & INLAND An overtaking situation at night would be one in which one vessel sees which light(s) of a vessel ahead?
⚓ A. Stern light
B. Both sidelights
C. One sidelight, the masthead lights and stern light
D. Masthead lights and sidelights

040319/RR04387 **RULE 13 (b)**
BOTH INTERNATIONAL & INLAND An overtaking situation would be one in which one vessel is approaching another from more than how many degrees abaft the beam?
A. 0°
⚓ B. 22.5°
C. 10°
D. None of the above

040320/RR04339 **RULE 13 (b)**
BOTH INTERNATIONAL & INLAND Two vessels are in an overtaking situation. Which of the lights on the overtaken vessel will the overtaking vessel see?
A. One masthead light and a sidelight
B. two masthead lights
⚓ C. Stern light only
D. Both sidelights

040321/RR00240 **RULE 13 (b)**
BOTH INTERNATIONAL & INLAND Vessel "A" is overtaking vessel "B" as shown in illustration D017RR below and will pass without changing course. Which light will vessel "A" observe on vessel "B"? See DIAGRAM D017RR
⚓ A. white stern light
B. yellow towing light
C. green sidelight
D. None of the above

040322/RR00229 **RULE 13 (b)**
BOTH INTERNATIONAL & INLAND Vessel "A" is overtaking vessel "B" as shown in illustration D017RR below. Which of the following describes vessel "A" in this scenario? See DIAGRAM D017RR
⚓ A. give-way vessel
B. stand-on vessel
C. overtaken vessel
D. None of the above

040323/RR04463 **RULE 13 (b)**
BOTH INTERNATIONAL & INLAND You are underway on vessel "B" approaching vessel "A", as shown in illustration D038RR below. You are unable to see any sidelights on vessel "A". What type of situation is this? See DIAGRAM D038RR
⚓ A. overtaking situation
B. meeting situation
C. special circumstances situation
D. crossing situation

040324/RR04086 **RULE 13 (c)**
BOTH INTERNATIONAL & INLAND You are on vessel "A" and approaching vessel "B" as shown in illustration D015RR below. You are not sure whether your vessel is crossing or overtaking vessel "B". You should take which of the following actions? See DIAGRAM D015RR
A. consider it to be a crossing situation
⚓ B. consider it to be an overtaking situation
C. consider it a crossing situation if you can cross ahead safely
D. change course to make the situation definitely either crossing or overtaking

040325/RR04551 **RULE 13 (d)**
BOTH INTERNATIONAL & INLAND The Rules state that a vessel overtaking another vessel is relieved of her duty to keep clear when _____.
A. she is forward of the other vessel's port beam
B. the overtaking situation becomes a crossing situation
⚓ C. she is past and clear of the other vessel
D. the other vessel is no longer in sight

040326/RR04443 **RULE 13 (d)**
BOTH INTERNATIONAL & INLAND Which statement is TRUE in an overtaking situation?
⚓ A. Any later change of bearing between the two vessels shall not make the overtaking vessel a crossing vessel.
B. An overtaking situation exists when one vessel is approaching another vessel from anywhere abaft the beam.
C. It is the duty of the vessel being overtaken to get out of the way.
D. All of the above

RULE 14 - HEAD-ON SITUATION

040327/RR04557   **RULE 14 (a)**
BOTH INTERNATIONAL & INLAND RULE 14 describes the action to be taken by vessels meeting head-on. Which of the following conditions must exist in order for this rule to apply?
A. Both vessels must be power-driven.
B. The situation must involve risk of collision.
C. They must be meeting on reciprocal or nearly reciprocal courses.
⚓ D. All of the above

040328/RR04053   **RULE 14 (a)**
BOTH INTERNATIONAL & INLAND Two power-driven vessels meeting in a "head-on" situation are directed by the Rules to _____.
⚓ A. alter course to starboard and pass port to port
B. slow to bare steerageway
C. alter course to port and pass starboard to starboard
D. decide on which side the passage will occur by matching whistle signals

040329/RR04327   **RULE 14 (a)**
BOTH INTERNATIONAL & INLAND Two vessels are approaching each other near head on. What action should be taken to avoid collision?
A. The first vessel to sight the other should give way.
⚓ B. Both vessels should alter course to starboard.
C. The vessel making the slower speed should give way.
D. Both vessels should alter course to port.

040330/RR04429   **RULE 14 (a)**
BOTH INTERNATIONAL & INLAND Two vessels are meeting head-on. How must the vessels pass?
A. Both vessels should alter course to port and pass starboard to starboard.
B. One vessel must alter course while the other must continue on its course.
⚓ C. Both vessels should alter course to starboard and pass port to port.
D. The vessels should determine which will alter course by sounding whistle signals.

040331/RR04537   **RULE 14 (a)**
BOTH INTERNATIONAL & INLAND Vessel "A" is on course 000°T. Vessel "B" is on a course such that she is involved in a head-on situation and is bearing 355°T, 2 miles away from vessel "A". To ensure a safe passing, vessel "A" should _____.
A. alter course to ensure a starboard to starboard passing
⚓ B. maneuver to ensure a port to port passing
C. maintain course
D. alter course to port

040332/RR04605   **RULE 14 (a)**
BOTH INTERNATIONAL & INLAND When two power-driven vessels are meeting head-on and there is a risk of collision, each shall _____.
A. stop her engines
B. sound the danger signal
⚓ C. alter course to starboard
D. back down

040333/RR04492   **RULE 14 (a) - (b)**
BOTH INTERNATIONAL & INLAND You sight another power-driven vessel dead-ahead showing both the red and green sidelights. The required action to take would be to _____.
A. alter your course to port
B. start a radar plot in order to ascertain his course
⚓ C. alter your course to starboard
D. carefully watch his compass bearing

040334/RR04384   **RULE 14 (a)**
BOTH INTERNATIONAL & INLAND Vessel "A" and vessel "B" (which is pushing ahead) are meeting head-on as shown in illustration D008RR below. How must the vessels pass? See DIAGRAM D008RR
A. Both vessels should alter course to port and pass starboard to starboard.
B. Vessel "A" must alter course while vessel "B" continues on its present course.
C. The vessels should determine which will alter course by exchanging whistle signals.
⚓ D. Both vessels should alter course to starboard and pass port to port.

040335/RR04662   **RULE 14 (a)**
BOTH INTERNATIONAL & INLAND Vessel "A" (towing) and vessel "B" are meeting as shown in illustration D012RR below. In this situation, which statement is TRUE? See DIAGRAM D012RR
A. Both vessels should alter course to port and pass starboard to starboard.
⚓ B. Both vessels should alter course to starboard and pass port to port.
C. Vessel "A" should hold course while vessel "B" alters course to starboard.
D. Vessel "A" is the stand-on in this situation.

040336/RR04348 **RULE 14 (a)**
BOTH INTERNATIONAL & INLAND You are on vessel "A" pushing a barge ahead and meeting vessel "B" as shown in illustration D012RR below. How should the vessels pass? See DIAGRAM D012RR
A. Both vessels must alter course to port and pass starboard to starboard.
⚓ B. Both vessels must alter course to starboard and pass port to port.
C. Vessel "A" should maintain course and vessel "B" alter course.
D. The vessels should determine which will alter course by sounding whistle signals.

040337/RR00189 **RULE 14 (a)**
BOTH INTERNATIONAL & INLAND You are on vessel "A" towing a barge alongside and meeting power-driven vessel "B" as shown in illustration D039RR below. Which action should you take? See DIAGRAM D039RR
A. Alter course to port
⚓ B. Alter course to starboard
C. Back down to reduce the strain on the lines
D. Maintain course and speed

040338/RR04313 **RULE 14 (a); RULE 23 (a)**
BOTH INTERNATIONAL & INLAND While underway at night, you sight a vessel ahead displaying the lights shown in illustration D071RR below. How should the vessels pass? See DIAGRAM D071RR
A. Both vessels should alter course to port and pass starboard to starboard.
⚓ B. Both vessels should alter course to starboard and pass port to port.
C. You should sound an appropriate overtaking signal.
D. Your vessel should hold course and speed and the other vessel should keep clear.

040339/RR04169 **RULE 14 (b)**
BOTH INTERNATIONAL & INLAND A "head on" situation shall be deemed to exist at night when a power-driven vessel sees another power-driven vessel ahead and _____.
⚓ A. both sidelights and masthead light(s) are visible
B. the vessels will pass closer than half a mile
C. one sidelight and the masthead light are visible
D. both vessels sound one prolonged blast

040340/RR04371 **RULE 14 (b)**
BOTH INTERNATIONAL & INLAND A head-on situation at night is one in which you see _____.
A. one sidelight and a masthead light of a vessel ahead of you
⚓ B. both sidelights of a vessel dead ahead of you
C. one sidelight, a masthead light, and a range light of a vessel ahead of you
D. one sidelight of a vessel ahead of you

040341/RR04473 **RULE 14 (b)**
BOTH INTERNATIONAL & INLAND A head-on situation at night is one in which you see dead ahead a vessel showing _____.
⚓ A. both sidelights of a vessel and her masthead light(s)
B. one sidelight and two masthead lights
C. one sidelight and a masthead light
D. one sidelight

040342/RR04586 **RULE 14 (b)**
BOTH INTERNATIONAL & INLAND What describes a head-on situation?
A. Seeing two forward white towing lights in a vertical line on a towing vessel directly ahead
⚓ B. Seeing both sidelights of a vessel directly ahead
C. Seeing one red light of a vessel directly ahead
D. Seeing both sidelights of a vessel directly off your starboard beam

040343/RR04417 **RULE 14 (b)**
BOTH INTERNATIONAL & INLAND What describes a head-on situation?
A. Seeing two forward white towing identification lights in a vertical line on a towing vessel directly ahead
B. Seeing a vessel displaying both sidelights ONLY dead ahead
⚓ C. Seeing both sidelights and masthead light(s) of a vessel dead ahead
D. Seeing both sidelights of a vessel directly off your starboard beam

RULE 15 - CROSSING SITUATION

040344/RR04569 **RULE 15**
BOTH INTERNATIONAL & INLAND When two power-driven vessels are crossing, the vessel which has the other to starboard must keep out of the way if _____.
A. the vessels will pass within half a mile of each other
B. she is the faster vessel
C. whistle signals have been sounded
⚓ D. the situation involves risk of collision

040345/RR04353 **RULE 15**
BOTH INTERNATIONAL & INLAND Every vessel that is to keep out of the way of another vessel must take positive early action to comply with this obligation and must _____.
A. avoid passing astern of the other vessel
B. sound one prolonged blast to indicate compliance
⚓ C. avoid crossing ahead of the other vessel
D. alter course to port for a vessel on her port side

040346/RR04599 **RULE 15**
BOTH INTERNATIONAL & INLAND underway at night you see the red sidelight of a vessel well off your port bow. Which statement is TRUE?
A. You are required to alter course to the right.
B. You are on a collision course with the other vessel.
⚓ C. You may maintain course and speed.
D. You must stop engines.

040347/RR04414 **RULE 15**
BOTH INTERNATIONAL & INLAND Every vessel which is directed by these Rules to keep out of the way of another vessel shall, if the circumstances of the case admit, avoid _____.
A. crossing astern of the other
B. passing port to port
C. passing starboard to starboard
⚓ D. crossing ahead of the other

040348/RR09116 **RULE 15**
BOTH INTERNATIONAL & INLAND Two power-driven vessels are crossing as shown in illustration D042RR below. Vessel "A" sounds one short blast on the whistle. What is Vessel "A" considered in this scenario? See DIAGRAM D042RR
A. the overtaking vessel
⚓ B. the give-way vessel
C. the stand-on vessel
D. None of the above

040349/RR04610 **RULE 15; RULE 8**
BOTH INTERNATIONAL & INLAND You are aboard the give-way vessel in a crossing situation. What should you NOT do in obeying the Rules?
A. Make a large course change to starboard
B. Slow your vessel
C. Back your vessel
⚓ D. Cross ahead of the stand-on vessel

040350/RR04640 **RULE 15; RULE 17**
BOTH INTERNATIONAL & INLAND When two power-driven vessels are crossing, which vessel is the stand-on vessel?
A. The vessel which is to port of the other vessel
⚓ B. The vessel which is to starboard of the other vessel
C. The vessel that sounds the first whistle signal
D. The larger vessel

040351/RR04562 **RULE 15 (a); RULE 17 (c)**
BOTH INTERNATIONAL & INLAND In a crossing situation, the vessel which has the other on her own starboard side shall _____.
A. reduce her speed
⚓ B. if the circumstances of the case admit, avoid crossing ahead of the other
C. change course to port to keep out of the way
D. All of the above

040352/RR04448 **RULE 15; RULE 17**
BOTH INTERNATIONAL & INLAND Vessel "A" is underway and pushing ahead when vessel "B" is sighted off the starboard bow as shown in illustration D005RR below. Which statement is TRUE? See DIAGRAM D005RR
A. Vessel "A" is the stand-on vessel because it is to the port side of vessel "B".
B. Neither vessel is the stand-on vessel.
C. Vessel "A" is the stand-on vessel because it is pushing ahead.
⚓ D. Vessel "B" is the stand-on vessel because it is to starboard of vessel "A".

040353/RR04453 **RULE 15; RULE 17**
BOTH INTERNATIONAL & INLAND Vessels "A" and "B" are crossing as shown in illustration D026RR below. Which statement is TRUE? See DIAGRAM D026RR
⚓ A. Vessel "A" must keep clear of vessel "B".
B. Vessel "B" should alter course to the right.
C. The vessels should pass starboard to starboard.
D. Vessel "B" should pass under the stern of vessel "A".

040354/RR04061 **RULE 15; RULE 17**
BOTH INTERNATIONAL & INLAND Vessels "A" and "B" are crossing as shown in illustration D030RR below. Which statement is TRUE? See DIAGRAM D030RR
⚓ A. Vessel "A" must keep clear of vessel "B".
B. Vessel "B" should alter course to the right.
C. Vessel "B" should pass astern of vessel "A".
D. The vessels should pass starboard to starboard.

040355/RR00248 **RULE 15 (a), RULE 17**
BOTH INTERNATIONAL & INLAND Vessels "I" and "II" are power-driven vessels. You are on vessel "I" as shown in illustration D036RR below. In this scenario you are which of the following? See DIAGRAM D036RR
⚓ A. stand-on vessel
B. give-way vessel
C. overtaking vessel
D. None of the above

040356/RR04062 **RULE 15; RULE 23 (a) (i), (a) (iii)**
BOTH INTERNATIONAL & INLAND You are in charge of a power-driven vessel navigating at night. You sight the red sidelight of another vessel on your port bow. The other vessel's after masthead light is to the right of her forward masthead light. You should _____.
A. stop engines
⚓ B. hold course and speed
C. sound the danger signal
D. alter course to port

040357/RR04458   **RULE 15; RULE 23 (a) (i) - (iii)**
BOTH INTERNATIONAL & INLAND You see the lights shown in illustration D050RR below on your port bow. What action should you take? See DIAGRAM D050RR
A. sound the danger signal
B. hold course and speed
C. alter course to port
D. stop engines

040358/RR00364   **RULE 15; RULE 34 (a) (i)**
BOTH INTERNATIONAL & INLAND Two power-driven vessels are crossing as shown in illustration D042RR below. Vessel "A" sounds one short blast on the whistle. Vessel "B" is which of the following in this scenario? See DIAGRAM D042RR
A. give-way vessel
B. overtaking vessel
C. burdened vessel
D. stand-on vessel

RULE 17 - ACTION BY THE STAND-ON VESSEL

040359/RR04388   **RULE 17 (a) (i); RULE 15**
BOTH INTERNATIONAL & INLAND A stand-on vessel is _____.
A. required to give way in a crossing situation
B. required to sound the first passing signal in a meeting situation
C. free to maneuver in any crossing or meeting situation as it has the right-of-way
D. required to maintain course and speed in a crossing situation but may take action to avoid collision

040360/RR04616   **RULE 17 (a) (i); RULE 15**
BOTH INTERNATIONAL & INLAND If your vessel is the stand-on vessel in a crossing situation _____.
A. you may change course and speed as the other vessel must keep clear
B. you must keep your course and speed
C. both vessels must keep their course and speed
D. the other vessel must keep her course and speed

040361/RR04474   **RULE 17 (a) (i); RULE 15**
BOTH INTERNATIONAL & INLAND In a crossing situation, what action should the stand-on vessel normally take?
A. take action to cross ahead of the other vessel
B. take action to pass astern of the other vessel
C. change course and increase speed
D. maintain course and speed

040362/RR04008   **RULE 17 (a) (ii); RULE 15**
BOTH INTERNATIONAL & INLAND If you are the stand-on vessel in a crossing situation, you may take action to avoid collision by your maneuver alone. When may this action be taken?
A. When you determine that your present course will cross ahead of the other vessel
B. When it becomes apparent to you that the give-way vessel is not taking appropriate action
C. Only when you have reached extremis
D. At any time you feel it is appropriate

040363/RR04228   **RULE 17 (a) (ii)**
BOTH INTERNATIONAL & INLAND When is a stand-on vessel FIRST allowed by the Rules to take action in order to avoid collision?
A. When the two vessels are less than half a mile from each other.
B. The stand-on vessel is never allowed to take action.
C. When the give-way vessel is not taking appropriate action to avoid collision.
D. When collision is imminent.

040364/RR09129   **RULE 17 (a) (ii)**
BOTH INTERNATIONAL & INLAND When is a stand-on vessel in a crossing situation allowed to take action?
A. on a collision course
B. the vessels will pass within one mile
C. the relative speed of the vessels indicates collision in less than six minutes
D. it becomes apparent to her that the give-way vessel is not taking appropriate action

040365/RR04332   **RULE 17 (a) (ii); RULE 15**
BOTH INTERNATIONAL & INLAND You are the stand-on vessel in a crossing situation. You may hold your course and speed until _____.
A. the other vessel gets to within half a mile of your vessel
B. the other vessel takes necessary action
C. action by the give-way vessel alone will not prevent collision
D. the other vessel gets to within a quarter mile of your vessel

040366/RR04625   **RULE 17 (a) (ii), (b)**
BOTH INTERNATIONAL & INLAND What must be TRUE in order for a stand-on vessel to take action to avoid collision by her maneuver alone?
A. She must determine that the give-way vessel is not taking appropriate action.
B. She must be in sight of the give-way vessel.
C. There must be risk of collision.
D. All of the above

040367/RR04470   **RULE 17 (a) (ii), (b)**
BOTH INTERNATIONAL & INLAND You are in charge of a stand-on vessel in a crossing situation. The other vessel is 1.5 miles to port and you believe that risk of collision exists. What action should you take?
A. take avoiding action immediately upon determining that risk of collision exists
B. take avoiding action only after giving the give-way vessel time to take action, and determining that her action is not appropriate
C. hold course and speed until the point of extremis, and then sound the danger signal, taking whatever action will best avoid collision
D. immediately sound the danger signal, and change course

040368/RR04383   **RULE 17 (a) (ii), (b)**
BOTH INTERNATIONAL & INLAND You are in charge of a stand-on vessel in a crossing situation. The other vessel is 1.5 miles to port. You believe that risk of collision exists. You should _____.
A. take avoiding action immediately upon determining that risk of collision exists
B. hold course and speed until the point of extremis, and then sound the danger signal, taking whatever action will best avert collision
C. take avoiding action only after providing the give-way vessel time to take action, and determining that her action is not appropriate
D. immediately sound the danger signal

040369/RR03683   **RULE 17 (b)**
BOTH INTERNATIONAL & INLAND The rules require that a stand-on vessel SHALL take action to avoid collision when she determines that _____.
A. the other vessel will cross ahead of her
B. the other vessel is not taking appropriate action
C. risk of collision exists
D. collision cannot be avoided by the give-way vessel's maneuver alone

040370/RR04418   **RULE 17 (b); RULE 7; RULE 8**
BOTH INTERNATIONAL & INLAND When two vessels are in immediate danger of collision, the stand-on vessel must _____.
A. sound a distress signal
B. abandon ship
C. assist in taking whatever action is necessary to avoid collision
D. hold course and speed

040371/RR04297   **RULE 17 (b)**
BOTH INTERNATIONAL & INLAND Which requirement must be met in order for a stand-on vessel to take action to avoid collision?
A. Risk of collision must exist.
B. The vessels must be within half a mile of each other.
C. The give-way vessel must have taken action first.
D. There are no requirements to be met. The stand-on vessel may take action anytime.

040372/RR04629   **RULE 17 (c); RULE 15**
BOTH INTERNATIONAL & INLAND For a stand-on vessel to take action to avoid collision she shall, if possible, NOT _____.
A. increase speed
B. decrease speed
C. turn to port for a vessel on her port side
D. turn to starboard for a vessel on her port side

040373/RR04048   **RULE 17 (c); RULE 15**
BOTH INTERNATIONAL & INLAND If it becomes necessary for a stand-on vessel to take action to avoid collision, she shall NOT, if possible, _____.
A. decrease speed
B. increase speed
C. turn to starboard for a vessel on her own port side
D. turn to port for a vessel on her own port side

040374/RR04454   **RULE 17 (c)**
BOTH INTERNATIONAL & INLAND In a crossing situation, a stand-on vessel which is forced to take action in order to avoid collision with a vessel on her own port side shall, if possible, avoid _____.
A. decreasing speed
B. increasing speed
C. turning to starboard
D. turning to port

040375/RR04351   **RULE 17 (c); RULE 15**
BOTH INTERNATIONAL & INLAND Two power-driven vessels are crossing so as to involve risk of collision. Which statement is TRUE, according to the Rules?
A. The vessel which has the other on her own port side shall keep out of the way.
B. The give-way vessel should keep the other vessel to her starboard.
C. If the give-way vessel takes action, she shall avoid changing course to starboard.
D. If the stand-on vessel takes action, she shall avoid changing course to port.

040376/RR04055　　　　　　**RULE 17 (c)**

BOTH INTERNATIONAL & INLAND When shall the stand-on vessel change course and speed?

A. After the give-way vessel sounds one blast in a crossing situation

B. The stand-on vessel may change course and speed at any time as it has the right-of-way

C. When the two vessels become less than half a mile apart

⚓ D. When action by the give-way vessel alone cannot prevent collision

040377/RR04316　　　　　　**RULE 17 (c)**

BOTH INTERNATIONAL & INLAND When shall the stand-on vessel in a crossing situation take action to avoid the other vessel?

⚓ A. When action by the give-way vessel alone will not prevent a collision

B. When the vessels become less than 1/2 mile apart

C. When a risk of collision exists

D. When the bearing to give-way vessel becomes steady

RULE 18 - RESPONSIBILITIES BETWEEN VESSELS

040378/RR04049　　　**RULE 18 (a); RULE 15; RULE 16**

BOTH INTERNATIONAL & INLAND Your power-driven vessel is NOT making way, but is not in any way disabled. Another power-driven vessel is approaching you on your starboard beam. Which statement is TRUE?

⚓ A. Your vessel is the give-way vessel in a crossing situation.

B. You should be showing the lights or shapes for a vessel restricted in her ability to maneuver.

C. You should be showing the lights or shapes for a vessel not under command.

D. The other vessel must give way since your vessel is stopped.

040379/RR04500　　　**RULE 18 (a); RULE 15; RULE 16**

BOTH INTERNATIONAL & INLAND Your power-driven vessel is stopped and making no way, but is not in any way disabled. Another vessel is approaching you on your starboard beam. Which statement is TRUE?

A. You should be showing the lights or shapes for a vessel not under command.

B. The other vessel must give way since your vessel is stopped.

⚓ C. Your vessel is the give-way vessel in a crossing situation.

D. You should be showing the lights or shapes for a vessel restricted in her ability to maneuver.

040380/RR04159　　　**RULE 18 (a) (i), (iii) - (iv)**

BOTH INTERNATIONAL & INLAND A power-driven vessel underway shall keep out of the way of a

_____.

A. sailing vessel

B. vessel not under command

C. vessel engaged in fishing

⚓ D. All of the above

040381/RR04173　　　**RULE 18 (a) (i) - (iii)**

BOTH INTERNATIONAL & INLAND A power-driven vessel underway shall keep out of the way of a vessel _____.

A. not under command

B. engaged in fishing

C. restricted in her ability to maneuver

⚓ D. All of the above

040382/RR04627　　**RULE 18 (a) (ii), (b) (ii), (c) (ii), (d) (i);**
　　　　　　　　　　　　　　　　　　　　　　　RULE 27 (b)

BOTH INTERNATIONAL & INLAND While underway you sight a vessel displaying the day-shapes shown in illustration D006RR below. What action should you take? See DIAGRAM D006RR

A. stop your vessel and sound passing signals

B. contact the vessel on VHF radiotelephone

C. provide assistance, the other vessel is in distress

⚓ D. stay clear, the other vessel cannot get out of the way

040383/RR04046　　　　　　**RULE 18 (a) (iii)**

BOTH INTERNATIONAL & INLAND Vessel "A", a power-driven vessel underway, sights vessel "B" which is a vessel underway and fishing as shown in illustration D014RR below. Which statement is true? See DIAGRAM D014RR

A. Vessel "A" must keep out of the way of vessel "B" because "B" is to port.

B. In this case, both vessels are required by the Rules to keep clear of each other.

⚓ C. Vessel "A" must keep out of the way of vessel "B" because "B" is fishing.

D. Vessel "B" must keep out of the way of vessel "A" because "A" is to starboard.

040384/RR04107　　　　　　**RULE 18 (a) (iv)**

BOTH INTERNATIONAL & INLAND A power-driven vessel has on her port side a sailing vessel which is on a collision course. The power-driven vessel is to

_____.

A. sound one blast and turn to starboard

B. maintain course and speed

C. stop her engines

⚓ D. keep clear, passing at a safe distance

040385/RR04224   **RULE 18 (a) (iv)**
BOTH INTERNATIONAL & INLAND A power-driven vessel has on her port side a sailing vessel which is on a collision course. What action is the power-driven vessel required to take?
A. sound one blast and turn to starboard
B. stop her engines
C. maintain course and speed
⚓ D. keep clear

040386/RR04638   **RULE 18 (a) (iv); RULE 3 (d);**
                           RULE 35 (a) - (b); RULE 13
BOTH INTERNATIONAL & INLAND A power-driven vessel is underway and fishing with trolling lines. This vessel _____.
A. must sound a one prolonged, two short blasts signal in restricted visibility
B. is the stand-on vessel when overtaking power-driven vessels
⚓ C. must keep out of the way of sailing vessels
D. All of the above

040387/RR04266   **RULE 18 (a) (iv);**
                                      RULE 15; RULE 13
BOTH INTERNATIONAL & INLAND On open waters, a power-driven vessel shall keep out of the way of which of the following?
A. a vessel on her port side that is crossing her course
B. a vessel that is overtaking her
C. a seaplane on the water
⚓ D. a sailing vessel

040388/RR04207   **RULE 18 (a) (iv)**
BOTH INTERNATIONAL & INLAND Your power-driven vessel is underway when you sight a sailing vessel on your port bow. Which vessel is the "stand-on" vessel?
A. Your vessel, because it is a power-driven vessel
⚓ B. The sailboat, because it is under sail
C. The sailboat, because it is to port of your vessel
D. Your vessel, because it is to starboard of the sailboat

040389/RR04068   **RULE 18 (a) (iv); RULE 15**
BOTH INTERNATIONAL & INLAND In illustration D002RR below, vessel I is a power-driven vessel. Vessel II is a sailing vessel with the wind dead aft. Which statement about this situation is correct? See DIAGRAM D002RR
⚓ A. Vessel I should keep out of the way of Vessel II.
B. The Rules of Special Circumstances applies, and neither vessel is the stand-on vessel.
C. Vessel II would normally be the stand-on vessel, but should stay out of the way in this particular situation.
D. Vessel II should keep out of the way of Vessel I.

040390/RR04094   **RULE 18 (a) (iv); RULE 17**
BOTH INTERNATIONAL & INLAND You are aboard vessel "A" which is towing on open waters when vessel "B", a sailing vessel, is sighted off your port bow as shown in illustration D020RR below. Which vessel is the stand-on? See DIAGRAM D020RR
A. Vessel "A" is the stand-on vessel because it is to starboard of vessel "B".
B. Vessel "A" is the stand-on vessel because it is towing.
⚓ C. Vessel "B" is the stand-on vessel because it is sailing.
D. Vessel "B" is the stand-on vessel because it is to port of vessel "A".

040391/RR04081   **RULE 18 (a) (iv); RULE 17**
BOTH INTERNATIONAL & INLAND You are aboard vessel "A" , a power-driven vessel, on open waters and vessel "B", a sailing vessel, is sighted off your port bow as shown in illustration D027RR below. Which vessel is the stand-on vessel? See DIAGRAM D027RR
A. Vessel "B" because it is to port of vessel "A"
B. Vessel "A" because it is to starboard of vessel "B"
⚓ C. Vessel "B" because it is sailing
D. Vessel "A" because it is towing

040392/RR04567   **RULE 18 (a); RULE 15**
BOTH INTERNATIONAL & INLAND In illustration D005RR below, vessel "A", which is pushing ahead, and vessel "B" are crossing. Which is the stand-on vessel? See DIAGRAM D005RR
⚓ A. Vessel "B" is the stand-on vessel because she is to starboard of vessel "A".
B. Vessel "A" is the stand-on vessel because she is pushing ahead.
C. Vessel "A" is the stand-on vessel because she is to port of vessel "B".
D. Neither vessel is the stand-on vessel in this situation.

040393/RR04124   **RULE 18 (a); RULE 15; RULE 17**
BOTH INTERNATIONAL & INLAND Vessel "A" is underway and pushing ahead when vessel "B" is sighted off the starboard bow as shown in illustration D028RR below. Which vessel is the stand-on vessel? See DIAGRAM D028RR
A. Vessel "A" is the stand-on vessel because it is to port.
B. Neither vessel is the stand-on vessel.
C. Vessel "A" is the stand-on vessel because it is pushing ahead.
⚓ D. Vessel "B" is the stand-on vessel because it is to starboard of vessel "A".

040394/RR09130   **RULE 18 (b)**
BOTH INTERNATIONAL & INLAND Except where specifically required by the rules, a sailing vessel is NOT required to keep out of the way of a _____.
A. vessel anchored
B. vessel setting a channel buoy
⚓ C. power-driven pilot vessel on station
D. vessel engaged in fishing

040395/RR04873   **RULE 18 (b) (i) - (ii), (a), (b) (iii);**
                                                    RULE 15
BOTH INTERNATIONAL & INLAND In a crossing situation on open waters, a sailing vessel shall keep out of the way of all the following vessels EXCEPT a vessel _____.
A. fishing
B. not under command
C. restricted in her ability to maneuver
⚓ D. engaged in towing

040396/RR04121   **RULE 18 (b) (i) - (iii), (a) (iv)**
BOTH INTERNATIONAL & INLAND A sailing vessel is NOT required to keep out of the way of a _____.
⚓ A. power-driven vessel
B. vessel not under command
C. vessel engaged in fishing
D. vessel restricted in her ability to maneuver

040397/RR04636   **RULE 18 (b) (i), (a) (iv), (b) (ii) - (iii)**
BOTH INTERNATIONAL & INLAND A vessel sailing shall keep out of the way of all of the following vessels except a vessel _____.
A. restricted in her ability to maneuver
B. engaged in fishing
⚓ C. engaged on pilotage duty
D. not under command

040398/RR04187   **RULE 18 (b) (i) - (ii), (a), (b) (iii);**
                                                    RULE 15
BOTH INTERNATIONAL & INLAND In a crossing situation on open waters, a sailing vessel shall keep out of the way of all the following vessels EXCEPT a _____.
A. vessel not under command
B. vessel restricted in her ability to maneuver
⚓ C. power-driven vessel approaching on her starboard side
D. vessel fishing

040399/RR04460   **RULE 18 (b) (ii), (b) (i), (b) (iii)**
BOTH INTERNATIONAL & INLAND Of the vessels listed, which must keep out of the way of all the others?
⚓ A. A sailing vessel
B. A vessel restricted in her ability to maneuver
C. A vessel engaged in fishing
D. A vessel not under command

040400/RR09000   **RULE 18 (b) (iii)**
BOTH INTERNATIONAL & INLAND In open waters, a vessel fishing is in a crossing situation with a vessel sailing. The sailing vessel is located on the fishing vessel's starboard side. Which vessel is the stand-on vessel?
A. The fishing vessel because it is to port of the sailing vessel.
B. The sailing vessel because it is sailing.
⚓ C. The fishing vessel because it is fishing.
D. The sailing vessel because it is to starboard of the fishing vessel.

040401/RR09131   **RULE 18 (b) (iii)**
BOTH INTERNATIONAL & INLAND Unless the rules require otherwise, a sailing vessel must keep out of the way of _____.
A. an overtaking vessel
⚓ B. a vessel trawling
C. another sailing vessel on a crossing course
D. a pilot vessel on station

040402/RR04280   **RULE 18 (b) (iii); RULE 15**
BOTH INTERNATIONAL & INLAND Vessels I and II are underway as shown in illustration D033RR below. Vessel I is a sailing vessel with the wind dead aft. Vessel II is a power-driven vessel trawling. Which statement is TRUE? See DIAGRAM D033RR
⚓ A. Vessel I is to keep clear because the other vessel is fishing.
B. Vessel II is to keep clear because the other vessel is tits starboard.
C. Vessel II is to keep clear because she is a power-driven vessel.
D. Both vessels are to take action to stay clear of each other.

040403/RR08023   **RULE 18 (c) (i)**
BOTH INTERNATIONAL & INLAND A fishing vessel is approaching a vessel not under command. Which statement is TRUE?
A. If the vessel not under command is a power-driven vessel, she must keep clear of the fishing vessel.
B. Both vessels are required to take action to stay clear of each other.
C. They must exchange whistle signals.
⚓ D. The fishing vessel must keep clear of the vessel not under command.

040404/RR04362   **RULE 18 (c) (i), (b) (iii), (a) (iii)**
BOTH INTERNATIONAL & INLAND A vessel underway and fishing shall keep out of the way of a _____.
A. vessel sailing
B. power-driven vessel underway
⚓ C. vessel not under command
D. vessel engaged on pilotage duty

040405/RR08114   **RULE 18 (c) (i)**
BOTH INTERNATIONAL & INLAND Which statement is TRUE concerning a situation involving a fishing vessel and a vessel not under command?
⚓ A. The fishing vessel must keep out of the way of the vessel not under command.
B. Both vessels are required to take action to stay clear of each other.
C. If the vessel not under command is a power-driven vessel, she must keep clear of the fishing vessel.
D. They are required to communicate by radiotelephone.

040406/RR04654   **RULE 18 (c) (ii) - (iii); RULE 9**
BOTH INTERNATIONAL & INLAND A vessel engaged in fishing shall keep out of the way of which of the following vessels?
⚓ A. restricted in her ability to maneuver
B. under sail
C. crossing a channel
D. All of the above

040407/RR04397   **RULE 18 (c) (ii), (b) (iii), (a)**
BOTH INTERNATIONAL & INLAND In a crossing situation, a vessel fishing must keep out of the way of a vessel which is _____.
A. engaged in pilotage duty
B. under sail
C. towing
⚓ D. restricted in her ability to maneuver

040408/RR04729   **RULE 18 (c) (ii)**
BOTH INTERNATIONAL & INLAND Which statement is TRUE, according to the Rules?
A. A vessel not under command shall keep out of the way of a vessel engaged in fishing.
B. A vessel engaged in fishing shall keep out of the way of a sailing vessel.
⚓ C. A vessel engaged in fishing while underway shall, so far as possible, keep out of the way of a vessel restricted in her ability to maneuver.
D. A vessel not under command shall keep out of the way of a vessel restricted in her ability to maneuver.

040409/RR04527   **RULE 18 (c) (ii); RULE 27 (b)**
BOTH INTERNATIONAL & INLAND You are fishing at night, and you sight a vessel showing three lights in a vertical line. The upper and lower lights are red and the middle light is white. Which statement is TRUE?
A. The other vessel is responsible to keep out of your way.
B. The rule of special circumstances applies.
C. The other vessel is at anchor.
⚓ D. You must keep out of the way of the other vessel.

040410/RR04632   **RULE 18 (e)**
BOTH INTERNATIONAL & INLAND The Rules state that a seaplane shall _____.
A. not be regarded as a vessel
B. proceed at a slower speed than surrounding vessels
C. when making way, show the lights for a vessel not under command
⚓ D. in general, keep well clear of all vessels

040411/RR04472   **RULE 18 (e)**
BOTH INTERNATIONAL & INLAND Which statement is TRUE concerning seaplanes on the water?
A. A seaplane should exhibit the lights for a vessel constrained by her draft.
⚓ B. A seaplane on the water shall, in general, keep well clear of all vessels.
C. In situations where a risk of collision exists, a seaplane should always give way.
D. A seaplane must show appropriate lights but need not exhibit shapes.

040412/RR04059   **RULE 18 (e)**
BOTH INTERNATIONAL & INLAND Which statement is TRUE concerning seaplanes on the water?
A. In situations where a risk of collision exists, a seaplane should always give way.
B. A seaplane must exhibit appropriate lights but need not exhibit shapes.
⚓ C. A seaplane on the water shall, in general, keep well clear of all vessels.
D. A seaplane should show the lights for a vessel constrained by her draft.

040413/RR04358   **RULE 18 (e)**
BOTH INTERNATIONAL & INLAND Which vessel should not impede the navigation of a power-driven vessel?
⚓ A. A seaplane
B. A vessel not under command
C. A vessel engaged in fishing
D. A sailing vessel

**PART B STEERING & SAILING RULES
SECTION SUBPART III
CONDUCT OF VESSELS
IN RESTRICTED VISIBILITY**

RULE 19 - CONDUCT IN RESTRICTED VISIBILITY

040414/RR04621   **RULE 19 (a)**
BOTH INTERNATIONAL & INLAND The steering and sailing rules for vessels in restricted visibility apply to vessels _____.
A. only if they are showing special purpose lights
B. only if they have operational radar
⚓ C. navigating in or near an area of restricted visibility
D. in sight of one another in fog

040415/RR00403　　　　　**RULE 19 (a); RULE 15**

BOTH INTERNATIONAL & INLAND Which vessel is the stand-on vessel when two vessels crossing in fog are NOT in sight of one another?

A. The vessel which has the other on her own port side

⚓ B. Neither vessel is the stand-on vessel.

C. The vessel which hears the other vessel's fog signal first

D. The vessel which has the other on her own starboard side

040416/RR04645　　　**RULE 19 (a) (b); RULE 35; RULE 7**

BOTH INTERNATIONAL & INLAND What is required of a vessel navigating near an area of restricted visibility?

A. If she detects another vessel by radar, she shall determine if risk of collision exists.

B. A power-driven vessel shall have her engines ready for immediate maneuver.

C. She must sound appropriate sound signals.

⚓ D. All of the above

040417/RR04097　　　　　　　　**RULE 19 (b)**

BOTH INTERNATIONAL & INLAND When navigating in restricted visibility, what action shall a power-driven vessel take?

A. when making way, sound one prolonged blast at intervals of not more than one minute

⚓ B. have her engines ready for immediate maneuver

C. stop her engines when hearing a fog signal forward of her beam, even if risk of collision does not exist

D. operate at a speed to be able to stop in the distance of her visibility

040418/RR04660　　　　　　　　**RULE 19 (d)**

BOTH INTERNATIONAL & INLAND In fog you observe your radar and determine that risk of collision exists with a vessel which is 2 miles off your port bow. You should _____.

A. hold course and speed until the other vessel is sighted

B. stop your engines

C. sound the danger signal at two minute intervals

⚓ D. take avoiding action as soon as possible

040419/RR04852　　　**RULE 19 (d); RULE 8 (a) - (d)**

BOTH INTERNATIONAL & INLAND What is TRUE when operating in fog and other vessels are detected by radar?

A. Long-range scanning will provide early warning of ALL other vessels within radar range.

B. You should make an ample change to port for a vessel crossing on the starboard bow.

C. You should determine the course and speed of all radar contacts at six minute intervals.

⚓ D. You should maneuver in ample time if a close-quarters situation is developing.

040420/RR04657　　　　　　　**RULE 19 (d) (ii)**

BOTH INTERNATIONAL & INLAND In restricted visibility, a vessel which detects by radar alone the presence of another vessel shall determine if a close-quarters situation is developing or risk of collision exists. If so, she shall _____.

A. sound the danger signal

B. when taking action, make only course changes

⚓ C. avoid altering course toward a vessel abaft the beam

D. All of the above

040421/RR04338　　　　　　　　**RULE 19 (e)**

BOTH INTERNATIONAL & INLAND A vessel hearing a fog signal forward of her beam has not determined if risk of collision exists. What shall she reduce speed to?

A. moderate speed

⚓ B. bare steerageway

C. safe speed

D. half speed

040422/RR04209　　　　　　　　**RULE 19 (e)**

BOTH INTERNATIONAL & INLAND Which statement concerning maneuvering in restricted visibility is FALSE?

A. A vessel which cannot avoid a close-quarters situation with a vessel forward of her beam shall reduce her speed to bare steerageway.

B. A vessel which hears a fog signal forward of the beam shall navigate with caution.

⚓ C. A vessel which hears a fog signal forward of her beam shall stop her engines.

D. If a vessel determines by radar that a close-quarters situation is developing, she shall take avoiding action in ample time.

040423/RR04233　　　　　　　　**RULE 19 (e)**

BOTH INTERNATIONAL & INLAND While underway in fog, you hear the fog signal of another vessel ahead. If a risk of collision exists, you must _____.

⚓ A. slow to bare steerageway and navigate with caution

B. continue on your course and speed until the other vessel is sighted

C. sound three short blasts and back your engines

D. stop your engines and navigate with caution

040424/RR04148　　　　　　　　**RULE 19 (e)**

BOTH INTERNATIONAL & INLAND You are in restricted visibility and hear a fog signal forward of the beam. Nothing appears on your radar screen. You must _____.

A. stop your engines

B. sound two prolonged blasts of the whistle

⚓ C. slow to bare steerageway

D. sound the danger signal

040425/RR04191   **RULE 19 (e)**
BOTH INTERNATIONAL & INLAND You are on watch in the fog. Your vessel is proceeding at a safe speed when you hear a fog signal ahead of you. The Rules require you to navigate with caution and take what action if danger of collision exists?
A. begin a radar plot
B. stop your engines
C. reduce to bare steerageway
D. slow to less than 2 knots

040426/RR04401   **RULE 19 (e)**
BOTH INTERNATIONAL & INLAND You are underway in heavy fog. You hear the fog signal of a vessel which is somewhere ahead of your vessel. You must _____.
A. slow to moderate speed and navigate with caution
B. stop engines and navigate with caution
C. maintain speed and sound the danger signal
D. slow to bare steerageway and navigate with caution

040427/RR04485   **RULE 19 (e)**
BOTH INTERNATIONAL & INLAND You are underway in reduced visibility. You hear the fog signal of another vessel about 20° on your starboard bow. Risk of collision may exist. You should _____.
A. alter course to starboard to pass around the other vessel
B. alter course to port to pass the other vessel on its portside
C. slow your engines and let the other vessel pass ahead of you
D. reduce your speed to bare steerageway

040428/RR04254   **RULE 19 (e)**
BOTH INTERNATIONAL & INLAND You are underway in restricted visibility and hear a fog signal forward of the beam. Nothing appears on your radar screen. You must take what action?
A. sound the danger signal
B. sound two prolonged blasts of the whistle
C. slow to bare steerageway
D. stop your engines

040429/RR04163   **RULE 19 (e)**
BOTH INTERNATIONAL & INLAND You are underway in restricted visibility. You hear the fog signal of another vessel about 22° on your starboard bow. If danger of collision exists you must _____.
A. alter the course to starboard to pass around the other vessel's stern
B. slow your engines and let the other vessel pass ahead of you
C. reduce your speed to bare steerageway
D. alter course to port to pass the other vessel on its port side

040430/RR01000   **RULE 19 (e)**
BOTH INTERNATIONAL & INLAND You hear the fog signal of another vessel forward of your beam. Risk of collision may exist. You MUST _____.
A. begin a radar plot
B. stop your engines
C. take all way off, if necessary
D. All of the above

040431/RR04177   **RULE 19 (e)**
BOTH INTERNATIONAL & INLAND Your vessel is underway in reduced visibility. You hear the fog signal of another vessel about 30° on your starboard bow. If danger of collision exists, you must _____.
A. slow your engines and let the other vessel pass ahead of you
B. reduce your speed to bare steerageway
C. alter course to port and pass the other vessel on its port side
D. alter course to starboard to pass around the other vessel's stern

PART C LIGHTS AND SHAPES

RULE 20 - APPLICATION

040432/RR04529   **RULE 20 (b); RULE 36**
BOTH INTERNATIONAL & INLAND A vessel may exhibit lights other than those prescribed by the Rules as long as the additional lights _____.
A. have a lesser range of visibility than the prescribed lights
B. do not impair the visibility or distinctive character of the prescribed lights
C. are not the same color as either side light
D. All of the above

040433/RR04507   **RULE 20 (b), (c)**
BOTH INTERNATIONAL & INLAND When must the lights required by the Rules be shown ?
A. from sunrise to sunset in restricted visibility
B. whenever a look-out is posted
C. at all times
D. ONLY from sunset to sunrise

040434/RR04681   **RULE 20 (b); RULE 36**
BOTH INTERNATIONAL & INLAND A vessel may exhibit lights other than those prescribed by the Rules as long as the additional lights _____.
A. are not the color of either sidelight
B. have a lesser range than the prescribed lights
C. do not interfere with the keeping of a proper look-out
D. All of the above

040435/RR04682   **RULE 20 (b); RULE 36**
BOTH INTERNATIONAL & INLAND A vessel may exhibit lights other than those prescribed by the Rules as long as the additional lights _____.
- A. do not interfere with the keeping of a proper look-out
- B. cannot be mistaken for the lights specified elsewhere in the Rules
- C. do not impair the visibility or distinctive character of the prescribed lights
- ⚓ D. All of the above

040436/RR04157   **RULE 20 (b); RULE 26**
BOTH INTERNATIONAL & INLAND Which vessel may exhibit identifying lights when not actually engaged in her occupation?
- A. A tug
- B. A fishing vessel
- C. A trawler
- ⚓ D. None of the above

040437/RR04416   **RULE 20 (c)**
BOTH INTERNATIONAL & INLAND Navigation lights must be displayed in all weathers from sunset to sunrise. They also _____.
- A. must be displayed when day signals are being used
- B. must be displayed when moored to a pier
- C. may be extinguished at night on open waters when another vessels are in the area
- ⚓ D. may be displayed during daylight

040438/RR04680   **RULE 20 (d)**
BOTH INTERNATIONAL & INLAND Day-shapes must be displayed _____.
- A. between sunset and sunrise
- B. during daylight hours in unrestricted visibility only
- ⚓ C. during daylight hours in any visibility
- D. only between 8 AM and 4 PM

040439/RR04556   **RULE 20 (d)**
BOTH INTERNATIONAL & INLAND Day-shapes MUST be shown _____.
- A. between sunset and sunrise
- B. during daylight hours except in restricted visibility
- C. ONLY between 8 AM and 4 PM daily
- ⚓ D. during daylight hours

RULE 21 - DEFINITIONS

040440/RR04542   **RULE 21 (a); RULE 24**
BOTH INTERNATIONAL & INLAND A vessel is towing and carrying the required lights on the masthead. What is the visibility arc of these lights?
- A. 112.5°
- B. 135.0°
- ⚓ C. 225.0°
- D. 360.0°

040441/RR04436   **RULE 21 (a)**
BOTH INTERNATIONAL & INLAND A white masthead light shows through an arc of how many degrees?
- A. 90°
- B. 112.5°
- ⚓ C. 225°
- D. 360°

040442/RR04136   **RULE 21 (a)**
BOTH INTERNATIONAL & INLAND The white masthead light required for a power-driven vessel under the Rules is visible over how many degrees of the horizon?
- ⚓ A. 225.0°
- B. 022.5°
- C. 360.0°
- D. 112.5°

040443/RR04333   **RULE 21 (b); RULE 22**
BOTH INTERNATIONAL & INLAND The arc of visibility for sidelights is from right ahead to _____.
- ⚓ A. 22.5° abaft the beam
- B. 22.5° forward of the beam
- C. 135° abaft the beam
- D. abeam

040444/RR00333   **RULE 21 (b)**
BOTH INTERNATIONAL & INLAND In illustration D023RR below Diagram "B" represents the arc of visibility of which of the following? See DIAGRAM D023RR
- A. red sidelight
- B. stern light
- C. yellow flashing light
- ⚓ D. green sidelight

040445/RR00327   **RULE 21 (b)**
BOTH INTERNATIONAL & INLAND In illustration D023RR below item "A" represents the arc of visibility of which of the following lights? See DIAGRAM D023RR
- A. green sidelight
- ⚓ B. red sidelight
- C. white masthead light
- D. stern light

040446/RR00325   **RULE 21 (b)**
BOTH INTERNATIONAL & INLAND In illustration D023RR below item "B" shows the arc of visibility of which of the following lights? See DIAGRAM D023RR
- A. white masthead light
- B. stern light
- C. red sidelight
- ⚓ D. green sidelight

040447/RR00335   **RULE 21 (b)**
BOTH INTERNATIONAL & INLAND In illustration D023RR below item "C" shows the arc of visibility of which of the following? See DIAGRAM D023RR
A. yellow flashing light
B. red sidelight
C. green sidelight
⚓ D. None of the above

040448/RR00328   **RULE 21 (b)**
BOTH INTERNATIONAL & INLAND In illustration D023RR below item "D" represents the arc of visibility of which of the following lights? See DIAGRAM D023RR
A. white masthead light
B. stern light
C. green sidelight
⚓ D. None of the above

040449/RR00324   **RULE 21 (b)**
BOTH INTERNATIONAL & INLAND In illustration D023RR below which item shows the arc of visibility of a green sidelight? See DIAGRAM D023RR
A. A
⚓ B. B
C. C
D. D

040450/RR00323   **RULE 21 (b)**
BOTH INTERNATIONAL & INLAND In illustration D023RR below which represents the arc of visibility of a red sidelight? See DIAGRAM D023RR
⚓ A. A
B. B
C. C
D. D

040451/RR04585   **RULE 21 (c); RULE 23 (a) (iv)**
BOTH INTERNATIONAL & INLAND While underway at night you are coming up on a vessel from astern. What lights would you expect to see?
⚓ A. One white light
B. Red and green sidelights
C. Two white lights
D. One white light and red and green sidelights

040452/RR04707   **RULE 21 (c); RULE 23 (a) (iv)**
BOTH INTERNATIONAL & INLAND While underway at night you are coming up on a vessel from astern. Which light(s) would you expect to see?
⚓ A. A stern light only
B. Both sidelights and the stern light
C. Sidelights only
D. two masthead lights

040453/RR04683   **RULE 21 (c)**
BOTH INTERNATIONAL & INLAND The stern light shall be positioned such that it will show from dead astern to how many degrees on each side of the stern of the vessel?
A. 22.5°
⚓ B. 67.5°
C. 112.5°
D. 135.0°

040454/RR04558   **RULE 21 (c)**
BOTH INTERNATIONAL & INLAND The stern light shall be positioned such that it will show from dead astern to how many degrees on each side of the stern of the vessel?
A. 135.0°
B. 112.5°
⚓ C. 67.5°
D. 22.5°

040455/RR04518   **RULE 21 (d)**
BOTH INTERNATIONAL & INLAND As defined in the Rules, a towing light is a yellow light having the same characteristics as a(n) _____.
A. all-round light
⚓ B. stern light
C. masthead light
D. sidelight

040456/RR08089   **RULE 21 (d)**
BOTH INTERNATIONAL & INLAND A towing light _____.
A. shows an unbroken light over an arc of the horizon of not less than 180° nor more than 225°
B. flashes at regular intervals of 50-70 flashes per minute
⚓ C. is yellow in color
D. All of the above

040457/RR04427   **RULE 21 (d)**
BOTH INTERNATIONAL & INLAND A towing light, according to the Rules, is a _____.
⚓ A. yellow light
B. blue light
C. white light
D. red light

040458/RR04116   **RULE 21 (d)**
BOTH INTERNATIONAL & INLAND The towing light is a(n) _____.
A. all-round yellow light
⚓ B. yellow light with the same characteristics as the stern light
C. yellow light with the same characteristics as the masthead light
D. flashing amber light

040459/RR04706   **RULE 21 (f)**
BOTH INTERNATIONAL & INLAND A "flashing light" is a light that _____.
A. is visible over an arc of the horizon of not less than 180° nor more than 225°
B. is yellow in color
C. flashes at regular intervals at a frequency of 120 flashes or more per minute
D. All of the above

040460/RR04087   **RULE 21 (f)**
BOTH INTERNATIONAL & INLAND A "flashing light", by the definition given in the rules, is a light that _____.
A. is red in color
B. is visible over an arc of the horizon of 360°
C. flashes at regular intervals at a frequency of 120 flashes or more per minute
D. All of the above

RULE 22 - VISIBILITY OF LIGHTS

040461/RR04684   **RULE 22; RULE 21 (b)**
BOTH INTERNATIONAL & INLAND You see a red sidelight bearing NW (315°). That vessel may be heading _____.
A. northeast (045°)
B. south (180°)
C. west (270°)
D. east (090°)

040462/RR04514   **RULE 22; RULE 21 (b)**
BOTH INTERNATIONAL & INLAND You are heading due east (090°) and observe a vessel's red sidelight on your port beam. The vessel may be heading _____.
A. north (000°)
B. southeast (135°)
C. southwest (225°)
D. northwest (315°)

040463/RR04702   **RULE 22; RULE 21 (b)**
BOTH INTERNATIONAL & INLAND You are heading due east (090°) and observe a vessel's red sidelight on your port beam. The vessel may be heading _____.
A. northwest (315°)
B. southeast (135°)
C. northeast (045°)
D. southwest (225°)

040464/RR04421   **RULE 22; RULE 21 (b)**
BOTH INTERNATIONAL & INLAND You see a red sidelight bearing NW (315°). That vessel may be heading _____.
A. southwest (225°)
B. west (270°)
C. northwest (315°)
D. east (090°)

040465/RR04044   **RULE 22; RULE 21 (b)**
BOTH INTERNATIONAL & INLAND You see a vessel's green sidelight bearing due east from you. The vessel might be heading _____.
A. southwest (225°)
B. east (090°)
C. northeast (045°)
D. northwest (315°)

040466/RR00162   **RULE 22; RULE 21 (b)**
BOTH INTERNATIONAL & INLAND You are on a vessel heading due north and see the lights shown in illustration D051RR below one point on your port bow. This vessel could be heading in what direction? See DIAGRAM D051RR
A. NW
B. SE
C. SW
D. NE

040467/RR00377   **RULE 22; RULE 21 (b)**
BOTH INTERNATIONAL & INLAND You are on a vessel heading due north and see the lights shown in illustration D051RR below, one point on your port bow. What direction could this vessel be heading in? See DIAGRAM D051RR
A. SW
B. NE
C. SE
D. NW

040468/RR00161   **RULE 22; RULE 21 (b)**
BOTH INTERNATIONAL & INLAND You are on a vessel heading due south and see the lights shown in illustration D051RR below one point on the port bow. What direction could this vessel be heading in? See DIAGRAM D051RR
A. SW
B. NW
C. SE
D. NE

040469/RR00166   **RULE 22; RULE 21 (b)**
BOTH INTERNATIONAL & INLAND You are on a vessel heading due south and see the lights shown in illustration D051RR below, one point on the port bow. What direction could this vessel be heading? See DIAGRAM D051RR
A. NE
B. SE
⚓ C. NW
D. SW

RULE 23 - POWER-DRIVEN VESSELS UNDERWAY

040470/RR04413   **RULE 23 (a) (i) - (ii)**
BOTH INTERNATIONAL & INLAND Which statement is TRUE concerning a 75-meter power-driven vessel underway at night?
A. She must exhibit only a forward masthead light.
B. She must exhibit an all-round white light at the stern.
C. She may exhibit a red light over a green light forward.
⚓ D. She must exhibit forward and after masthead lights.

040471/RR04517   **RULE 23 (a) (i) - (ii)**
BOTH INTERNATIONAL & INLAND Which vessel must exhibit forward and after masthead lights when underway?
A. A 100-meter vessel engaged in fishing
B. A 200-meter sailing vessel
⚓ C. A 50-meter power-driven vessel
D. All of the above

040472/RR04614   **RULE 23; RULE 20 (b)**
BOTH INTERNATIONAL & INLAND Which vessel may show identifying lights when not actually engaged in her occupation?
A. A fishing vessel
B. A pilot vessel
C. A mineclearance vessel
⚓ D. None of the above

040473/RR04723   **RULE 23 (a) (i), (a) (iii)**
BOTH INTERNATIONAL & INLAND You see a vessel displaying ONLY the lights shown in illustration D045RR below. This vessel could be which of the following? See DIAGRAM D045RR
A. pilot vessel on pilotage duty
B. vessel engaged in launching or recovering aircraft
⚓ C. power-driven vessel underway
D. vessel engaged in fishing at anchor

040474/RR04709   **RULE 23 (a) (i), (a) (iii)**
BOTH INTERNATIONAL & INLAND At night, a vessel displaying the lights shown in illustration D052RR below is doing which of the following? See DIAGRAM D052RR
A. engaged in dredging
B. towing a submerged object
⚓ C. underway
D. pushing ahead

040475/RR09105   **RULE 23 (a) (i), (a) (iii)**
BOTH INTERNATIONAL & INLAND At night, a vessel displaying the lights shown in illustration D052RR below represents which of the following? See DIAGRAM D052RR
A. a vessel dredging
⚓ B. a vessel underway
C. a vessel at anchor
D. a vessel aground

040476/RR04582   **RULE 23 (a) (i), (a) (iii)**
BOTH INTERNATIONAL & INLAND At night, a vessel displaying the lights shown in illustration D052RR below. Which of the following describes this vessel? See DIAGRAM D052RR
⚓ A. underway
B. aground
C. at anchor
D. transferring dangerous cargo

040477/RR04540   **RULE 23 (a) (i), (a) (iii)**
BOTH INTERNATIONAL & INLAND The lights shown in illustration D058RR below represent which of the following? See DIAGRAM D058RR
A. sailboat
⚓ B. power-driven vessel of less than 50 meters in length
C. fishing vessel at anchor
D. vessel being towed

040478/RR00170   **RULE 23 (a) (i), (a) (iii); RULE 15**
BOTH INTERNATIONAL & INLAND You are on a vessel and see ahead the lights shown in illustration D059RR below. These lights indicate which of the following? See DIAGRAM D059RR
A. vessel meeting head-on
B. vessel being overtaken
⚓ C. vessel crossing from your port
D. vessel crossing from your starboard

040479/RR00172   RULE 23 (a) (i), (a) (iii); RULE 15
BOTH INTERNATIONAL & INLAND You are on watch and sight a vessel showing only the lights in illustration D059RR below. What type of vessel do these lights represent? See DIAGRAM D059RR
⚓ A. power-driven vessel
    B. sailing vessel
    C. mineclearance vessel
    D. vessel engage in trawling

040480/RR00175   RULE 23 (a) (i) - (iii); RULE 14 (b)
BOTH INTERNATIONAL & INLAND You see the display of lights shown in illustration D071RR below. These lights indicate what type of vessel? See DIAGRAM D071RR
    A. trawling
⚓ B. approaching head-on
    C. fishing with nets extending more than 150 meters
    D. dredging

040481/RR04260   RULE 23 (a) (ii)
BOTH INTERNATIONAL & INLAND The minimum length of a power-driven vessel that must show forward and after masthead lights is _____.
⚓ A. 50 meters
    B. 100 meters
    C. 75 meters
    D. 30 meters

040482/RR04352   RULE 23 (a) (ii)
BOTH INTERNATIONAL & INLAND What is the minimum vessel length which must show two white masthead lights, one forward and one aft, when underway at night?
    A. 7 meters
⚓ B. 50 meters
    C. 100 meters
    D. 20 meters

040483/RR04296   RULE 23 (a) (ii), (a) (i)
BOTH INTERNATIONAL & INLAND Which power-driven vessel is NOT required to carry a light in the position of the after masthead light?
    A. A vessel of 60 meters in length towing astern
⚓ B. A vessel of 45 meters in length trolling
    C. A pushing vessel and a vessel being pushed, in a composite unit and 100 meters in length
    D. Any vessel constrained by her draft

040484/RR04618   RULE 23 (a) (iii)
BOTH INTERNATIONAL & INLAND Which vessel would exhibit sidelights when underway and not making way?
⚓ A. A power-driven vessel
    B. A vessel engaged in fishing
    C. A vessel engaged in dredging
    D. A vessel not under command

040485/RR00234   RULE 23 (a) (iv); RULE 13 (b); RULE 21 (c)
BOTH INTERNATIONAL & INLAND Vessel "A" is overtaking vessel "B" as shown in illustration D017RR below. Which color light will vessel "A" observe on vessel "B"? See DIAGRAM D017RR
    A. Flashing red
    B. Green
    C. Yellow over yellow
⚓ D. White

040486/RR04117   RULE 23 (b)
BOTH INTERNATIONAL & INLAND An all-round flashing yellow light may be exhibited by a(n) _____.
⚓ A. air-cushion vessel
    B. vessel laying cable
    C. vessel not under command
    D. vessel towing a submerged object

040487/RR04612   RULE 23 (b)
BOTH INTERNATIONAL & INLAND An all-round flashing yellow light may be exhibited by a(n) _____.
    A. vessel towing a submerged object
    B. vessel not under command
⚓ C. air-cushion vessel in the nondisplacement mode
    D. vessel engaged in diving operations

040488/RR00233   RULE 23 (b)
BOTH INTERNATIONAL & INLAND Vessel "A" is overtaking vessel "B" as shown in illustration D017RR below, and will pass without changing course. Vessel "B" is an air-cushion vessel operating in the nondisplacement mode. Which light will vessel "A" observe from vessel "B"? See DIAGRAM D017RR
⚓ A. flashing yellow light
    B. flashing white light
    C. flashing red light
    D. Green light

040489/RR00109   RULE 23 (b)
BOTH INTERNATIONAL & INLAND Vessel "A" is overtaking vessel "B" as shown in illustration D017RR below. Vessel "B" is an air-cushion vessel operating in the nondisplacement mode. In addition to a steady white light which other light will vessel "A" observe on vessel "B"? See DIAGRAM D017RR
    A. Flashing white light
    B. Steady green light
⚓ C. Flashing yellow light
    D. Flashing red light

040490/RR04354   **RULE 23 (d) (i) International;**
RULE 23 (d) Inland
BOTH INTERNATIONAL & INLAND At night, a power-driven vessel less than 12 meters in length may, instead of the normal navigation lights, show sidelights and one _____.
A. yellow light
B. flashing white light
C. flashing yellow light
⚓ D. white light

040491/RR04441   **RULE 23 (d) (i)**
BOTH INTERNATIONAL & INLAND At night, power-driven vessels less than 12 meters in length may, instead of the underway lights for vessels under 50 meters, show which lights?
A. Masthead light only
B. Stern light only
C. Sidelights and stern light
⚓ D. One all-round white light and sidelights

040492/RR04001   **RULE 23 (d) (i)**
BOTH INTERNATIONAL & INLAND The maximum length of a power-driven vessel which may show an all-round white light and sidelights instead of a masthead light, sidelights and a stern light is _____.
A. 19.9 meters
B. 6.9 meters
⚓ C. 11.9 meters
D. 9.9 meters

RULE 24 - TOWING AND PUSHING

040493/RR04170   **RULE 24 (a) (i)**
BOTH INTERNATIONAL & INLAND A 20-meter vessel is towing another vessel astern. The length of the tow from the stern of the towing vessel to the stern of the tow is 75 meters. How many white towing masthead lights shall the towing vessel show at night?
A. 1
⚓ B. 2
C. 3
D. 4

040494/RR04100   **RULE 24 (a) (i), (d)**
BOTH INTERNATIONAL & INLAND A 45-meter vessel is pulling a 210-meter tow. She may exhibit _____.
⚓ A. three masthead lights forward and one aft
B. three masthead lights aft and none forward
C. a masthead light forward, and two masthead lights in a vertical line aft
D. two masthead lights forward and no after masthead light

040495/RR04480   **RULE 24 (a) (i)**
BOTH INTERNATIONAL & INLAND A power-driven vessel towing another vessel astern (tow less than 200 meters) shall show _____.
A. three masthead lights in a vertical line instead of either the forward or after masthead light
⚓ B. two masthead lights in a vertical line instead of either the forward or after masthead lights
C. two towing lights in a vertical line at the stern
D. a small white light aft of the funnel

040496/RR04166   **RULE 24 (a) (i)**
BOTH INTERNATIONAL & INLAND A power-driven vessel towing another vessel astern (tow less than 200 meters) shall show _____.
A. two towing lights in a vertical line at the stern
⚓ B. two masthead lights in a vertical line instead of either the forward or after masthead lights
C. a small white light abaft the funnel
D. three masthead lights in a vertical line instead of either the forward or after masthead lights

040497/RR04623   **RULE 24 (a) (i)**
BOTH INTERNATIONAL & INLAND A towing vessel 35 meters in length, with a tow 100 meters astern, must show a minimum of how many masthead lights?
A. 1
⚓ B. 2
C. 3
D. 4

040498/RR04205   **RULE 24 (a) (i)**
BOTH INTERNATIONAL & INLAND A towing vessel is towing two barges astern. The length of the tow from the stern of the tug to the stern of the last barge is 250 meters. The towing vessel is 45 meters in length. How many white masthead lights should be displayed on the tugboat at night?
A. 1
B. 2
⚓ C. 3
D. 4

040499/RR04082   **RULE 24 (a) (i)**
BOTH INTERNATIONAL & INLAND Which vessel must exhibit three white masthead lights in a vertical line?
A. A vessel being towed
B. Any vessel towing astern
⚓ C. A vessel whose tow exceeds 200 meters astern
D. A vessel not under command, at anchor

040500/RR04129   **RULE 24 (a) (i), (c)**
BOTH INTERNATIONAL & INLAND Which vessel MUST show two masthead lights in a vertical line?
A. A vessel not under command
B. A vessel engaged in dredging
⚓ C. A power-driven vessel less than 50 meters in length with a 20-meter tow
D. A sailing vessel towing a small vessel astern

040501/RR04184   **RULE 24 (a) (i) - (ii)**
BOTH INTERNATIONAL & INLAND You are approaching another vessel at night. You can see both red and green sidelights and, above the level of the sidelights, three white lights in a vertical line. The vessel may be _____.
A. underway and dredging
B. not under command
⚓ C. towing a tow more than 200 meters astern
D. trawling

040502/RR04222   **RULE 24 (a) (i)**
BOTH INTERNATIONAL & INLAND You are towing two barges astern. The length of the tow from the stern of the tug to the stern of the last barge is 150 meters. How many white towing identification lights should be displayed on the tugboat at night?
A. 1
⚓ B. 2
C. 3
D. 4

040503/RR00379   **RULE 24 (a) (i) - (iv); RULE 27 (c)**
BOTH INTERNATIONAL & INLAND A seagoing tug has a tow greater than 200 meters as shown in illustration D024RR below and is severely restricted in her ability to deviate from her course. Which lights would be displayed from the towing vessel? See DIAGRAM D024RR
⚓ A. Three white masthead lights, red-white-red all-round lights, sidelights, stern light and a towing light
B. Three white masthead lights, two all-round red lights, sidelights, stern light and a towing light
C. Three white masthead lights, red-white-red all-round lights, sidelights and two towing lights
D. None of the above

040504/RR00290   **RULE 24 (a) (i) - (iv); RULE 27 (c)**
BOTH INTERNATIONAL & INLAND The tow shown in illustration D024RR below is greater than 200 meters in length and severely restricts the tow vessel's ability to deviate from her course. Which day shape(s) would be displayed by day from the vessel(s)? See DIAGRAM D024RR
A. diamond on the barges
B. diamond on the towing vessel
C. ball-diamond-ball on the towing vessel
⚓ D. All of the above

040505/RR00292   **RULE 24 (a) (i) - (iv); RULE 27 (c)**
BOTH INTERNATIONAL & INLAND The tug shown in illustration D024RR below is greater than 50 meters and severely restricted in her ability to deviate from her course. Which lights would be displayed from the towing vessel? See DIAGRAM D024RR
A. Two white masthead lights, red-white-red all round lights, sidelights, stern light and a towing light
B. Three white masthead lights, two all round red lights, sidelights, stern light and a towing light
C. Three white masthead lights, red-white-red all round lights, sidelights and two towing lights
⚓ D. None of the above

040506/RR00176   **RULE 24 (a) (i) - (ii); RULE 14 (b)**
BOTH INTERNATIONAL & INLAND You see the display of lights shown in illustration D064RR below. These lights could indicate which of the following? See DIAGRAM D064RR
A. tug unable to maneuver as required by the Rules
B. 60-meter tug pushing a barge ahead
C. range marking a channel beneath a drawbridge
⚓ D. 40-meter tug with tow exceeding 200 meters

040507/RR00177   **RULE 24 (a) (i) - (ii); RULE 14 (b)**
BOTH INTERNATIONAL & INLAND You see the display of lights shown in illustration D064RR below. This could indicate which of the following? See DIAGRAM D064RR
A. 55-meter tug towing astern, length of tow exceeds 200 meters
B. dredge working at anchor
⚓ C. 65-meter tug towing astern, length of tow 150 meters
D. dredge restricted in its ability to maneuver

040508/RR04331   **RULE 24 (a) (i) - (iv)**
BOTH INTERNATIONAL & INLAND You see the lights shown in illustration D077RR below. This could be which of the following? See DIAGRAM D077RR
A. A pipeline
B. A stationary dredge
⚓ C. A vessel towing barges astern
D. A vessel pushing barges ahead

040509/RR00298   **RULE 24 (a) (i) - (iv), (d)**
BOTH INTERNATIONAL & INLAND A vessel displaying the lights shown in illustration D079RR below could be which of the following? See DIAGRAM D079RR
A. vessel constrained by her draft
B. law enforcement vessel
C. vessel not under command
⚓ D. vessel towing astern

040510/RR00288   **RULE 24 (a); RULE 27 (c)**
BOTH INTERNATIONAL & INLAND The tow shown in illustration D024RR below is less than 200 meters in length and severely restricted in her ability to deviate from her course. Which dayshape(s) would be displayed by day from the vessel(s)? See DIAGRAM D024RR
A. diamond on the towing vessel
⚓ B. ball-diamond-ball on the towing vessel
C. diamond on the last barge
D. All of the above

040511/RR04711   **RULE 24 (a) (ii)**
BOTH INTERNATIONAL & INLAND Which vessel would exhibit sidelights when underway and not making way?
A. A vessel not under command
⚓ B. A vessel towing astern
C. A vessel engaged in dredging operations
D. A vessel trawling

040512/RR04201   **RULE 24 (a) (iii) - (iv)**
BOTH INTERNATIONAL & INLAND A power-driven vessel towing astern shall show _____.
A. two towing lights in a vertical line
B. a small white light in lieu of the stern light
C. two towing lights in addition to the stern light
⚓ D. a towing light in a vertical line above the stern light

040513/RR04152   **RULE 24 (a) (iii) - (iv)**
BOTH INTERNATIONAL & INLAND A power-driven vessel with a 150-meter stern tow shall display _____.
A. two towing lights in a vertical line
B. a red light over a white light at the masthead
⚓ C. a towing light above the stern light
D. three masthead lights in a vertical line

040514/RR04180   **RULE 24 (a) (iii) - (iv)**
BOTH INTERNATIONAL & INLAND A power-driven vessel, when towing astern, shall show _____.
⚓ A. a towing light in a vertical line above the stern light
B. two towing lights in a vertical line
C. two towing lights in addition to the stern light
D. a small white light in lieu of the stern light

040515/RR04337   **RULE 24 (a) (iii) - (iv)**
BOTH INTERNATIONAL & INLAND A vessel showing a yellow light over a white light at night is a vessel _____.
A. in distress
B. engaged in fishing
C. engaged in piloting
⚓ D. towing astern

040516/RR04601   **RULE 24 (a) (iii) - (iv)**
BOTH INTERNATIONAL & INLAND A vessel towing a barge astern would show, at the stern _____.
A. two towing lights in a vertical line
B. only a stern light
C. two white lights in a vertical line
⚓ D. a towing light above the stern light

040517/RR04267   **RULE 24 (a) (iii) - (iv)**
BOTH INTERNATIONAL & INLAND You are overtaking a vessel at night and you see a yellow light showing above the stern light of the overtaken vessel. The overtaken vessel is _____.
⚓ A. towing astern
B. a pilot vessel
C. pushing ahead or towing alongside
D. underway and dredging

040518/RR00294   **RULE 24 (a) (iii) - (iv), (e) (ii)**
BOTH INTERNATIONAL & INLAND The display of lights shown in illustration D048RR below could represent which of the following? See DIAGRAM D048RR
A. a vessel not under command
⚓ B. tug and a barge being towed astern
C. sailing vessel
D. a submarine on the surface

040519/RR04175   **RULE 24 (a) (iii) - (iv)**
BOTH INTERNATIONAL & INLAND A vessel displaying the lights shown in illustration D060RR below is which of the following? See DIAGRAM D060RR
A. being towed
B. broken down
C. fishing
⚓ D. towing

040520/RR04225   **RULE 24 (a) (iv)**
BOTH INTERNATIONAL & INLAND A single towing light will be carried above a vessel's stern light under which of the following situations?
A. at any time when towing
B. if the towing vessel is part of a composite unit
⚓ C. only if she is towing astern
D. only if the tow exceeds 200 meters

040521/RR04143   **RULE 24 (a) (iv)**
BOTH INTERNATIONAL & INLAND Which statement is true concerning a towing light when a towing vessel is towing astern?
⚓ A. The towing light is shown above the stern light.
B. The towing light is shown below the stern light.
C. When a towing light is shown, no stern light is necessary.
D. When a stern light is shown, no towing light is necessary.

040522/RR04445   **RULE 24 (a) (iv)**
BOTH INTERNATIONAL & INLAND Which vessel must show a towing light above the stern light?
⚓ A. A vessel with a 150-meter tow astern
   B. A vessel towing alongside
   C. A vessel pushing three barges ahead
   D. None of the above

040523/RR04606   **RULE 24 (a) (v)**
BOTH INTERNATIONAL & INLAND A power-driven vessel when towing and the length of the tow exceeds 200 meters shall exhibit during daylight hours where they can best be seen which of the following shapes?
⚓ A. a diamond shape
   B. one cone, apex upward
   C. two cones, apexes together
   D. a black ball

040524/RR04155   **RULE 24 (a) (v)**
BOTH INTERNATIONAL & INLAND A vessel towing is showing three forward white masthead lights in a vertical line. This means that the length of the _____.
⚓ A. tow is greater than 200 meters
   B. tow is less than 200 meters
   C. towing vessel is less than 50 meters
   D. towing vessel is greater than 50 meters

040525/RR04461   **RULE 24 (a) (v)**
BOTH INTERNATIONAL & INLAND During the day, a vessel with a tow over 200 meters in length will show _____.
   A. a black ball
⚓ B. a diamond shape
   C. one cone, apex upward
   D. two cones, apexes together

040526/RR04398   **RULE 24 (a) (v)**
BOTH INTERNATIONAL & INLAND A tug boat displaying the day-shape shown in illustration D010RR below is which of the following? See DIAGRAM D010RR
⚓ A. has a tow that exceeds 200 meters in length
   B. is at anchor
   C. has a tow that is carrying dangerous cargo
   D. is not under command

040527/RR04328   **RULE 24 (a) (v)**
BOTH INTERNATIONAL & INLAND A vessel displaying the day-shape shown in illustration D010RR below is which of the following? See DIAGRAM D010RR
   A. has a tow that is carrying dangerous cargo
   B. is not under command
⚓ C. has a tow that exceeds 200 meters in length
   D. is at anchor

040528/RR04363   **RULE 24 (a) (v)**
BOTH INTERNATIONAL & INLAND A vessel displaying the day-shape shown in illustration D010RR below is which of the following? See DIAGRAM D010RR
   A. broken down
   B. anchored
   C. fishing
⚓ D. towing

040529/RR04040   **RULE 24 (a) (v)**
BOTH INTERNATIONAL & INLAND Which of the day-shapes shown in illustration D016RR below indicates a vessel with a tow exceeding 200 meters in length? See DIAGRAM D016RR
   A. A
⚓ B. B
   C. C
   D. D

040530/RR04072   **RULE 24, RULE 23 (a) (i), (a) (iv)**
BOTH INTERNATIONAL & INLAND A 30-meter tug is underway and NOT towing. At night, this vessel must show sidelights and _____.
   A. a stern light ONLY
⚓ B. one masthead light and a stern light
   C. three masthead lights and a stern light
   D. two masthead lights and a stern light

040531/RR04634   **RULE 24, RULE 23 (a) (i), (a) (iv)**
BOTH INTERNATIONAL & INLAND Your tug is underway at night and NOT towing. What light(s) should your vessel show aft to other vessels coming up from astern?
   A. One white light and one yellow light
   B. Two white lights
   C. One white light and two yellow lights
⚓ D. One white light

040532/RR00152   **RULE 24 (a) - (f); RULE 27 (c)**
BOTH INTERNATIONAL & INLAND The vessel showing the day shape in illustration D022RR below is which of the following? See DIAGRAM D022RR
   A. A vessel engaged in mine clearance operations
   B. A trawler shooting nets in the direction indicated
   C. A fishing vessel with gear extending more than 150 meters horizontally
⚓ D. A tug with a tow exceeding 200 meters unable to deviate from course

040533/RR04425   **RULE 24 (b)**
BOTH INTERNATIONAL & INLAND A power-driven vessel exhibits the same lights as a _____.
   A. vessel towing, when not underway
⚓ B. pushing vessel and a vessel being pushed, when they are in a composite unit
   C. vessel towing astern
   D. sailing vessel

040534/RR04573   **RULE 24 (b)**
BOTH INTERNATIONAL & INLAND A power-driven vessel shows the same lights as a _____.
A. vessel towing astern
B. pushing vessel and a vessel being pushed, when they are rigidly connected in a composite unit
C. sailing vessel
D. vessel engaged in towing, when not underway

040535/RR04042   **RULE 24 (b)**
BOTH INTERNATIONAL & INLAND A towing vessel pushing a barge ahead and rigidly connected in a composite unit shall show the lights of _____.
A. a vessel pushing ahead
B. a power-driven vessel, not towing
C. a barge being pushed ahead
D. either answer A or answer B

040536/RR04150   **RULE 24 (c) (i)**
BOTH INTERNATIONAL & INLAND A towing vessel 30 meters in length is pushing barges ahead. How many white masthead lights is the vessel REQUIRED to show at night?
A. One
B. Two
C. Three
D. Four

040537/RR04710   **RULE 24 (c) (ii)**
BOTH INTERNATIONAL & INLAND Which vessel would exhibit sidelights when underway and not making way?
A. A vessel engaged in dredging
B. A vessel pushing ahead
C. A vessel not under command
D. A vessel trawling

040538/RR05100   **RULE 24 (c) (iii)**
BOTH INTERNATIONAL & INLAND Lighting requirements in INLAND waters are different from those for international waters for _____.
A. vessels pushing ahead
B. barges being towed astern
C. vessels not under command
D. All of the above

040539/RR00388   **RULE 24 (c) (iii)**
BOTH INTERNATIONAL & INLAND Lighting requirements in INLAND waters are different from those in international waters for _____.
A. vessels being towed alongside
B. barges being pushed ahead
C. vessels pushing ahead
D. All of the above

040540/RR04111   **RULE 24 (d), (a) (i) - (iv)**
BOTH INTERNATIONAL & INLAND A 50-meter vessel is towing astern and the length of the tow is 100 meters. In addition to sidelights, which lights may she show to fully comply with the Rules?
A. A masthead light forward, two masthead lights aft, a stern light, and a towing light above the stern light
B. Two masthead lights forward, a stern light, and a towing light above the stern light
C. Three masthead lights forward, one masthead light aft, and two towing lights in a vertical line at the stern
D. No masthead light forward, two masthead lights aft, a stern light, and a towing light above the stern light

040541/RR04137   **RULE 24 (d)**
BOTH INTERNATIONAL & INLAND Which statement is TRUE concerning lights and shapes for towing vessels?
A. If a tow exceeds 200 meters in length, the towing vessel will display a black ball during daylight.
B. If the towing vessel is over 50 meters in length, she must carry forward and after masthead lights.
C. When towing astern, a vessel will carry her identification lights at the masthead in addition to her regular masthead light.
D. When towing astern, the towing vessel may show either a stern light or a towing light, but not both.

040542/RR04412   **RULE 24 (d), (a) (i) - (ii)**
BOTH INTERNATIONAL & INLAND A vessel displaying the lights shown in illustration D063RR below is which of the following? See DIAGRAM D063RR
A. underway and more than 50 meters in length
B. towing astern
C. fishing
D. not under command

040543/RR00178   **RULE 24 (d)**
BOTH INTERNATIONAL & INLAND Which display of lights shown in illustration D072RR below indicates a 65-meter tug towing a barge astern, length of tow 120 meters? See DIAGRAM D072RR
A. A
B. B
C. C
D. D

040544/RR04395   **RULE 24 (d), (a) (i) - (ii)**
BOTH INTERNATIONAL & INLAND What do the lights displayed in illustration D073RR indicate? See DIAGRAM D073RR
A. fishing vessel trolling
B. vessel laying submarine cable
⚓ C. vessel towing astern
D. vessel dredging

040545/RR04210   **RULE 24 (e) (i) - (ii)**
BOTH INTERNATIONAL & INLAND A vessel being towed astern shall show at night _____.
⚓ A. sidelights and a stern light
B. only the required masthead lights
C. a stern light only
D. the lights required for a power-driven vessel underway

040546/RR04346   **RULE 24 (e) (i) - (ii)**
BOTH INTERNATIONAL & INLAND A vessel being towed at night must show _____.
A. a white all-round light, only
⚓ B. sidelights and a stern light
C. forward and after masthead lights
D. a flashing yellow light, only

040547/RR04304   **RULE 24 (e) (i)**
BOTH INTERNATIONAL & INLAND A vessel being towed will show _____.
A. a forward masthead light
⚓ B. sidelights and a stern light
C. a towing light
D. All of the above

040548/RR04220   **RULE 24 (e) (i);**
*** Comment ***
Sternlight is also required.

BOTH INTERNATIONAL & INLAND A vessel towed astern shall show _____.
A. masthead lights
⚓ B. sidelights
C. a special flashing light
D. All of the above

040549/RR04004   **RULE 24 (e) (i) - (ii)**
BOTH INTERNATIONAL & INLAND At night, a barge being towed astern must display _____.
A. red and green sidelights only
⚓ B. sidelights and a stern light
C. one all-round white light
D. a white stern light only

040550/RR04258   **RULE 24 (e) (i) - (ii)**
BOTH INTERNATIONAL & INLAND At night, a broken down vessel being towed would show the same lights as _____.
⚓ A. a barge
B. a power-driven vessel underway
C. a vessel at anchor
D. the towing vessel

040551/RR04491   **RULE 24 (e) (i) - (iii), (f)**
BOTH INTERNATIONAL & INLAND Barges being towed at night _____.
A. must be lighted only if towed astern
B. need not be lighted
C. must be lighted only if manned
⚓ D. must be lighted at all times

040552/RR00259   **RULE 24 (e) (i) - (iii), (f)**
BOTH INTERNATIONAL & INLAND Barges being towed at night must exhibit navigation lights _____.
A. only if towed astern
⚓ B. at all times
C. only if manned
D. Need not be lighted

040553/RR04261   **RULE 24 (e) (i) - (ii)**
BOTH INTERNATIONAL & INLAND What light(s), if any, would you show at night if your vessel was broken down and being towed astern by another vessel?
A. None
B. Same lights as for a power-driven vessel underway
C. A white light forward and a white light aft
⚓ D. The colored sidelights and a white stern light

040554/RR04196   **RULE 24 (e) (i) - (ii)**
BOTH INTERNATIONAL & INLAND What lights must be shown on a barge being towed astern at night?
A. A white light fore and aft
⚓ B. Sidelights and a stern light
C. A white light at each corner
D. A stern light only

040555/RR04234   **RULE 24 (e) (i) - (ii)**
BOTH INTERNATIONAL & INLAND What lights, if any, would you exhibit at night if your vessel were broken down and being towed by another vessel?
A. None
⚓ B. The colored sidelights and a white stern light
C. A white light forward and a white light aft
D. Same lights as for a power-driven vessel underway

040556/RR04560   **RULE 24 (e) (i) - (iii)**
BOTH INTERNATIONAL & INLAND When towing more than one barge astern at night _____.
A. only the last barge on the tow must be lighted
B. only manned barges must be lighted
⚓ C. each barge in the tow must be lighted
D. only the first and the last barges in the tow must be lighted

040557/RR04133   **RULE 24 (e) (i) - (iii)**
BOTH INTERNATIONAL & INLAND Which statement is TRUE when you are towing more than one barge astern at night?
A. All barges, except unmanned barges, must be lighted.
B. Only the last barge in the tow must be lighted.
C. Only the first and last barges in the tow must be lighted.
⚓ D. All barges in the tow must be lighted.

040558/RR04409   **RULE 24 (e) (ii)**
*** Comment ***
Sternlight is also required.

BOTH INTERNATIONAL & INLAND A vessel or object being towed astern shall display a(n) _____.
A. after masthead light
⚓ B. stern light
C. forward masthead light
D. All of the above

040559/RR04603   **RULE 24 (e) (ii), (f) (ii)**
BOTH INTERNATIONAL & INLAND In addition to sidelights what light should a vessel being towed astern show?
⚓ A. A stern light
B. Not under command lights
C. Range lights
D. A masthead light

040560/RR04626   **RULE 24 (e) (iii)**
BOTH INTERNATIONAL & INLAND A vessel being towed astern, where the length of the tow exceeds 200 meters, will exhibit _____.
A. no day-shape
B. a ball on each end of the tow
C. two balls in a vertical line
⚓ D. a diamond shape where it can best be seen

040561/RR04131   **RULE 24 (e) (iii)**
BOTH INTERNATIONAL & INLAND What day-shape should a vessel being towed exhibit if the tow EXCEEDS 200 meters?
A. Two balls
B. One ball
⚓ C. One diamond
D. Two diamonds

040562/RR04716   **RULE 24 (e) (iii)**
BOTH INTERNATIONAL & INLAND Which day-shape should a vessel being towed exhibit if the tow EXCEEDS 200 meters?
A. A ball
⚓ B. A diamond
C. A cone, apex downward
D. A cone, apex upward

040563/RR04631   **RULE 24 (f) (i)**
BOTH INTERNATIONAL & INLAND two barges are being pushed ahead by a tugboat. Which statement is TRUE concerning lights on the barges?
A. Each vessel should show at least one white light.
⚓ B. The barges should be lighted as one vessel.
C. The barges should be lighted as separate units.
D. Each vessel should show sidelights.

040564/RR04194   **RULE 24 (g) (i)**
BOTH INTERNATIONAL & INLAND At night, you are towing a partly submerged vessel, 20 meters in length and 4 meters in breadth. What lights must you display on the towed vessel?
A. A white light at the stern
B. two red lights in a vertical line at the after end
C. Two white lights side by side at the stern
⚓ D. A white light at the forward end and a white light at the after end

040565/RR04003   **RULE 24 (g) (i) - (v); RULE 36**
BOTH INTERNATIONAL & INLAND What is used to show the presence of a partly submerged object being towed?
A. A diamond shape on the towed object
B. A searchlight from the towing vessel in the direction of the tow
C. An all-round light at each end of the towed object
⚓ D. All of the above

040566/RR00375   **RULE 24 (g) (i)**
BOTH INTERNATIONAL & INLAND The tow shown in illustration D024RR below is made up of inconspicuous, partly submerged vessels and is 150 meters in length. The towed vessels are less than 25 meters in breadth and less than 100 meters in length. Which lights would be displayed from the towed vessels? See DIAGRAM D024RR
A. Sidelights and stern light on each vessel towed
B. One all round white light at each end and one all round white light at the extremities of its breadth of each vessel towed
C. One all round white light at the after end of each vessel towed
⚓ D. One all round white light at or near each end of each vessel towed

040567/RR04394   **RULE 24 (g) (iv)**
BOTH INTERNATIONAL & INLAND A partly submerged vessel or object being towed, which is not readily noticeable, shall show _____.
A. a black ball
B. yellow lights at each end
C. two red lights in a vertical line
⚓ D. a diamond shape

040568/RR04215   **RULE 24 (g) (iv)**
BOTH INTERNATIONAL & INLAND An inconspicuous, partly submerged vessel or object being towed, where the length of tow is 100 meters, shall show _____.
A. yellow lights at each end
B. two red lights in a vertical line
⚓ C. a diamond shape
D. a black ball

040569/RR04309   **RULE 24 (g) (iv)**
BOTH INTERNATIONAL & INLAND What day-shape must be shown on a partly submerged vessel which is being towed?
A. One black ball
B. A cone
C. two black balls in a vertical line
⚓ D. A diamond

040570/RR04530   **RULE 24 (g) (iv)**
BOTH INTERNATIONAL & INLAND Which statement is TRUE concerning a partly submerged vessel being towed?
A. It must show a yellow light at each end
⚓ B. A diamond shape will be carried at the aftermost extremity of the tow
C. It will show red lights along its length
D. All of the above

040571/RR00024   **RULE 24 (g) (iv)**
BOTH INTERNATIONAL & INLAND Which of the day-shapes shown in illustration D016RR below would you show on the after end of an inconspicuous partially submerged vessel or object being towed less than 200 meters in length? See DIAGRAM D016RR
A. A
⚓ B. B
C. C
D. No day-shape would be shown.

040572/RR00091   **RULE 24 (g) (iv)**
BOTH INTERNATIONAL & INLAND Which of the day-shapes shown in illustration D016RR below would you show on the after end of an inconspicuous partially submerged vessel or object being towed over 200 meters in length? See DIAGRAM D016RR
A. A
⚓ B. B
C. C
D. No day-shape would be shown.

040573/RR04584   **RULE 24 (g) (v); RULE 36**
BOTH INTERNATIONAL & INLAND A vessel that is not equipped with towing lights should show that it has a vessel in tow by _____.
⚓ A. shining a searchlight on the towline of the towed vessel
B. sounding one prolonged followed by two short blasts at intervals of not more than 2 minutes
C. continuously sounding its horn
D. None of the above; a vessel shall not engage in towing at night without proper navigation lights

040574/RR04611   **RULE 24 (i) International;
                                              RULE 24 (j) Inland**
BOTH INTERNATIONAL & INLAND A vessel, which does not normally engage in towing operations, is towing a vessel in distress. Which of the following statements is True?
A. may show the lights for a vessel not under command
B. must show the lights for a vessel towing
⚓ C. need not show the lights for a vessel engaged in towing, if it is impractical to do so
D. must show a yellow light above the stern light

RULE 25 - SAILING VESSELS UNDERWAY AND VESSELS UNDER OARS

040575/RR04639   **RULE 25 (a) (i)**
BOTH INTERNATIONAL & INLAND At night you sight a vessel displaying a single green light. This is a _____.
⚓ A. sailing vessel
B. small motorboat underway
C. vessel drifting
D. vessel at anchor

040576/RR04476   **RULE 25 (a) (i)**
BOTH INTERNATIONAL & INLAND At night you sight a vessel displaying one green light. What is indicated by this light configuration?
⚓ A. sailboat underway
B. vessel drifting
C. vessel at anchor
D. small motorboat underway

040577/RR04390   **RULE 25 (a) (i) - (ii)**
BOTH INTERNATIONAL & INLAND What light(s) must sailboats twenty meters in length show when underway at night?
A.   Red and green sidelights
B.   A stern light
C.   One all-round white light
⚓ D.   Red and green sidelights and a stern light

040578/RR04165   **RULE 25 (a) (i) - (ii)**
BOTH INTERNATIONAL & INLAND Which statement is TRUE of a 30-meter sailing vessel underway?
⚓ A.   She must show sidelights and a stern light in restricted visibility.
B.   If she is using propelling machinery, she shall show forward a shape consisting of two cones, apexes together.
C.   She need not show a stern light if she is showing all-round lights on the mast.
D.   She may show an all-round white light at the top of the mast.

040579/RR00181   **RULE 25 (a) (i) - (ii)**
BOTH INTERNATIONAL & INLAND At night, you see the display of lights shown in illustration D074RR below. These lights indicate which of the following? See DIAGRAM D074RR
A.   12-meter fishing vessel
B.   vessel not under command
C.   8-meter power-driven vessel
⚓ D.   sailing vessel

040580/RR04193   **RULE 25 (a) (ii)**
BOTH INTERNATIONAL & INLAND A 20-meter sailing vessel underway must exhibit a _____.
A.   combined lantern
⚓ B.   stern light
C.   red light over a green light at the masthead
D.   All of the above

040581/RR04214   **RULE 25 (a) (ii)**
BOTH INTERNATIONAL & INLAND A sailing vessel of over 20 meters in length underway must show a _____.
⚓ A.   stern light
B.   white masthead light
C.   combined lantern
D.   red light over a green light at the masthead

040582/RR00392   **RULE 25 (a)**
BOTH INTERNATIONAL & INLAND You see ONLY the light shown in illustration D080RR below. What type of vessel could this be? See DIAGRAM D080RR
A.   vessel engaged in fishing
⚓ B.   sailing vessel
C.   law enforcement vessel
D.   vessel on pilotage duty

040583/RR04231   **RULE 25 (b)**
BOTH INTERNATIONAL & INLAND A 15-meter sailing vessel would be required to show _____.
⚓ A.   sidelights, and stern light, but they may be in a combined lantern on the mast
B.   separate sidelights and stern light
C.   sidelights, stern light, and a red light over a green light on the mast
D.   sidelights only

040584/RR04373   **RULE 25 (b)**
BOTH INTERNATIONAL & INLAND A lantern combining the two sidelights and stern light may be shown on a _____.
A.   25-meter pilot vessel
⚓ B.   10-meter sailing vessel
C.   20-meter vessel engaged in fishing and making way
D.   25-meter power-driven vessel engaged in trolling

040585/RR04649   **RULE 25 (b)**
BOTH INTERNATIONAL & INLAND Which vessel may carry her sidelights and stern light in one combined lantern?
A.   a 20-meter vessel engaged in fishing and making way
B.   a 25-meter power-driven vessel trolling
⚓ C.   a 15-meter sailing vessel
D.   a 15-meter sail vessel propelled by machinery

040586/RR04032   **RULE 25 (b)**
BOTH INTERNATIONAL & INLAND Which vessel may combine her sidelights and stern light in one lantern on the fore and aft centerline of the vessel?
A.   A 28-meter sailing vessel
B.   A 25-meter power-driven vessel
C.   Any non-self-propelled vessel
⚓ D.   A 16-meter sailing vessel

040587/RR04300   **RULE 25 (b)**
BOTH INTERNATIONAL & INLAND At night, you see a vessel displaying the light shown in illustration D046RR below. This could be which of the following? See DIAGRAM D046RR
⚓ A.   sailing
B.   fishing and anchored
C.   a pilot boat making way
D.   fishing and making way

040588/RR04179 **RULE 25 (c)**
BOTH INTERNATIONAL & INLAND A sailing vessel is NOT allowed to show the all-round red over green lights on the mast if _____.
⚓ A. her sidelights and stern light are combined in one lantern and shown on the mast
B. she is showing a stern light
C. she is showing sidelights
D. her sidelights are combined and shown on the fore and aft centerline of the vessel

040589/RR09104 **RULE 25 (c)**
BOTH INTERNATIONAL & INLAND What light configuration may a sailing vessel underway exhibit?
A. a green light over a red light at the masthead
B. two white lights in a vertical line at the stern
⚓ C. a red light over a green light at the masthead
D. a special flashing light at the bow

040590/RR09103 **RULE 25 (c), (a) (i), (a) (iii), (a) (iv)**
BOTH INTERNATIONAL & INLAND Your 18-meter vessel is under sail at night displaying sidelights, stern light, and a red light over a green light at the masthead. If you start the auxiliary engine and engage the propeller, you must _____.
A. show two green lights instead of a red and green at the masthead
⚓ B. turn off the red over green, turn on the white masthead light
C. display a white light in sufficient time to prevent collision
D. turn your stern light off

040591/RR00153 **RULE 25 (c)**
BOTH INTERNATIONAL & INLAND You are underway at night and you sight the lights shown in illustration D047RR below. You know these lights indicate which of the following? See DIAGRAM D047RR
A. fishing vessel engaged in fishing
B. trawler dragging nets
⚓ C. sailing vessel
D. dredge at work

040592/RR04245 **RULE 25 (c)**
BOTH INTERNATIONAL & INLAND Underway at night, a vessel displaying the lights shown in illustration D062RR below is which of the following? See DIAGRAM D062RR
⚓ A. under sail
B. a pilot boat
C. engaged in fishing
D. mine sweeping

040593/RR04506 **RULE 25 (d) (ii), (b)**
BOTH INTERNATIONAL & INLAND A lantern combining the sidelights and stern light MAY be shown on a _____.
A. sailing vessel of 25 meters in length
⚓ B. 6-meter vessel under oars
C. 20-meter vessel engaged in fishing and making way
D. 25-meter power-driven vessel engaged in trolling

040594/RR04076 **RULE 25 (d) (ii)**
BOTH INTERNATIONAL & INLAND If a rowboat underway does NOT show the lights specified for a sailing vessel underway, it shall show which of the following?
A. combined lantern showing green to starboard and red to port and shown in sufficient time to prevent collision
B. all-round yellow light from sunset to sunrise
C. combined lantern showing green to starboard and red to port and shown from sunset to sunrise
⚓ D. white light exhibited in sufficient time to prevent collision

040595/RR04637 **RULE 25 (d) (ii)**
BOTH INTERNATIONAL & INLAND Which statement is TRUE concerning a vessel under oars?
A. She must show a day-shape of a black cone.
⚓ B. She is allowed to show the same lights as a sailing vessel.
C. She must show a flashing all-round white light.
D. She must show a stern light.

040596/RR04490 **RULE 25 (d) (ii)**
BOTH INTERNATIONAL & INLAND Which vessel would be required to show a white light from a lantern exhibited in sufficient time to prevent collision?
A. A 9-meter sailing vessel
B. A small vessel fishing
C. A 6-meter motorboat
⚓ D. A rowboat

040597/RR00389 **RULE 25 (d) (ii)**
BOTH INTERNATIONAL & INLAND You see ONLY the light shown in illustration D080RR below. This could be what type of vessel? See DIAGRAM D080RR
⚓ A. under oars
B. engaged in fishing
C. towing
D. not under command

040598/RR00390   **RULE 25 (d) (ii)**
BOTH INTERNATIONAL & INLAND You see ONLY the light shown in illustration D080RR below. This could be which of the following vessels? See DIAGRAM D080RR
A. engaged in fishing
B. towing
C. not under command
⚓ D. under oars

040599/RR04050   **RULE 25 (e)**
BOTH INTERNATIONAL & INLAND A 22-meter sailing vessel when also being propelled by machinery shall show during daylight hours a _____.
A. basket
B. black diamond
C. black ball
⚓ D. black cone

040600/RR04498   **RULE 25 (e)**
BOTH INTERNATIONAL & INLAND In the daytime, you see a large sailing vessel on the beam. You know that she is also propelled by machinery if she shows _____.
A. a basket
B. a black ball
⚓ C. a black cone
D. two black cones

040601/RR04357   **RULE 25 (e)**
BOTH INTERNATIONAL & INLAND What day shape shall a vessel 15 meters in length, proceeding under sail as well as being propelled by machinery, exhibit?
A. two cones with their apexes together
B. a basket
⚓ C. a cone with its apex downward
D. one black ball

040602/RR04444   **RULE 25 (e)**
BOTH INTERNATIONAL & INLAND Which vessel must exhibit a conical shape, apex downwards?
A. A 20-meter vessel restricted in her ability to maneuver
⚓ B. A 15-meter vessel proceeding under sail when also being propelled by machinery
C. A 10-meter vessel engaged in fishing
D. All of the above

040603/RR04399   **RULE 25 (e)**
BOTH INTERNATIONAL & INLAND Which vessel would display a cone, apex downward?
A. A vessel engaged in diving operations
B. A fishing vessel with outlying gear
⚓ C. A vessel proceeding under sail and machinery
D. A vessel being towed

040604/RR09106   **RULE 25 (e)**
BOTH INTERNATIONAL & INLAND You are under sail with the auxiliary engine running and the propeller engaged on a 15 meter sail vessel. Which statement is TRUE?
A. You are considered a sailing vessel as long as sail propulsion affects the vessel's maneuverability.
B. You must display two green lights in a vertical line at or near the masthead.
⚓ C. This condition is indicated by a conical shape, apex downwards.
D. You should maintain course and speed when approaching a power-driven vessel.

040605/RR09101   **RULE 25 (e)**
BOTH INTERNATIONAL & INLAND Your 18-meter vessel is propelled by sail and power. What action is required when the engine is stopped?
A. Remove the black balls (one at the masthead and one on each spreader).
B. Display a black cylindrical shape at the masthead.
C. Display a black diamond shape forward.
⚓ D. Remove the black cone shape from forward.

040606/RR00128   **RULE 25 (e)**
BOTH INTERNATIONAL & INLAND You are on a sailing vessel. While under sail you decide to use your engine to assist in propulsion. Which of the day signals shown in illustration D016RR below would you display? See DIAGRAM D016RR
A. D
B. C
C. B
⚓ D. None of these day signals are correct.

040607/RR04628   **RULE 25 (e)**
BOTH INTERNATIONAL & INLAND A sailing vessel displaying the day-shape shown in illustration D035RR is indicating that she is which of the following? See DIAGRAM D035RR
⚓ A. being propelled by power as well as sail
B. fishing as well as sailing
C. on a starboard tack
D. close-hauled and has difficulty maneuvering

RULE 26 - FISHING VESSELS

040608/RR04171   **RULE 26 (a)**
BOTH INTERNATIONAL & INLAND A vessel engaged in fishing, and at anchor, shall show _____.
A. sidelights and a stern light
B. an anchor light
C. three lights in a vertical line, the highest and lowest being red, and the middle being white
⚓ D. None of the above

040609/RR04185   **RULE 26 (a)**
BOTH INTERNATIONAL & INLAND A vessel engaged in fishing, and at anchor, should exhibit _____.

A. three lights in a vertical line, the highest and lowest being red, and the middle being white
B. an anchor light
C. sidelights and stern light
⚓ D. None of the above

040610/RR04722   **RULE 26 (a)**
BOTH INTERNATIONAL & INLAND Which vessel, when anchored at night, is not required to show anchor lights?
⚓ A. A vessel engaged in fishing
B. A vessel engaged on pilotage duty
C. A vessel engaged in survey operations
D. A power-driven vessel

040611/RR04644   **RULE 26 (b) (i)**
BOTH INTERNATIONAL & INLAND A vessel engaged in trawling will show identification lights of _____.

A. two red lights in a vertical line
⚓ B. a green light over a white light
C. a white light over a red light
D. a red light over a white light

040612/RR04345   **RULE 26 (b) (i)**
BOTH INTERNATIONAL & INLAND A vessel showing a green light over a white light in a vertical line above the level of the sidelights is _____.
A. engaged in underwater construction
B. under sail and power
C. a pilot vessel
⚓ D. trawling

040613/RR04047   **RULE 26 (b) (i)**
BOTH INTERNATIONAL & INLAND A vessel trawling will display a _____.
A. red light over a white light
B. white light over a green light
⚓ C. green light over a white light
D. yellow light over a red light

040614/RR04158   **RULE 26 (b) (i)**
BOTH INTERNATIONAL & INLAND A 25-meter vessel trawling will show the dayshape(s) consisting of _____.

A. two balls
⚓ B. two cones, apexes together
C. a cone, apex downward
D. a basket

040615/RR04120   **RULE 26 (b) (i), (c) (i)**
BOTH INTERNATIONAL & INLAND A vessel engaged in fishing during the day would show _____.
⚓ A. two cones, apexes together
B. one black ball
C. two cones with bases together
D. a cone, apex downward

040616/RR04139   **RULE 26 (b) (i)**
BOTH INTERNATIONAL & INLAND What type of vessel or operation is indicated by a vessel displaying two cones with the apexes together?
A. Sailing
⚓ B. Trawling
C. Minesweeping
D. Dredging

040617/RR04106   **RULE 26 (b) (i)**
BOTH INTERNATIONAL & INLAND What type of vessel or operation is indicated by a vessel showing two cones with the apexes together?
⚓ A. Vessel trawling
B. Mineclearing
C. Sailing vessel
D. Dredge

040618/RR04186   **RULE 26 (b) (i), (c) (i)**
BOTH INTERNATIONAL & INLAND A vessel fishing should display which of the day signals shown in illustration D001RR below? See DIAGRAM D001RR
A. A
⚓ B. B
C. C
D. D

040619/RR00116   **RULE 26 (b) (i), (c) (i)**
BOTH INTERNATIONAL & INLAND You are on a 30-meter fishing vessel. Which of the day shapes shown in illustration D016RR below must you show while engaged in fishing? See DIAGRAM D016RR
A. A
B. B
⚓ C. C
D. D

040620/RR00135   **RULE 26 (b) (i), (c) (i)**
BOTH INTERNATIONAL & INLAND You are on a 30-meter trawler. Which day signal shown in illustration D016RR below must you show while trawling? See DIAGRAM D016RR
A. A
B. B
⚓ C. C
D. None of these day signals are correct.

040621/RR04487   **RULE 26 (b) (i), (c) (i)**
BOTH INTERNATIONAL & INLAND A vessel displaying the day-shape shown in illustration D034RR below is doing which of the following? See DIAGRAM D034RR
A. anchored
B. being towed
C. towing
⚓ D. fishing

040622/RR04653   **RULE 26 (b) (i), (c) (i)**
BOTH INTERNATIONAL & INLAND Which of the following describes a vessel showing the day-shape in illustration D034RR below? See DIAGRAM D034RR
A. has a tow which exceeds 200 meters in length
B. is not under command
C. is engaged in surveying or underwater work
⚓ D. is fishing

040623/RR04408   **RULE 26 (b) (i) - (ii), (a)**
BOTH INTERNATIONAL & INLAND A fishing vessel displaying the lights shown in illustration D067RR below is doing which of the following? See DIAGRAM D067RR
A. underway but not fishing
⚓ B. fishing by trawling
C. tending a small fishing boat
D. anchored

040624/RR04286   **RULE 26 (b) (i), (b) (iii)**
BOTH INTERNATIONAL & INLAND Which of the following describes a vessel which is underway at night and displaying the lights shown in illustration D069RR below? See DIAGRAM D069RR
A. a pilot boat
⚓ B. engaged in trawling
C. under sail
D. minesweeping

040625/RR04499   **RULE 26 (b) (i), (b) (iii)**
BOTH INTERNATIONAL & INLAND At night, the lights shown in illustration D076RR would indicate a vessel engaged in which of the following operations? See DIAGRAM D076RR
⚓ A. trawling
B. laying submarine cable
C. dredging
D. towing astern

040626/RR04658   **RULE 26 (b) (ii)**
BOTH INTERNATIONAL & INLAND A 60-meter vessel which is trawling is required to show which of the following?
A. two masthead lights at night.
B. a conical shape, apex downwards during the day.
⚓ C. one masthead light at night.
D. a red light over a white light in a vertical line at night.

040627/RR04503   **RULE 26 (b) (ii)**
BOTH INTERNATIONAL & INLAND Which vessel must show a masthead light abaft of and higher than her identifying lights?
A. A 55-meter vessel fishing
⚓ B. A 55-meter vessel trawling
C. A 20-meter vessel engaged on pilotage duty
D. A 100-meter vessel not under command

040628/RR00183   **RULE 26 (b) (ii)**
BOTH INTERNATIONAL & INLAND Which vessel must show an after masthead light, if over 50 meters in length?
A. A vessel not under command
⚓ B. A vessel trawling
C. A vessel at anchor
D. A vessel engaged in fishing

040629/RR04496   **RULE 26 (b) (iii), (c) (iii)**
BOTH INTERNATIONAL & INLAND A vessel which is fishing is required to show sidelights and a stern light only when _____.
⚓ A. underway and making way
B. anchored
C. underway
D. dead in the water

040630/RR04199   **RULE 26 (b) (iii), (c) (iii)**
BOTH INTERNATIONAL & INLAND A vessel which is fishing must show sidelights and a stern light only when _____.
⚓ A. underway and making way
B. anchored
C. underway
D. dead in the water

040631/RR04574   **RULE 26 (b) (iii), (c) (iii)**
BOTH INTERNATIONAL & INLAND Which vessel shall NOT show her sidelights?
A. A vessel engaged in underwater operations
⚓ B. A fishing vessel that is not making way
C. A vessel that is not under command making way
D. A sailing vessel which is becalmed

040632/RR04655   **RULE 26 (b) (iii), (c) (iii)**
BOTH INTERNATIONAL & INLAND Which vessels shall turn off their sidelights?
⚓ A. All fishing vessels that are not making way
B. All vessels that are not under command
C. All sailing vessels which are becalmed
D. All vessels engaged in underwater operations

040633/RR04405   **RULE 26 (c) (i)**

BOTH INTERNATIONAL & INLAND A vessel underway but not making way and fishing other than trawling will show which lights?

- A. A red light over a white light, sidelights, and a stern light
- B. A white light over a red light
- C. A white light over a red light, sidelights, and a stern light
- D. A red light over a white light

040634/RR04237   **RULE 26 (c) (i)**

BOTH INTERNATIONAL & INLAND At night, which lights would you see on a vessel engaged in fishing, other than trawling?

- A. Two red lights, one over the other
- B. A white light over a red light
- C. A red light over a white light
- D. A green light over a red light

040635/RR00185   **RULE 26 (c) (i) - (ii)**

BOTH INTERNATIONAL & INLAND You see the display of lights shown in illustration D054RR below, this could be which of the following? See DIAGRAM D054RR

- A. fishing vessel with outlying gear more than 150 meters
- B. fishing vessel at anchor
- C. fishing vessel adrift and fishing with handlines
- D. pilot vessel with a motor launch alongside

040636/RR04270   **RULE 26 (c) (i)**

BOTH INTERNATIONAL & INLAND A vessel displaying the lights shown in illustration D070RR below is which of the following? See DIAGRAM D070RR

- A. motorboat
- B. sailboat
- C. fishing vessel
- D. pilot boat

040637/RR04251   **RULE 26 (c) (i)**

BOTH INTERNATIONAL & INLAND At night, if you see a vessel ahead displaying the lights shown in illustration D070RR below what action should you take? See DIAGRAM D070RR

- A. change course to the right as the vessel is crossing your bow
- B. stay clear as the vessel is fishing
- C. provide assistance as the vessel is in distress
- D. stay clear as the vessel is transferring dangerous cargo

040638/RR00322   **RULE 26 (c) (i), (c) (iii); RULE 9 (c)**

BOTH INTERNATIONAL & INLAND The vessel whose lights are shown in illustration D082RR below is navigating in a narrow channel. Which statement about this vessel is TRUE? See DIAGRAM D082RR

- A. It may anchor in the channel or fairway
- B. It shall not impede the passage of any other vessel navigating within the channel or fairway
- C. It shows two balls
- D. It is the stand-on vessel

040639/RR04647   **RULE 26 (c) (i), (c) (iii)**

BOTH INTERNATIONAL & INLAND What type of vessel displays the lights as shown in illustration D082RR? See DIAGRAM D082RR

- A. a pilot boat
- B. anchored
- C. fishing
- D. sailing

040640/RR00318   **RULE 26 (c) (i), (c) (iii)**

BOTH INTERNATIONAL & INLAND Which dayshape(s) would be displayed by the vessel engaged in the operation indicated by the lights shown in illustration D082RR below? See DIAGRAM D082RR

- A. a cylinder
- B. a diamond
- C. two cones with apexes together
- D. a ball, a diamond and another ball

040641/RR09107   **RULE 26 (c) (i), (c) (iii)**

BOTH INTERNATIONAL & INLAND Which of the following describes a vessel at night displaying the lights shown in illustration D082RR below?

- A. sailing
- B. trawling
- C. fishing
- D. a pilot boat

040642/RR04142   **RULE 26 (c) (ii)**

BOTH INTERNATIONAL & INLAND A vessel engaged in fishing must display a light in the direction of any gear that extends outward more than 150 meters. The color of this light is _____.

- A. white
- B. yellow
- C. red
- D. green

040643/RR04656   **RULE 26 (c) (ii)**

BOTH INTERNATIONAL & INLAND A vessel fishing at night, with gear extending more than 150 meters horizontally outwards, will show in the direction of the gear _____.

- A. one yellow light
- B. two vertical white lights
- C. one white light
- D. two vertical yellow lights

040644/RR04403   **RULE 26 (c) (ii)**
BOTH INTERNATIONAL & INLAND What day-shape must be shown by a vessel over 20 meters fishing which has gear extending more than 150 meters horizontally outward from it?
A. One diamond shape
⚓ B. One cone with its apex upwards
C. One black ball
D. One basket

040645/RR00118   **RULE 26 (c) (iii)**
BOTH INTERNATIONAL & INLAND You are on a vessel engaged in fishing, other than trawling, and have gear extending more than 150 meters horizontally from the vessel. Which of the day-shapes shown in illustration D016RR below must you show in the direction of the outlying gear? See DIAGRAM D016RR
A. A
B. B
C. C
⚓ D. D

RULE 27 - VESSELS NOT UNDER COMMAND AND RESTRICTED IN ABILITY TO MANEUVER

040646/RR04312   **RULE 27 (a) (i)**
BOTH INTERNATIONAL & INLAND A power-driven vessel "not under command" at night must show which lights in a vertical line?
A. Three red
⚓ B. Two red
C. Two white
D. Three white

040647/RR04597   **RULE 27 (a) (i) - (ii)**
BOTH INTERNATIONAL & INLAND A vessel not under command shall display _____.
A. three red lights at night and three black balls during daylight
B. two red lights at night and three black balls during daylight
⚓ C. two red lights at night and two black balls during daylight
D. three red lights at night and two black balls during daylight

040648/RR04464   **RULE 27 (a) (i)**
BOTH INTERNATIONAL & INLAND A vessel not under command, underway but not making way, would show _____.
⚓ A. two all-round red lights in a vertical line
B. a stern light
C. sidelights
D. All of the above

040649/RR04176   **RULE 27 (a) (i)**
BOTH INTERNATIONAL & INLAND Two all-round red lights displayed in a vertical line are shown by a vessel _____.
⚓ A. not under command
B. being towed
C. pushing a barge ahead
D. at anchor

040650/RR04147   **RULE 27 (a) (i), (a) (iii)**
BOTH INTERNATIONAL & INLAND Which vessel would have no white lights visible when meeting her head-on?
A. A vessel restricted in her ability to maneuver
B. A vessel trawling
⚓ C. A vessel not under command
D. A vessel mineclearing

040651/RR00157   **RULE 27 (a) (i), (a) (iii)**
BOTH INTERNATIONAL & INLAND Which of the following describes a vessel exhibiting the lights shown in illustration D049RR below? See DIAGRAM D049RR
A. on pilotage duty
B. engaged in fishing
C. restricted in her ability to maneuver
⚓ D. not under command

040652/RR04162   **RULE 27 (a) (i)**
BOTH INTERNATIONAL & INLAND Which of the following describes a vessel exhibiting the lights shown in illustration D083RR below? See DIAGRAM D083RR
⚓ A. not under command
B. fishing
C. being towed
D. towing

040653/RR00421   **RULE 27 (a) (i), (a) (iii)**
BOTH INTERNATIONAL & INLAND Which of the following describes a vessel exhibiting the lights shown in illustration D084RR below? See DIAGRAM D084RR
A. showing improper lights
B. towing
C. dredging
⚓ D. not under command

040654/RR04013   **RULE 27 (a) (ii)**
BOTH INTERNATIONAL & INLAND Which of the following describes a vessel displaying the day-shapes shown in illustration D007RR below? See DIAGRAM D007RR
A. a minesweeper
⚓ B. broken down
C. transferring dangerous cargo
D. fishing

040655/RR04376   **RULE 27 (a) (iii)**
BOTH INTERNATIONAL & INLAND A power-driven vessel "not under command" at night must show her sidelights when _____.
- A. moored to a buoy
- ⚓ B. making headway
- C. at anchor
- D. making no headway

040656/RR04262   **RULE 27 (a) (iii), (a) (i)**
BOTH INTERNATIONAL & INLAND A vessel not under command making way at night would show _____.
- A. anchor lights and sidelights
- ⚓ B. two all-round red lights in a vertical line, sidelights, and a stern light
- C. two all-round red lights in a vertical line
- D. two all-round white lights in a vertical line, sidelights and a stern light

040657/RR04197   **RULE 27 (a) (iii)**
BOTH INTERNATIONAL & INLAND A vessel which is unable to maneuver due to some exceptional circumstance, shall show two red lights in a vertical line and _____.
- A. during the day, three balls in a vertical line
- ⚓ B. when making way at night, sidelights and a stern light
- C. when making way at night, masthead lights, sidelights, and a stern light
- D. during the day, three shapes, the highest and lowest being balls and the middle being a diamond

040658/RR04127   **RULE 27 (a) (iii)**
BOTH INTERNATIONAL & INLAND A vessel will NOT show sidelights when _____.
- A. making way, not under command
- B. underway but not making way
- C. trolling underway
- ⚓ D. not under command, not making way

040659/RR04112   **RULE 27 (a) (iii), (a) (i)**
BOTH INTERNATIONAL & INLAND A vessel, which is unable to maneuver due to some exceptional circumstance, shall exhibit _____.
- A. during the day, three shapes, the highest and lowest being balls and the middle being a
- B. during the day, three balls in a vertical line
- ⚓ C. when making way at night, two all-round red lights, sidelights, and a stern light
- D. when making way at night, masthead lights, sidelights, and a stern light

040660/RR04206   **RULE 27 (b) (i)**
BOTH INTERNATIONAL & INLAND At night, a vessel shall indicate that she is restricted in her ability to maneuver by showing in a vertical line two _____.
- A. red lights and two white lights
- ⚓ B. red lights with a white light in between
- C. white lights with a red light in between
- D. red lights

040661/RR04650   **RULE 27 (b) (i)**
BOTH INTERNATIONAL & INLAND Which lights would be shown at night by a vessel which is restricted in her ability to deviate from her course?
- ⚓ A. Three lights in a vertical line, the highest and lowest red and the middle white
- B. Three red lights in a vertical line
- C. Three lights in a vertical line, the highest and lowest white and the middle red
- D. Three white lights in a vertical line

040662/RR04720   **RULE 27 (b) (i), (b) (iii)**
BOTH INTERNATIONAL & INLAND Which of the following describes a vessel exhibiting the lights shown in illustration D056RR below? See DIAGRAM D056RR
- A. at anchor and dredging
- ⚓ B. underway and laying cable
- C. underway and carrying dangerous cargo
- D. towing a barge alongside

040663/RR04149   **RULE 27 (b) (i), (b) (iii)**
BOTH INTERNATIONAL & INLAND A vessel displaying the lights shown in illustration D057RR below is doing which of the following? See DIAGRAM D057RR
- A. towing and making way
- ⚓ B. restricted in her ability to maneuver and not making way
- C. a pilot vessel underway and making way on pilotage duty
- D. engaged in fishing and not making way

040664/RR04659   **RULE 27 (b) (ii)**
BOTH INTERNATIONAL & INLAND A vessel servicing a pipeline during the day shall display _____.
- A. three black balls in a vertical line
- B. three shapes in a vertical line; the highest and lowest are red balls, and the middle one is a white diamond
- ⚓ C. three black shapes in a vertical line; the highest and lowest are balls, and the middle one is a diamond
- D. two black balls in a vertical line

040665/RR04420   **RULE 27 (b) (ii)**
BOTH INTERNATIONAL & INLAND A vessel transferring provisions or cargo at sea shall display during the day _____.
A. two black balls in a vertical line
B. three black shapes in a vertical line; the highest and lowest shall be balls and the middle one a diamond
C. three black balls in a vertical line
D. three shapes in a vertical line; the highest and lowest shall be red balls and the middle a white diamond

040666/RR04513   **RULE 27 (b) (ii)**
BOTH INTERNATIONAL & INLAND By day, you sight a vessel displaying three shapes in a vertical line. The top and bottom shapes are balls, and the middle shape is a diamond. It could be a _____.
A. mineclearing vessel
B. trawler
C. vessel engaged in replenishment at sea
D. vessel trolling

040667/RR04274   **RULE 27 (b) (ii)**
BOTH INTERNATIONAL & INLAND During the day, a vessel picking up a submarine cable shall carry _____.
A. three shapes; the highest and lowest shall be black balls and the middle shall be a black diamond
B. three shapes, the highest and lowest shall be red balls, and the middle shall be a white diamond
C. three shapes; the highest and lowest shall be black balls, and the middle shall be a red diamond
D. two black balls

040668/RR04311   **RULE 27 (b) (ii)**
BOTH INTERNATIONAL & INLAND Which vessel would show 3 day-shapes in a vertical line, the highest and lowest being balls and the middle shape being a diamond?
A. Vessel constrained by her draft
B. Vessel not under command
C. Vessel minesweeping
D. Vessel restricted in her ability to maneuver

040669/RR04012   **RULE 27 (b) (ii)**
BOTH INTERNATIONAL & INLAND A vessel which displays the day signal shown in illustration D006RR below may be engaged in which of the following? See DIAGRAM D006RR
A. fishing
B. submarine cable laying
C. mineclearance
D. pilotage duty

040670/RR04360   **RULE 27 (b) (ii)**
BOTH INTERNATIONAL & INLAND While underway, you see a vessel displaying the day-shapes shown in illustration D006RR below. Which action should you take? See DIAGRAM D006RR
A. Stay clear, the other vessel is maneuvering with difficulty
B. Stop your vessel and sound passing signals
C. Maintain course and speed
D. Provide assistance, the other vessel is in distress

040671/RR04189   **RULE 27 (b) (ii)**
BOTH INTERNATIONAL & INLAND You see a vessel displaying the day signal shown in illustration D006RR below. The vessel may be which of the following? See DIAGRAM D006RR
A. aground
B. fishing with trawls
C. not under command
D. laying cable

040672/RR04288   **RULE 27 (b) (iii)**
BOTH INTERNATIONAL & INLAND A vessel is carrying three lights in a vertical line. The highest and lowest of these are red and the middle light is white. Which statement is always TRUE?
A. During the day, she would display three balls in a vertical line.
B. If at anchor, she need not show anchor lights while displaying identifying lights.
C. Her fog signal would consist of a rapid ringing of a bell for five seconds every minute.
D. If making way, she would show masthead lights at night.

040673/RR04483   **RULE 27 (b) (iii), (b) (i)**
BOTH INTERNATIONAL & INLAND A vessel restricted in her ability to maneuver shall _____.
A. keep out of the way of a vessel engaged in fishing
B. when operating in restricted visibility, sound a whistle signal of two prolonged and one short blast
C. show a day-shape of two diamonds in a vertical line
D. turn off her sidelights when not making way

040674/RR04069   **RULE 27 (b) (iii)**
BOTH INTERNATIONAL & INLAND Which lights are shown by a vessel restricted in her ability to maneuver to indicate that the vessel is making way?
A. Sidelights and stern light only
B. Sidelights only
C. Masthead lights, sidelights and stern light
D. Masthead lights and sidelights only

040675/RR04641   **RULE 27 (b) (iii)**
BOTH INTERNATIONAL & INLAND Which vessel must exhibit forward and after white masthead lights when making way?
A. A 75-meter vessel restricted in her ability to maneuver
B. A 45-meter vessel engaged in towing
C. A 150-meter vessel engaged in fishing
D. A 100-meter sailing vessel

040676/RR00376 **RULE 27 (b) (iii); RULE 23 (a) (ii)**
BOTH INTERNATIONAL & INLAND Which vessel must show forward and after masthead lights when making way?
A. A 45-meter vessel engaged in towing
B. A 100-meter sailing vessel
C. A 150-meter vessel engaged in fishing
D. A 75-meter vessel restricted in her ability to maneuver

040677/RR04468   **RULE 27 (b) (iii)**
BOTH INTERNATIONAL & INLAND You see a vessel displaying three lights in a vertical line. The highest and lowest lights are red and the middle light is white. She is also showing a white light at the stern, which is lower than the forward light. It could be a _____.
A. vessel aground
B. pilot vessel with port side to you
C. vessel not under command
D. survey vessel

040678/RR04365   **RULE 27 (b) (iv)**
BOTH INTERNATIONAL & INLAND An anchored vessel is servicing an aid to navigation and is restricted in her ability to maneuver. Which lights will she show?
A. Three lights in a vertical line, the highest and lowest red and the middle white, and anchor lights
B. Three lights in a vertical line, the highest and lowest red and the middle white, ONLY
C. Anchor lights ONLY
D. Anchor lights and sidelights ONLY

040679/RR06500   **RULE 27 (c)**
BOTH INTERNATIONAL & INLAND A vessel towing astern and her tow are severely restricted in their ability to change course. When making way, the towing vessel will show ONLY which of the following light configurations?
A. the lights for a vessel restricted in her ability to maneuver
B. sidelights, stern light, and towing light
C. the masthead lights for a towing vessel
D. All of the above

040680/RR04404 **RULE 27 (c); RULE 24 (a) - (f)**
BOTH INTERNATIONAL & INLAND A vessel towing astern in an operation which severely restricts the towing vessel and her tow in their ability to change course shall, when making way, exhibit _____.
A. sidelights, stern light and towing light
B. the masthead lights for a towing vessel
C. the lights for a vessel restricted in its ability to maneuver
D. All of the above

040681/RR04471 **RULE 27 (c); RULE 24 (a) - (f)**
BOTH INTERNATIONAL & INLAND A vessel towing astern in an operation which severely restricts the towing vessel and her tow in their ability to deviate from their course shall, when making way, show _____.
A. the lights for a vessel restricted in its ability to maneuver
B. sidelights, stern light and towing light
C. the masthead lights for a towing vessel
D. All of the above

040682/RR04534 **RULE 27 (c); RULE 24 (a) - (f)**
BOTH INTERNATIONAL & INLAND A vessel towing where the tow prevents her from changing course shall carry _____.
A. the lights for a towing vessel and the lights for a vessel not under command
B. only the lights for a vessel restricted in her ability to maneuver
C. the lights for a towing vessel and the lights for a vessel restricted in her ability to maneuver
D. only the lights for a vessel towing

040683/RR04369   **RULE 27 (c)**
BOTH INTERNATIONAL & INLAND If a towing vessel and her tow are severely restricted in their ability to deviate from their course, they may show lights in addition to their towing identification lights. These additional lights may be shown if the tow is _____.
A. towed astern
B. pushed ahead
C. towed alongside
D. All of the above

040684/RR04661   RULE 27 (c); RULE 24 (a) - (f)
BOTH INTERNATIONAL & INLAND Which statement is TRUE concerning a towing vessel which, due to the nature of her work, is unable to keep out of the way of another vessel?
A. By day, she shall carry a black cylinder shape.
B. By night, she would show the same lights as a vessel not under command.
C. By day, she would show the same shapes as a vessel restricted in her ability to maneuver.
D. By day, she shall carry two black balls in a vertical line.

040685/RR00151   RULE 27 (c); RULE 24
BOTH INTERNATIONAL & INLAND Which vessel is indicated by the day signal shown in illustration D022RR? See DIAGRAM D022RR
A. A vessel engaged in underwater operations with a diver down
B. A tug with a tow exceeding 200 meters which limits her ability to maneuver
C. A dredge indicating the side with the obstruction
D. A fishing vessel with gear extending more than 150 meters horizontally

040686/RR04475   RULE 27 (d); RULE 23 (a) (i), (a) (iv)
BOTH INTERNATIONAL & INLAND A self-propelled dredge not engaged in dredging but proceeding to a dredging location at night would _____.
A. not be required to show any lights
B. be required to show the lights characteristic of a dredge
C. be required to show the lights of a power-driven vessel underway
D. be required to show the lights of a stationary dredge

040687/RR04646   RULE 27 (d) (i)
BOTH INTERNATIONAL & INLAND By night, you sight the lights of a vessel engaged in underwater operations. If an obstruction exists on the port side of the vessel, it will be marked by _____.
A. a single red light
B. two red lights in a vertical line
C. a floodlight
D. any visible lights

040688/RR04652   RULE 27 (d) (i) - (ii)
BOTH INTERNATIONAL & INLAND Which of the following describes a vessel exhibiting the day-shapes shown in illustration D018RR below? See DIAGRAM D018RR
A. dredging
B. not under command
C. towing astern with a tow greater than 200 meters in length
D. carrying dangerous cargo

040689/RR04067   RULE 27 (d) (ii)
BOTH INTERNATIONAL & INLAND At night, which lights are required to be shown by a dredge on the side of the dredge which another vessel may pass?
A. two red lights
B. Two green lights
C. One white light
D. One red light

040690/RR04099   RULE 27 (d) (ii)
BOTH INTERNATIONAL & INLAND During the day, a dredge will indicate the side on which it is safe to pass by displaying _____.
A. a single black ball
B. two diamonds in a vertical line
C. no shape is shown during the day
D. two balls in a vertical line

040691/RR04510   RULE 27 (d) (ii)
BOTH INTERNATIONAL & INLAND You are approaching a vessel dredging during the day and see two balls in a vertical line on the port side of the dredge. These shapes mean that _____.
A. you should pass on the port side of the dredge
B. the dredge is not under command
C. the dredge is moored
D. to here is an obstruction on the port side of the dredge

040692/RR04721   RULE 27 (d) (iii)
BOTH INTERNATIONAL & INLAND Which vessel when anchored at night, would not be required to show anchor lights?
A. A vessel engaged in mine clearance
B. A vessel engaged in survey operations
C. A vessel engaged on pilotage duty
D. A vessel engaged in underwater operations

040693/RR04595   RULE 27 (d) (iii)
BOTH INTERNATIONAL & INLAND Which vessel, when anchored at night, would NOT be required to show anchor lights?
A. A vessel on pilotage duty
B. A vessel restricted in her ability to maneuver
C. A power-driven vessel
D. A vessel dredging

040694/RR04624   **RULE 27 (d)**
*** Comment ***
Shows no anchor lights in accordance with the provisions of 27 (d) (iii)

BOTH INTERNATIONAL & INLAND Which of the following describes a vessel exhibiting the lights shown in illustration D56RR below? See DIAGRAM D056RR
A. transferring dangerous cargo at a berth
B. restricted in her ability to maneuver, underway but not making way
C. fishing at anchor
⚓ D. dredging while underway

040695/RR00179   **RULE 27 (d); RULE 23 (a) (i) - (iv)**
BOTH INTERNATIONAL & INLAND Which display of lights shown in illustration D072RR below indicates a dredge underway and not dredging? See DIAGRAM D072RR
A. A
⚓ B. B
C. C
D. D

040696/RR04223   **RULE 27 (b), (d), (e)**
BOTH INTERNATIONAL & INLAND Which vessel may show three lights in a vertical line, the top and bottom being red and the middle being white?
A. A pilot vessel
B. A vessel trawling
⚓ C. A vessel engaged in diving operations
D. All of the above

040697/RR04447   **RULE 27 (e) (ii)**
BOTH INTERNATIONAL & INLAND A rigid replica of the International Code flag "A" may be shown by a vessel _____.
A. engaged in underway replenishment
⚓ B. engaged in diving operations
C. pulling a submarine cable
D. transferring explosives

040698/RR04608   **RULE 27 (e) (ii)**
BOTH INTERNATIONAL & INLAND A vessel showing a rigid replica of the International Code flag "A" is engaged in _____.
A. fishing
B. dredging
C. mineclearance operations
⚓ D. diving operations

040699/RR04126   **RULE 27 (e) (ii)**
BOTH INTERNATIONAL & INLAND By day, when it is impracticable for a small vessel engaged in diving operations to display the shapes for a vessel engaged in underwater operations, she shall display _____.
A. a black cylinder
B. two red balls in a vertical line
⚓ C. a rigid replica of the International Code flag "A"
D. three black balls in a vertical line

040700/RR04818   **RULE 27 (f)**
BOTH INTERNATIONAL & INLAND A vessel engaged in mine clearance operations shows special identity lights _____.
A. which means that other vessels should not approach closer than 500 meters on either side of the vessel
⚓ B. in addition to the lights required for a power-driven vessel
C. that are green and show through an arc of the horizon of 225°
D. All of the above

040701/RR04089   **RULE 27 (f)**
BOTH INTERNATIONAL & INLAND A vessel engaged in mineclearing shows special identity lights _____.
A. which mean that other vessels should not approach within 1000 meters of the mineclearing vessel
B. in addition to the lights required for a power-driven vessel
C. which are green and show all-round
⚓ D. All of the above

040702/RR04860   **RULE 27 (f)**
BOTH INTERNATIONAL & INLAND A vessel engaged in mine clearance operations shows special identity lights _____.
A. that are 225° green lights
B. instead of the masthead lights
⚓ C. which mean that other vessels should not approach within 1000 meters
D. All of the above

040703/RR04635   **RULE 27 (f)**
BOTH INTERNATIONAL & INLAND A vessel conducting mineclearing operations will show _____.
A. three balls in a vertical line
B. one diamond near the foremast head and one ball at each fore yard
C. two balls in a vertical line
⚓ D. one ball near the foremast and one ball at each fore yard

040704/RR04128   **RULE 27 (f)**
BOTH INTERNATIONAL & INLAND Which display indicates a vessel conducting mine clearance operations?
A. Three balls in a vertical line
B. One ball near the foremast and one ball at each yardarm
C. Two balls in a vertical line
D. One diamond near the foremast and one ball at each yardarm

040705/RR04719   **RULE 27 (f)**
BOTH INTERNATIONAL & INLAND The lights shown in illustration D068RR mean that another vessel should pass within what distance? See DIAGRAM D068RR
A. 1000 meters
B. 1500 meters
C. 500 meters
D. 2000 meters

RULE 29 - PILOT VESSELS

040706/RR04253   **RULE 29 (a) (i) - (iii)**
BOTH INTERNATIONAL & INLAND A pilot vessel on pilotage duty shall show identity lights _____.
A. at any time while underway
B. while alongside a vessel
C. while at anchor
D. All of the above

040707/RR04323   **RULE 29 (a) (i) - (ii)**
BOTH INTERNATIONAL & INLAND A vessel is displaying ONLY the lights shown in illustration D053RR. What type of vessel is this? See DIAGRAM D053RR
A. vessel engaged on pilotage duty underway
B. vessel engaged in fishing
C. vessel under sail
D. power-driven vessel underway

040708/RR00195   **RULE 29 (a) (i) - (ii)**
BOTH INTERNATIONAL & INLAND At night, you see the lights shown. This would indicate a vessel _____. See illustration D078RR. See DIAGRAM D078RR
A. not under command
B. on pilotage duty and underway
C. restricted in her ability to maneuver
D. engaged in fishing and making way

040709/RR04011   **RULE 29 (a) (ii)**
BOTH INTERNATIONAL & INLAND A pilot vessel on pilotage duty at night will show sidelights and a stern light _____.
A. only when the identifying lights are not being shown
B. only when making way
C. when at anchor
D. at any time when underway

040710/RR04714   **RULE 29 (a) (ii)**
BOTH INTERNATIONAL & INLAND Which vessel would exhibit sidelights when underway and not making way?
A. A pilot vessel
B. A vessel engaged in dredging
C. A vessel not under command
D. A vessel trawling

040711/RR04494   **RULE 29 (a) (iii)**
BOTH INTERNATIONAL & INLAND An anchored vessel on pilotage duty must show which light(s) at night?
A. A white light over a red light only
B. A white light over a red light and anchor lights
C. Anchor lights only
D. A stern light only

040712/RR04580   **RULE 29 (a) (i), (a) (iii)**
BOTH INTERNATIONAL & INLAND A vessel is displaying ONLY the lights shown in illustration D045RR. What type of vessel could this be? See DIAGRAM D045RR
A. vessel engaged in dredging at anchor with an obstruction on one side
B. vessel engaged in fishing
C. pilot vessel less than 50 meters, underway and NOT engaged on pilotage duty
D. vessel aground less than 50 meters

040713/RR04432   **RULE 29 (a) (iii)**
BOTH INTERNATIONAL & INLAND A vessel is displaying ONLY the lights shown in illustration D061RR. What type of vessel is this? See DIAGRAM D061RR
A. a fishing vessel aground
B. fishing
C. a pilot vessel at anchor
D. fishing and hauling her nets

RULE 30 - VESSELS ANCHORED AND VESSELS AGROUND

040714/RR04077   **RULE 30 (a) (i)**
BOTH INTERNATIONAL & INLAND A vessel at anchor shall display, between sunrise and sunset, on the forward part of the vessel where it can best be seen _____.
A.   two orange and white balls
B.   two black balls
⚓ C.   one black ball
D.   one red ball

040715/RR04402   **RULE 30 (a) (i)**
BOTH INTERNATIONAL & INLAND A vessel at anchor will show a _____.
A.   cone
⚓ B.   ball
C.   cylinder
D.   double cone, apexes together

040716/RR04486   **RULE 30 (a) (i)**
BOTH INTERNATIONAL & INLAND What day-shape would a vessel at anchor show during daylight?
⚓ A.   One black ball
B.   Two black balls
C.   Three black balls
D.   No signal

040717/RR04457   **RULE 30 (a) (i)**
BOTH INTERNATIONAL & INLAND If you anchor your 25-meter vessel in a harbor, what light(s) must you show?
A.   All the deck house lights
B.   One all-round red light
C.   Two all-round white lights
⚓ D.   One all-round white light

040718/RR04520   **RULE 30 (a) (i)**
BOTH INTERNATIONAL & INLAND When anchoring a 20-meter vessel at night, you must show _____.
A.   one all-round white light and the stern light
⚓ B.   one all-round white light
C.   one all-round white light and a flare-up light
D.   two all-round white lights

040719/RR04489   **RULE 30 (a) (i) - (ii)**
BOTH INTERNATIONAL & INLAND Which statement is TRUE concerning a vessel of 150 meters in length, at anchor?
A.   She may show an all-round white light where it can best be seen
⚓ B.   She must show all-round white lights forward and aft
C.   The showing of working lights is optional
D.   None of the above

040720/RR04074   **RULE 30 (a) (i) - (ii), (c)**
BOTH INTERNATIONAL & INLAND Which statement is TRUE concerning a vessel of 75 meters in length, at anchor?
A.   She must show an all-round white light forward
B.   She may use her working lights to illuminate her decks
C.   She must show a second all-round white light aft
⚓ D.   All of the above

040721/RR04596   **RULE 30 (a) (i)**
BOTH INTERNATIONAL & INLAND A vessel displaying the day-shape shown in illustration D013RR below is doing which of the following? See DIAGRAM D013RR
A.   being towed
⚓ B.   anchored
C.   towing
D.   fishing

040722/RR00102   **RULE 30 (a) (i)**
BOTH INTERNATIONAL & INLAND Which of the day-shapes shown in illustration D016RR below must you show when at anchor? See DIAGRAM D016RR
⚓ A.   A
B.   B
C.   C
D.   D

040723/RR04335   **RULE 30 (a) (i) - (ii)**
BOTH INTERNATIONAL & INLAND At night a vessel displaying the lights shown in illustration D065RR is doing which of the following? See DIAGRAM D065RR
⚓ A.   anchored
B.   fishing
C.   being towed
D.   drifting

040724/RR04437   **RULE 30 (b)**
BOTH INTERNATIONAL & INLAND What is the minimum length of an anchored vessel which is required to show a white light both forward and aft?
A.   150 meters
B.   200 meters
⚓ C.   50 meters
D.   100 meters

040725/RR04607   **RULE 30 (b)**
BOTH INTERNATIONAL & INLAND What is the minimum length of vessels required to show two anchor lights?
A.   40 meters
⚓ B.   50 meters
C.   60 meters
D.   70 meters

040726/RR09001   **RULE 30 (b)**
BOTH INTERNATIONAL & INLAND You are on a 25-meter vessel at anchor. What lights are you required to show?
A. the sidelights and a stern light
B. one all-round white light and the sidelights
C. two all-round white lights
⚓ D. one all-round white light

040727/RR04393   **RULE 30 (c)**
BOTH INTERNATIONAL & INLAND Which light(s) is(are) AMONG those shown by a 200-meter vessel at anchor?
A. In the forepart of the vessel, a 135° white light
B. In the forepart of the vessel, a 225° white light
⚓ C. Any available working lights to illuminate the decks
D. In the after part of the vessel, a 135° white light

040728/RR04466   **RULE 30 (c)**
BOTH INTERNATIONAL & INLAND Which lights shall a 200-meter vessel exhibit when at anchor?
A. In the forepart of the vessel, a 112.5-degree white light
B. In the forepart of the vessel, a 225-degree white light
C. In the after part of the vessel, a 112.5-degree white light
⚓ D. Working lights to illuminate the decks

040729/RR04613   **RULE 30 (c)**
BOTH INTERNATIONAL & INLAND Working lights shall be used to illuminate the decks of a vessel _____.
A. constrained by her draft
⚓ B. over 100 meters at anchor
C. not under command
D. All of the above

040730/RR04559   **RULE 30 (d) (i)**
BOTH INTERNATIONAL & INLAND A vessel aground at night is required to show two red lights in a vertical line as well as _____.
A. sidelights and a stern light
B. restricted in her ability to maneuver lights
⚓ C. anchor lights
D. not under command lights

040731/RR04052   **RULE 30 (d) (i)**
BOTH INTERNATIONAL & INLAND The lights displayed in illustration D044RR below would be shown by a vessel described by which of the following? See DIAGRAM D044RR
A. not under command and is making way
⚓ B. aground
C. not under command and is dead in the water
D. laying or picking up navigation marks

040732/RR04317   **RULE 30 (d) (ii)**
BOTH INTERNATIONAL & INLAND What signal would a vessel aground show during daylight?
A. One black ball
B. Two black balls
⚓ C. Three black balls
D. Four black balls

040733/RR04281   **RULE 30 (d) (ii)**
BOTH INTERNATIONAL & INLAND A vessel 30 meters in length and aground would display a day-shape consisting of _____.
A. one black ball
B. two black balls in a vertical line
C. a cylinder
⚓ D. three black balls in a vertical line

040734/RR04374   **RULE 30 (d) (ii)**
BOTH INTERNATIONAL & INLAND A vessel aground would show the same day-shape as a _____.
A. vessel towing a submerged object
B. dredge underway and dredging
C. hydrographic survey vessel at anchor and surveying
⚓ D. None of the above

040735/RR04439   **RULE 30 (d) (ii)**
BOTH INTERNATIONAL & INLAND Signals required for vessels aground include _____.
⚓ A. by day, three black balls in a vertical line
B. a short, a prolonged, and a short blast
C. by night, the anchor lights for a vessel of her length, and three red lights in a vertical line
D. All of the above

040736/RR04247   **RULE 30 (d) (ii)**
BOTH INTERNATIONAL & INLAND What day-shape is to be shown by a vessel aground?
A. Two black balls in a vertical line
⚓ B. Three black balls in a vertical line
C. A cylinder
D. two cones with their apexes together

040737/RR04226   **RULE 30 (d) (ii), (f)**
BOTH INTERNATIONAL & INLAND Which day-shape must be shown by a vessel 25 meters in length aground during daylight hours?
A. One black ball
B. two black balls
⚓ C. Three black balls
D. Four black balls

040738/RR04553   **RULE 30 (d) (ii)**
BOTH INTERNATIONAL & INLAND Which day-shape would a vessel aground show during daylight?
A.   Four black balls
B.   Two black balls
C.   One black ball
⚓ D.   Three black balls

040739/RR04235   **RULE 30 (d) (ii)**
BOTH INTERNATIONAL & INLAND Which of the following describes a vessel displaying the day-shapes shown in illustration D011RR below? See DIAGRAM D011RR
A.   towing
⚓ B.   aground
C.   conducting underwater operations
D.   drifting

040740/RR04583   **RULE 30 (e)**
BOTH INTERNATIONAL & INLAND An anchor ball need NOT be exhibited by an anchored vessel if she is _____.
A.   rigged for sail
B.   under 50 meters in length, and anchored in an anchorage
⚓ C.   less than 7 meters in length, and not in or near an area where other vessels normally navigate
D.   over 150 meters in length

040741/RR04144   **RULE 30 (e)**
BOTH INTERNATIONAL & INLAND At night, a vessel which is less than 7 meters in length and anchored in an area where other vessels do not normally navigate is _____.
A.   required to show a flare-up light
B.   required to show sidelights and a stern light
C.   required to show one white light
⚓ D.   not required to show any anchor lights

PART D SOUND AND LIGHT SIGNALS

RULE 32 - DEFINITIONS

040742/RR04578   **RULE 32 (b)**
BOTH INTERNATIONAL & INLAND A "short blast" on the whistle has a duration of _____.
A.   4 to 6 seconds
⚓ B.   1 second
C.   8 to 12 seconds
D.   12 to 15 seconds

040743/RR04130   **RULE 32 (b)**
BOTH INTERNATIONAL & INLAND The duration of each blast of the whistle signals used in meeting and crossing situations is _____.
A.   2 or 4 seconds
⚓ B.   about 1 second
C.   8 to 10 seconds
D.   4 to 6 seconds

040744/RR04422   **RULE 32 (c)**
BOTH INTERNATIONAL & INLAND Each prolonged blast on whistle signals used by a power-driven vessel in fog, whether making way or underway but not making way, is _____.
A.   two to four seconds
⚓ B.   four to six seconds
C.   eight to ten seconds
D.   about one second

040745/RR04033   **RULE 32 (c)**
BOTH INTERNATIONAL & INLAND The duration of a prolonged blast of the whistle is _____.
A.   2 to 4 seconds
⚓ B.   4 to 6 seconds
C.   8 to 10 seconds
D.   6 to 8 seconds

040746/RR04377   **RULE 32 (c)**
BOTH INTERNATIONAL & INLAND The term "prolonged blast" means a blast of _____.
A.   two to four seconds duration
B.   six to eight seconds duration
C.   eight to ten seconds duration
⚓ D.   four to six seconds duration

RULE 33 - EQUIPMENT FOR SOUND SIGNALS

040747/RR04419   **RULE 33 (a)**
BOTH INTERNATIONAL & INLAND A vessel 25 meters in length must have which sound signaling appliance onboard?
A.   Whistle only
B.   None is required
⚓ C.   Whistle and bell only
D.   Whistle, bell, and gong

040748/RR04524   **RULE 33 (a)**
BOTH INTERNATIONAL & INLAND What equipment for fog signals is required for a vessel 20 meters in length?
A.   Bell only
B.   Whistle only
C.   Whistle, bell, and gong
⚓ D.   Whistle and bell only

040749/RR04115   **RULE 33 (a)**
BOTH INTERNATIONAL & INLAND What is the minimum sound signaling equipment required aboard a vessel 24 meters in length?
- A.   Any means of making an efficient sound signal
- B.   A bell only
- C.   A bell and a whistle
- D.   A whistle only

040750/RR04554   **RULE 33 (a)**
BOTH INTERNATIONAL & INLAND Which vessel must have a gong, or other equipment which will make the sound of a gong?
- A.   Any vessel over 50 meters
- B.   Any vessel over 100 meters
- C.   A sailing vessel
- D.   A power-driven vessel over 75 meters

040751/RR04663   **RULE 33 (a); ANNEX III**
BOTH INTERNATIONAL & INLAND Which statement is TRUE regarding equipment for bell & gong signals?
- A.   Signals must be able to be sounded manually and automatically.
- B.   A vessel of less than 12 meters in length need not have any sound signaling equipment.
- C.   Any vessel over 12 meters in length must be provided with a gong.
- D.   Manual sounding of the signals must always be possible.

040752/RR04548   **RULE 33 (a); ANNEX III**
BOTH INTERNATIONAL & INLAND Which statement is TRUE regarding equipment for sound signals?
- A.   Manual sounding of the bell and gong must always be possible.
- B.   A vessel of less than 12 meters in length need not have any sound signaling equipment.
- C.   Automatic sounding of the signals is not permitted.
- D.   Any vessel over 12 meters in length must be provided with a gong.

040753/RR04547   **RULE 33 (b)**
BOTH INTERNATIONAL & INLAND What is the minimum sound signaling equipment required aboard a vessel 10 meters in length?
- A.   A bell only
- B.   Any means of making an efficient sound signal
- C.   A whistle only
- D.   A bell and a whistle

RULE 34 - MANEUVERING AND WARNING SIGNALS

*** COMMENT ***

THE MANEUVERING AND WARNING SIGNALS REQUIRED BY RULE 34 (a) INTERNATIONAL ARE TO BE SOUNDED BY VESSELS ONLY WHEN INSIGHT OF ONE ANOTHER. SEE RULE 34 (a) INTERNATIONAL. THE MANEUVERING AND WARNING SIGNALS REQUIRED BY RULE 34 (a) INLAND ARE TO BE SOUNDED BY POWER-DRIVEN VESSELS ONLY WHEN INSIGHT OF ONE ANOTHER. SEE RULE 34 (a) INTERNATIONAL & INLAND.

040754/RR04588   **RULE 34 (a); RULE 35 (b)**
BOTH INTERNATIONAL & INLAND While underway in fog, you hear a vessel ahead sound two prolonged blasts on the whistle. You should _____.
- A.   sound whistle signals only if you change course
- B.   sound only fog signals until the other vessel is sighted
- C.   not sound any whistle signals until the other vessel is sighted
- D.   sound two blasts and change course to the left

040755/RR04667   **RULE 34 (a) (i)**
BOTH INTERNATIONAL & INLAND While underway and in sight of another vessel, less than one half mile away, you put your engines on astern propulsion. Which statement concerning whistle signals is TRUE?
- A.   You must sound three short blasts on the whistle.
- B.   You need not sound any whistle signals.
- C.   You must sound one blast if backing to starboard.
- D.   You must sound whistle signals only if the vessels are meeting.

040756/RR04544   **RULE 34 (a) (i); RULE 15 (a)**
BOTH INTERNATIONAL & INLAND You are approaching another vessel on crossing courses. She is approximately half a mile distant and is presently on your starboard bow. You believe she will cross ahead of you. She then sounds a whistle signal of five short blasts. You should _____.
- A.   make a large course change, accompanied by the appropriate whistle signal, and slow down if necessary
- B.   reduce speed slightly to make sure she will have room to pass
- C.   wait for another whistle signal from the other vessel
- D.   answer the signal and hold course and speed

040757/RR04336   **RULE 34 (a) (i)**
BOTH INTERNATIONAL & INLAND While underway and in sight of another vessel crossing less than .5 mile away, you put your engines full speed astern. Which statement concerning whistle signals is TRUE?
A. You need not sound any whistle signals.
B. You must sound one blast if backing to starboard.
C. You must sound whistle signals only if the vessels are meeting.
⚓ D. You must sound three short blasts on the whistle.

040758/RR04364   **RULE 34 (a) (i)**
BOTH INTERNATIONAL & INLAND The whistle signal for a vessel operating astern propulsion is _____ .
A. one long blast
B. one prolonged blast
⚓ C. three short blasts
D. four or more short blasts

040759/RR00360   **RULE 34 (a) (i); RULE 15 (a)**
BOTH INTERNATIONAL & INLAND Two power-driven vessels are crossing as shown in illustration D042RR below. Vessel "A" sounds one short blast on the whistle. You are on vessel "B" and doubt that sufficient action is being taken by vessel "A" . What action should you take? See DIAGRAM D042RR
⚓ A. sound at least five short and rapid blasts
B. sound one short blast and maintain course and speed
C. maintain course and speed
D. alter course to the right or slow down

040760/RR00361   **RULE 34 (a) (i); RULE 15 (a)**
BOTH INTERNATIONAL & INLAND Two power-driven vessels are crossing as shown in illustration D042RR below. Vessel "A" sounds two short blasts on the whistle. You are on vessel "B" and are in doubt that sufficient action is being taken by vessel "A" to avoid collision. What action should you take? See DIAGRAM D042RR
A. maintain course and speed
⚓ B. sound five or more short and rapid blasts
C. alter course to the left and increase speed
D. None of the above

040761/RR09108   **RULE 34 (a) (iii)**
BOTH INTERNATIONAL & INLAND Two power-driven vessels are crossing as shown in illustration D042RR below. Vessel "A" sounds three short blasts on the whistle. What is the meaning of this signal? See DIAGRAM D042RR
A. vessel "A" proposes to cross ahead of the other vessel
B. vessel "A" is sounding the danger signal
C. vessel "A" intends to hold course and speed
⚓ D. vessel "A" is backing engines

040762/RR04511   **RULE 34 (b) (i) - (ii), (d)**
BOTH INTERNATIONAL & INLAND Which statement is TRUE concerning the light used with whistle signals?
⚓ A. Its purpose is to supplement short blasts of the whistle
B. Use of such a light is required
C. The light shall have the same characteristics as a masthead light
D. All of the above

040763/RR04671   **RULE 34 (b) (i) - (ii), (d)**
BOTH INTERNATIONAL & INLAND Which statement is TRUE concerning the light used with whistle signals?
A. Use of such a light is required.
B. The light shall have the same characteristics as a masthead light.
⚓ C. It is only used to supplement short blasts of the whistle.
D. All of the above

040764/RR04278   **RULE 34 (b) (i)**
BOTH INTERNATIONAL & INLAND A light signal consisting of three flashes means _____ .
A. "I desire to overtake you"
⚓ B. "I am operating astern propulsion"
C. "I am in doubt as to your actions"
D. "My engines are full speed astern"

040765/RR04021   **RULE 34 (b) (i)**
BOTH INTERNATIONAL & INLAND A light signal of three flashes means _____ .
⚓ A. "I am operating astern propulsion"
B. "I desire to overtake you"
C. "My engines are full speed astern"
D. "I am in doubt as to your actions"

040766/RR04294   **RULE 34 (b) (i)**
BOTH INTERNATIONAL & INLAND At night you observe a vessel ahead show three flashes of a white light. This signal indicates that the vessel ahead is _____ .
A. intending to overtake another vessel
B. in distress
⚓ C. operating astern propulsion
D. approaching a bend in the channel

040767/RR04676   RULE 34 (d), (c) (i); RULE 9 (d), (e) (i)
BOTH INTERNATIONAL & INLAND You are underway in a narrow channel and are being overtaken by a vessel astern. The overtaking vessel sounds a signal indicating her intention to pass you on your starboard side. If such an action appears dangerous, you should sound _____.
A. one prolonged, one short, one prolonged, and one short blast in that order
⚓ B. five short and rapid blasts
C. one prolonged followed by one short blast
D. three short and rapid blasts

040768/RR04208   **RULE 34 (d)**
BOTH INTERNATIONAL & INLAND Five or more short blasts on a vessel's whistle indicates that she is _____.
A. the stand-on vessel and will maintain course and speed
⚓ B. in doubt that another vessel is taking sufficient action to avoid a collision
C. altering course to starboard
D. altering course to port

040769/RR04295   **RULE 34 (d)**
BOTH INTERNATIONAL & INLAND The use of the danger signal _____.
A. replaces directional signals
B. makes the other vessel the stand-on vessel
C. is the same as a "MAYDAY" signal
⚓ D. indicates doubt as to another vessels actions

040770/RR04232   **RULE 34 (d)**
BOTH INTERNATIONAL & INLAND The use of the signal consisting of five or more short blasts on the ship's whistle _____.
A. makes it necessary to slow or stop
B. replaces directional signals
C. makes the other vessel the give-way vessel
⚓ D. indicates doubt as to the other vessel's action

040771/RR04101   **RULE 34 (d)**
BOTH INTERNATIONAL & INLAND Which statement is TRUE concerning the danger signal?
A. Indicates that the vessel is in distress
B. Is used to indicate a course change
⚓ C. May be supplemented by an appropriate light signal
D. May be sounded by the stand-on vessel only

040772/RR04780   **RULE 34 (d)**
BOTH INTERNATIONAL & INLAND You are the stand-on vessel in a crossing situation. If you think the give-way vessel is NOT taking sufficient action to avoid collision, you should sound _____.
A. two short blasts, alter to port, and pass astern
B. one short blast and maintain course
⚓ C. the danger signal
D. no signal and maneuver at will

040773/RR04372   **RULE 34 (d)**
BOTH INTERNATIONAL & INLAND You are the stand-on vessel in a crossing situation. If you think the give-way vessel is NOT taking sufficient action to avoid collision, you should sound _____.
A. no signal and maneuver at will
B. one short blast and maintain course
C. two short blasts, alter to port, and pass astern
⚓ D. five short and rapid blasts

040774/RR04535   **RULE 34 (d)**
BOTH INTERNATIONAL & INLAND Which statement is TRUE concerning the danger signal?
A. Distress signals may be used in place of the danger signal.
⚓ B. When any vessel fails to understand the intentions of an approaching vessel she must sound the danger signal.
C. The danger signal consists of 4 or more short blasts of the whistle.
D. Only the stand-on vessel can sound the danger signal.

040775/RR04449   **RULE 34 (d)**
BOTH INTERNATIONAL & INLAND In a crossing situation, which vessel may sound the danger signal?
A. Stand-on vessel
⚓ B. Either vessel
C. Give-way vessel
D. Neither vessel

040776/RR04675   **RULE 34 (d)**
BOTH INTERNATIONAL & INLAND In a meeting situation, which vessel may sound the danger signal?
A. Stand-on vessel
⚓ B. Either vessel
C. Give-way vessel
D. Neither vessel

040777/RR04673   **RULE 34 (d)**
BOTH INTERNATIONAL & INLAND Which vessel may sound the danger signal?
A. The stand-on vessel in a crossing situation
B. A vessel at anchor
C. The give-way vessel in a crossing situation
⚓ D. All of the above

040778/RR04122   **RULE 34 (d)**
BOTH INTERNATIONAL & INLAND Which vessel may sound the danger signal?
A. The give-way vessel in a crossing situation
B. A vessel at anchor
C. Either vessel in a meeting situation
⚓ D. All of the above

040779/RR04546   **RULE 34 (d)**
BOTH INTERNATIONAL & INLAND Which vessel may use the danger signal?
A. The vessel to starboard when two power-driven vessels are crossing
B. Either of two power-driven vessels meeting head-on
C. A vessel engaged in fishing, crossing the course of a sailing vessel
⚓ D. All of the above

040780/RR04007   **RULE 34 (d)**
BOTH INTERNATIONAL & INLAND If you do NOT understand the course or intention of an approaching vessel you should sound _____.
A. not less than five prolonged blasts
⚓ B. not less than five short blasts
C. one prolonged blast
D. one short blast

040781/RR04479   **RULE 34 (d)**
BOTH INTERNATIONAL & INLAND What signal indicates doubt that sufficient action is being taken by another vessel to avoid collision?
A. Three short and rapid blasts of the whistle
B. Three long blasts of the whistle
⚓ C. Five short and rapid blasts of the whistle
D. One prolonged blast followed by three short blasts of the whistle

040782/RR04103   **RULE 34 (d)**
BOTH INTERNATIONAL & INLAND Which is the danger signal?
A. One prolonged blast on the whistle
B. A continuous sounding of the fog signal
C. Firing a gun every minute
⚓ D. Five or more short rapid blasts on the whistle

040783/RR04415   **RULE 34 (d)**
BOTH INTERNATIONAL & INLAND Which signal may be used by a vessel that is in doubt as to whether sufficient action is being taken by another vessel to avoid collision?
A. A continuous sounding of the fog horn
⚓ B. Five or more short rapid blasts on the whistle
C. One prolonged blast on the whistle
D. Firing a gun every minute

040784/RR04738   **RULE 34 (d), (a) (i)**
BOTH INTERNATIONAL & INLAND You are the stand-on vessel in a crossing situation. If you think the give-way vessel is NOT taking sufficient action to avoid collision, you should sound _____.
⚓ A. the danger signal
B. two short blasts, alter to port, and pass astern
C. no signal and maneuver at will
D. one short blast and maintain course

040785/RR04482   **RULE 34 (d), (c) (i); RULE 9 (d), (e) (i)**
BOTH INTERNATIONAL & INLAND You are underway in a narrow channel and you are being overtaken by a vessel astern. The overtaking vessel sounds a signal indicating his intention to pass your vessel on your starboard side. If such an action appears dangerous you should sound _____.
A. one prolonged, one short, one prolonged, and one short blast in that order
⚓ B. five short and rapid blasts
C. three short and rapid blasts
D. one prolonged followed by one short blast

040786/RR04563   **RULE 34 (d), (c) (i) - (ii)**
BOTH INTERNATIONAL & INLAND You are on vessel "A" as shown in illustration D032RR below, and hear vessel "B" sound a signal indicating her intention to overtake you. You feel it is not safe for vessel "B" to overtake you at the present time. What action should you take? See DIAGRAM D032RR
A. not answer the whistle signal from vessel "B"
⚓ B. sound five or more short rapid blasts
C. sound three blasts of the whistle
D. sound two short blasts

040787/RR04677   **RULE 34 (d), (c) (i); RULE 9 (e) (i)**
BOTH INTERNATIONAL & INLAND You are on vessel "A", as shown in illustration D032RR below and hear vessel "B" sound a signal indicating his intention to overtake you. You feel it is not safe for vessel "B" to overtake you at the present time. What action should you take? See DIAGRAM D032RR
A. sound three blasts of the whistle
B. not answer the whistle signal from vessel "B"
⚓ C. sound five or more short and rapid blasts
D. sound two short blasts

040788/RR00244   **RULE 34 (d); RULE 9 (b), (d)**
BOTH INTERNATIONAL & INLAND You are on a 15-meter vessel "A" in a narrow channel as shown in illustration D032RR below. Vessel "B", a large tanker which can safely navigate only within the channel, sounds five short and rapid blasts. What action should you take? See DIAGRAM D032RR
A. not answer the whistle signal from vessel "B"
B. maintain course and speed
C. sound one prolonged followed by two short blasts
⚓ D. not impede the passage of vessel "B"

040789/RR04509   **RULE 34 (e)**
BOTH INTERNATIONAL & INLAND A vessel nearing a bend or an area of a channel or fairway where other vessels may be hidden by an obstruction shall _____.
A. post a look-out
B. take all way off
C. sound a prolonged blast
D. sound the danger signal

040790/RR04302   **RULE 34 (e)**
BOTH INTERNATIONAL & INLAND A vessel nearing a bend or an area of a channel or fairway where other vessels may be obscured by an intervening obstruction shall sound _____.
A. two short blasts
B. one prolonged blast
C. one long blast
D. the danger signal

040791/RR04380   **RULE 34 (e)**
BOTH INTERNATIONAL & INLAND A vessel nearing a bend where other vessels may be obscured shall sound _____.
A. one short blast
B. one prolonged blast
C. one long blast
D. two short blasts

040792/RR04084   **RULE 34 (e)**
BOTH INTERNATIONAL & INLAND If you are approaching a bend, and hear a whistle signal of one prolonged blast from around the bend, you should answer with a signal of _____.
A. a prolonged blast
B. a long blast
C. one short, one prolonged, and one short blast
D. a short blast

040793/RR04212   **RULE 34 (e)**
BOTH INTERNATIONAL & INLAND While underway your vessel approaches a bend in a river where, due to the bank, you cannot see around the bend. You should _____.
A. sound the danger signal
B. keep to the starboard side of the channel and sound one short blast
C. sound one prolonged blast
D. slow your vessel to bare steerageway

040794/RR04488   **RULE 34 (e)**
BOTH INTERNATIONAL & INLAND You are approaching a bend in a channel. You cannot see around the bend because of the height of the bank. You should _____.
A. sound a whistle blast of 4 to 6 seconds duration
B. stay in the middle of the channel
C. stop engines and navigate with caution
D. sound passing signals to any other vessel that may be on the other side of the bend

040795/RR04565   **RULE 34 (e)**
BOTH INTERNATIONAL & INLAND You are approaching a bend in a river where, due to the bank, you cannot see around the other side. A vessel on the other side of the bend sounds one prolonged blast. You should _____.
A. sound a prolonged blast
B. sound the danger signal
C. not sound any signal until you sight the other vessel
D. sound passing signals

040796/RR04239   **RULE 34 (e)**
BOTH INTERNATIONAL & INLAND You are on a vessel nearing a bend in the channel where, because of the height of the bank, you cannot see a vessel approaching from the opposite direction. You should sound _____.
A. one long blast
B. one prolonged blast
C. five or more short blasts
D. one short blast

040797/RR04198   **RULE 34 (e)**
BOTH INTERNATIONAL & INLAND You are underway and approaching a bend in the channel where vessels approaching from the opposite direction cannot be seen. You should sound _____.
A. one blast, 8 to10 seconds in duration
B. three blasts, 4 to 6 seconds in duration
C. one continuous blast until you are able to see around the bend
D. one blast, 4 to 6 seconds in duration

040798/RR04006   **RULE 34 (e)**
BOTH INTERNATIONAL & INLAND Your vessel is approaching a bend. You hear a prolonged blast from around the bend. You should _____.
A. sound the danger signal
B. stop your engines and drift
C. answer with one prolonged blast
D. back your engines

RULE 35 - SOUND SIGNALS IN RESTRICTED VISIBILITY

040799/RR09109　　　　　　　**RULE 35 (a)**
BOTH INTERNATIONAL & INLAND You are proceeding under sail with the auxiliary engine running and the propeller engaged. Which statement is TRUE?
A. In fog you must sound one prolonged blast at two minute intervals when making way.
B. By day, you must display a black diamond shape forward.
C. If most of the propelling power comes from the sails, your vessel is considered a sailing vessel.
D. You must display a red light over a green light at the masthead.

040800/RR00402　　　　　　　**RULE 35 (a)**
BOTH INTERNATIONAL & INLAND While underway in fog, you hear a prolonged blast from another vessel. This signal indicates a _____.
A. sailboat making way
B. power-driven vessel making way, towing
C. power-driven vessel making way
D. vessel being towed

*** COMMENT ***

MORSE CODE LETTER "H" (. . . .). SIGNAL LETTER "H" (HOTEL) IS SOUNDED BY VESSELS ENGAGED IN PILOTAGE DUTIES. SEE RULE 35 (k) INTERNATIONAL & INLAND.

040801/RR04602　　　　　　　**RULE 35 (a), (k)**
BOTH INTERNATIONAL & INLAND A fog signal consisting of one prolonged blast followed by four short blasts would indicate the presence of a _____.
A. vessel being towed
B. power-driven pilot vessel on station underway
C. vessel at anchor warning of her location
D. fishing vessel engaged in trawling

040802/RR04701　　　　　　　**RULE 35 (a), (k)**
BOTH INTERNATIONAL & INLAND A fog signal of one prolonged blast followed by four short blasts would mean the presence of a _____.
A. vessel being towed
B. fishing vessel trawling
C. power-driven pilot vessel on station underway
D. vessel at anchor warning of her location

040803/RR04462　　　　　　　**RULE 35 (a), (k)**
BOTH INTERNATIONAL & INLAND A fog signal of one prolonged blast followed by four short blasts would mean the presence of a _____.
A. fishing vessel trawling
B. vessel at anchor warning of her location
C. power-driven pilot vessel on station underway
D. vessel being towed

040804/RR04615　　　　　　　**RULE 35 (a), (k)**
BOTH INTERNATIONAL & INLAND A pilot vessel may continue to sound an identity signal if she is _____.
A. being towed
B. underway, but not making way
C. aground
D. not engaged in pilotage duty

040805/RR04519　　　　　　　**RULE 35 (a)**
*** PROTEST ***
THE PREFERRED ANSWER ASSUMES AN UNTASKED POWER-DRIVEN VESSEL.

BOTH INTERNATIONAL & INLAND A vessel underway and making way in fog shall sound every 2 minutes _____.
A. one prolonged blast and three short blasts
B. one prolonged blast
C. three distinct blasts
D. two prolonged blasts

040806/RR04340　　　　　　　**RULE 35 (a)**
BOTH INTERNATIONAL & INLAND While underway and making way your vessel enters fog. Which fog signal should you sound every 2 minutes?
A. A prolonged blast and three short blasts
B. Two prolonged blasts
C. Three short blasts
D. One prolonged blast

040807/RR04190　　　　　　　**RULE 35 (a)**
BOTH INTERNATIONAL & INLAND A power-driven vessel making way through the water sounds a fog signal of _____.
A. two prolonged blasts at intervals of not more than 2 minutes
B. two prolonged blasts at intervals of not more than one minute
C. one prolonged blast at intervals of not more than one minute
D. one prolonged blast at intervals of not more than 2 minutes

040808/RR04428　　　　　　　**RULE 35 (a)**
BOTH INTERNATIONAL & INLAND Which signal shall a power-driven vessel sound when making way in fog?
A. Three short blasts every 2 minutes
B. One prolonged and two short blasts every 2 minutes
C. One prolonged blast every 2 minutes
D. One short blast every 2 minutes

040809/RR00187   **RULE 35 (a)**
BOTH INTERNATIONAL & INLAND You are in charge of a power-driven vessel making way in dense fog. You observe what appears to be another vessel on radar half a mile distant on your port bow and closing. You must take which of the following actions?
⚓ A. sound one prolonged blast
B. sound the danger signal
C. sound one short, one prolonged, and one short blast
D. exchange passing signals

040810/RR04204   **RULE 35 (a) - (c)**
BOTH INTERNATIONAL & INLAND Fog signals, required under the Rules for vessels underway, shall be sounded _____.
A. only when vessels are in sight of each other
⚓ B. at intervals of not more than 2 minutes
C. only on the approach of another vessel
D. at intervals of not more than one minute

040811/RR00238   **RULE 35; RULE 9**
BOTH INTERNATIONAL & INLAND Vessels "A" and "B" are meeting in a narrow channel as shown in illustration D029RR below but are not in sight of one another due to restricted visibility. Which statement is TRUE concerning whistle signals between the vessels? See DIAGRAM D029RR
A. Both vessels should sound two short blasts.
B. Both vessels should sound one short blast.
C. Vessel "A" should sound one short blast and vessel "B" should sound two short blasts.
⚓ D. None of the above statements is TRUE.

040812/RR04770   **RULE 35 (b); RULE 34 (a)**
BOTH INTERNATIONAL & INLAND While underway in fog, you hear a vessel ahead sound two prolonged blasts on the whistle. You should _____.
A. not sound any whistle signals until the other vessel is sighted
⚓ B. sound only fog signals until the other vessel is sighted
C. sound two blasts and change course to the left
D. sound whistle signals only if you change course

040813/RR05000   **RULE 35 (b); RULE 34 (a)**
BOTH INTERNATIONAL & INLAND While underway in fog, you hear a vessel ahead sound two prolonged blasts on the whistle. You should _____.
A. not sound any whistle signals until the other vessel is sighted
B. sound two blasts and change course to the left
⚓ C. sound only fog signals until the other vessel is sighted
D. sound whistle signals only if you change course

040814/RR04695   **RULE 35 (b); RULE 34 (a)**
BOTH INTERNATIONAL & INLAND While underway in fog, you hear a vessel ahead sound two short blasts on the whistle. You should _____.
A. sound two short blasts and change course to the left
⚓ B. sound only fog signals until the other vessel is sighted
C. sound whistle signals only if you change course
D. not sound any whistle signals until the other vessel is sighted

040815/RR04078   **RULE 35 (b); RULE 19 (c)**
BOTH INTERNATIONAL & INLAND You are making headway in fog and hear a fog signal of two prolonged blasts on your starboard quarter. You should _____.
A. change course to the left
B. change course to the right
⚓ C. hold your course and speed
D. stop your vessel

040816/RR04243   **RULE 35 (b)**
BOTH INTERNATIONAL & INLAND In reduced visibility, you hear two prolonged blasts of a whistle. This signal is sounded by a _____.
A. sailing vessel on the port tack
B. vessel not under command
C. vessel fishing with nets
⚓ D. power-driven vessel dead in the water

040817/RR04285   **RULE 35 (b)**
BOTH INTERNATIONAL & INLAND While underway in fog you hear another vessel sounding two prolonged blasts every 2 minutes. This signal indicates a vessel _____.
⚓ A. drifting
B. making way through the water
C. towing
D. anchored

040818/RR04303   **RULE 35 (b)**
BOTH INTERNATIONAL & INLAND In fog, you hear apparently forward of your beam a fog signal of 2 prolonged blasts in succession every 2 minutes. This signal indicates a _____.
A. vessel being pushed ahead
B. vessel restricted in her ability to maneuver
C. power-driven vessel making way through the water
⚓ D. power-driven vessel underway but stopped and making no way through the water

040819/RR04014   **RULE 35 (b)**

BOTH INTERNATIONAL & INLAND A power-driven vessel underway in fog making NO way must sound what signal?

A. One prolonged and two short blasts
B. One prolonged blast
⚓ C. Two prolonged blasts
D. One long blast

040820/RR04359   **RULE 35 (b)**

BOTH INTERNATIONAL & INLAND Your vessel is underway but stopped and making no way through the water when fog sets in. Which fog signal should you sound?

A. One prolonged blast and two short blasts on the whistle
B. One short, one prolonged, and one short blast on the whistle
C. One prolonged blast on the whistle
⚓ D. Two prolonged blasts on the whistle

040821/RR04426   **RULE 35 (b)**

BOTH INTERNATIONAL & INLAND A power-driven vessel is underway in fog but is stopped and making no way through the water. What is the required fog signal?

A. One prolonged blast at not more than one minute intervals
⚓ B. Two prolonged blasts at not more than two minute intervals
C. One prolonged blast at not more than two minute intervals
D. Two prolonged blasts at not more than one minute intervals

040822/RR04276   **RULE 35 (b)**

BOTH INTERNATIONAL & INLAND While underway your vessel enters fog. You stop your engines and the vessel is dead in the water. Which fog signal should you sound?

A. Three short blasts every 2 minutes
B. One prolonged blast every 2 minutes
⚓ C. Two prolonged blasts every 2 minutes
D. One prolonged and three short blasts every 2 minutes

040823/RR04531   **RULE 35 (b)**

*** *PROTEST* ***

THE PREFERRED ANSWER ASSUMES AN UNTASKED POWER-DRIVEN VESSEL.

BOTH INTERNATIONAL & INLAND Your vessel enters fog. You stop your engines, and the vessel is dead in the water. Which fog signal should you sound?

⚓ A. Two prolonged blasts every 2 minutes
B. One prolonged and two short blasts every 2 minutes
C. One prolonged blast every 2 minutes
D. Three short blasts every 2 minutes

*** *COMMENT* ***

MORSE CODE LETTER "D" (- . .) IS THE DOING SOMETHING SIGNAL. EXAMPLES: NOT UNDER COMMAND, RAM, CONSTRAINED BY DRAFT, SAILING, FISHING, OR TOWING. SEE RULE 35 (c) INTERNATIONAL & INLAND.

040824/RR04356   **RULE 35 (c)**

BOTH INTERNATIONAL & INLAND A vessel engaged in fishing underway sounds the same fog signal as a _____.

A. vessel being towed
⚓ B. vessel restricted in her ability to maneuver at anchor
C. sailing vessel at anchor
D. power-driven vessel stopped and making no way through the water

040825/RR04192   **RULE 35 (c)**

BOTH INTERNATIONAL & INLAND In restricted visibility, a vessel fishing with nets shall sound at intervals of 2 minutes _____.

⚓ A. one prolonged followed by two short blasts
B. two prolonged blasts in succession
C. one prolonged blast
D. one prolonged followed by three short blasts

040826/RR04080   **RULE 35 (c)**

BOTH INTERNATIONAL & INLAND You are underway, in fog, when you hear a whistle signal of one prolonged blast followed by two short blasts. This signal could indicate a vessel _____.

A. being towed
B. aground
⚓ C. not under command
D. All of the above

040827/RR04686   **RULE 35 (c)**
BOTH INTERNATIONAL & INLAND If underway in low visibility and sounding fog signals, what changes would you make in the fog signal IMMEDIATELY upon losing the power plant and propulsion?
A. Begin sounding two prolonged blasts at two minute intervals.
B. Begin sounding one prolonged blast followed by three short blasts at two minute intervals.
⚓ C. Begin sounding one prolonged blast followed by two short blasts at two minute intervals.
D. No change should be made in the fog signal.

040828/RR04572   **RULE 35 (c)**
BOTH INTERNATIONAL & INLAND You are underway in low visibility and sounding fog signals. What changes would you make in the fog signal immediately upon losing propulsion?
A. Begin sounding two prolonged blasts at two minute intervals.
B. No change should be made in the fog signal.
⚓ C. Begin sounding one prolonged blast followed by two short blasts at two minute intervals.
D. Begin sounding one prolonged blast followed by three short blasts at two minute intervals.

040829/RR04257   **RULE 35 (c)**
BOTH INTERNATIONAL & INLAND Which vessel is required to sound a fog signal of one prolonged followed by two short blasts?
A. A vessel not under command
B. A sailing vessel, underway
C. A vessel restricted in its ability to maneuver, at anchor
⚓ D. All of the above

040830/RR04293   **RULE 35 (c)**
BOTH INTERNATIONAL & INLAND Which vessel is to sound a fog signal of one prolonged followed by two short blasts?
A. A vessel restricted in its ability to maneuver, at anchor
B. A sailing vessel underway
C. A vessel not under command
⚓ D. All of the above

040831/RR04528   **RULE 35 (c)**
BOTH INTERNATIONAL & INLAND Which vessel is to sound a fog signal of one prolonged followed by two short blasts?
A. A vessel restricted in her ability to maneuver when carrying out her work at anchor
B. A sailing vessel, underway
C. A vessel not under command
⚓ D. All of the above

040832/RR04000   **RULE 35 (c)**
BOTH INTERNATIONAL & INLAND Your vessel is 75 meters in length and restricted in her ability to maneuver. Visibility is restricted. What signal do you sound if you are carrying out your work at anchor?
⚓ A. One prolonged blast followed by two short blasts on the whistle at intervals of not more than 2 minutes
B. Five seconds ringing of a bell and five second sounding of a gong at intervals of not more than one minute
C. Four short blasts on the whistle at intervals of not more than 2 minutes
D. Five seconds ringing of a bell at intervals of not more than one minute

040833/RR04230   **RULE 35 (c)**
BOTH INTERNATIONAL & INLAND In restricted visibility, a vessel restricted in her ability to maneuver, at anchor, would sound a fog signal of _____.
A. the rapid ringing of a bell for five seconds every minute
⚓ B. one prolonged and two short blasts every 2 minutes
C. two prolonged and two short blasts every 2 minutes
D. two prolonged and one short blast every 2 minutes

040834/RR04025   **RULE 35 (c)**
BOTH INTERNATIONAL & INLAND A sailing vessel with the wind abaft the beam is navigating in fog. She should sound _____.
A. three short blasts
⚓ B. one prolonged and two short blasts
C. two prolonged blasts
D. one prolonged blast

040835/RR04056   **RULE 35 (c)**
BOTH INTERNATIONAL & INLAND A sailing vessel with the wind abaft the beam is navigating in restricted visibility. She should sound _____.
⚓ A. one prolonged and two short blasts
B. one prolonged blast
C. three short blasts
D. two prolonged blasts

040836/RR04066   **RULE 35 (c)**
BOTH INTERNATIONAL & INLAND The wind is ESE, and a sailing vessel is steering NW. Which fog signal should she sound?
⚓ A. One prolonged and two short blasts at two minute intervals
B. One blast at one minute intervals
C. One blast at two minute intervals
D. Two blasts at one minute intervals

040837/RR04109   **RULE 35 (c)**
BOTH INTERNATIONAL & INLAND A vessel towing in fog shall sound a fog signal of _____.
A. two prolonged blasts every 2 minutes
B. one prolonged blast every 2 minutes
⚓ C. one prolonged and two short blasts every 2 minutes
D. one prolonged blast every one minute

040838/RR04213   **RULE 35 (c)**
BOTH INTERNATIONAL & INLAND Which statement concerning whistle signals is FALSE?
A. When a pushing vessel and a vessel pushed are connected in a composite unit, the unit sounds the fog signal of a power-driven vessel.
B. A pilot vessel may sound an identity signal on the whistle.
C. A vessel at anchor may sound one short, one prolonged, and one short blast.
⚓ D. A vessel engaged in towing in fog shall sound a fog signal at intervals of one minute.

040839/RR04265   **RULE 35 (c)**
BOTH INTERNATIONAL & INLAND While underway and pushing a barge ahead, your vessel enters a heavy rain storm. You should sound _____.
A. two prolonged blasts every 2 minutes
B. one prolonged and three short blasts every 2 minutes
C. a prolonged blast every 2 minutes
⚓ D. one prolonged and two short blasts every 2 minutes

040840/RR04141   **RULE 35 (c)**
BOTH INTERNATIONAL & INLAND While underway and towing, your vessel enters fog. Which fog signal should you sound?
A. One prolonged blast
⚓ B. One prolonged blast and two short blasts
C. Two prolonged blasts
D. Three distinct blasts

040841/RR04151   **RULE 35 (c)**
BOTH INTERNATIONAL & INLAND While underway in fog you hear a vessel sound one prolonged blast followed by two short blasts. What does this signal indicate?
A. A vessel aground
B. A vessel being towed
C. A pilot vessel engaged on pilotage duty
⚓ D. A vessel towing

040842/RR04164   **RULE 35 (c)**
BOTH INTERNATIONAL & INLAND While underway in fog you hear a whistle signal consisting of one prolonged blast followed immediately by two short blasts. This signal is sounded in fog by _____.
A. pilot vessels
⚓ B. vessels underway and towing
C. vessels in danger
D. vessels at anchor, not engaged in fishing

040843/RR04123   **RULE 35 (c)**
BOTH INTERNATIONAL & INLAND While underway in fog, you hear a vessel sound one prolonged blast followed by two short blasts on the whistle. What does this signal indicate?
⚓ A. A vessel towing
B. A vessel engaged in pilotage duty
C. A vessel aground
D. A vessel being towed

040844/RR04178   **RULE 35 (c)**
BOTH INTERNATIONAL & INLAND You are underway in fog and you hear one prolonged blast followed by two short blasts. This is a vessel _____.
A. aground in a fairway
B. stopped and making no way through the water
C. engaged on pilotage duty
⚓ D. towing

040845/RR04598   **RULE 35 (d) International;
                                 RULE 35 (c) Inland**
BOTH INTERNATIONAL & INLAND A vessel engaged in fishing while at anchor shall sound a fog signal of _____.
⚓ A. one prolonged and two short blasts at two minute intervals
B. a sounding of the bell and gong at one minute intervals
C. a rapid ringing of the bell for five seconds at one minute intervals
D. one prolonged and three short blasts at one minute intervals

040846/RR04687   **RULE 35 (d) International;
                                 RULE 35 (c) Inland**
BOTH INTERNATIONAL & INLAND A vessel engaged in fishing while at anchor shall sound a fog signal of _____.
⚓ A. one prolonged and two short blasts at two minute intervals
B. a sounding of the bell and gong at one minute intervals
C. one prolonged and three short blasts at two minute intervals
D. a rapid ringing of the bell for five seconds at one minute intervals

040847/RR04244　　　　　RULE 35 (d) International;
　　　　　　　　　　　　　　　RULE 35 (c) Inland

BOTH INTERNATIONAL & INLAND A 200-meter vessel restricted in her ability to maneuver, at anchor, will sound a fog signal of _____.

A. one prolonged followed by three short blasts every minute

B. one prolonged followed by three short blasts every 2 minutes

⚓ C. one prolonged followed by two short blasts every 2 minutes

D. a 5 second ringing of a bell forward and a 5 second sounding of a gong aft at intervals of 1 minute

040848/RR04688　　　　　RULE 35 (d) International;
　　　　　　　　　　　　　　　RULE 35 (c) Inland

BOTH INTERNATIONAL & INLAND What is the fog signal for a vessel 75 meters in length, restricted in her ability to maneuver, at anchor?

A. Four short blasts at intervals of not more than 2 minutes

B. Five second ringing of a bell at intervals of not more than one minute

C. Five second ringing of a bell and five second sounding of a gong at intervals of not more than one minute

⚓ D. One prolonged blast followed by two short blasts at intervals of not more than 2 minutes

040849/RR04564　　　　　RULE 35 (d) International;
　　　　　　　　　　　　　　　RULE 35 (c) Inland

BOTH INTERNATIONAL & INLAND Which vessel sounds the same fog signal when underway or at anchor?

A. A sailing vessel

⚓ B. A vessel restricted in her ability to maneuver

C. A vessel not under command

D. A vessel constrained by her draft

040850/RR04689　　　　　RULE 35 (d) International;
　　　　　　　　　　　　　　　RULE 35 (c) Inland

BOTH INTERNATIONAL & INLAND Which vessel sounds the same fog signal when underway or at anchor?

A. A vessel constrained by her draft

B. A vessel not under command

C. A sailing vessel

⚓ D. A vessel restricted in her ability to maneuver

*** COMMENT ***

MORSE CODE LETTER "B" (- . . .). SIGNAL LETTER "B" MEANS BARGE. "B" IS SOUNDED BY THE LAST BARGE IN THE TOW WHEN MANNED. SEE RULE 35(e) INTERNATIONAL & 35 (d) INLAND.

040851/RR04697　　　　　　　　　　RULE 35 (e)

BOTH INTERNATIONAL & INLAND A tug is towing three barges astern in restricted visibility. The second vessel of the tow should sound _____.

A. one prolonged and three short blasts

B. one prolonged and two short blasts

C. one short blast

⚓ D. no fog signal

040852/RR04241　　　　　　　　　　RULE 35 (e)

BOTH INTERNATIONAL & INLAND A tug is towing three manned barges in line in fog. The first vessel of the tow should sound _____.

A. one prolonged, one short, and one prolonged blast

⚓ B. no fog signal

C. one prolonged and three short blasts

D. one short blast

040853/RR04620　　　　　　　　　　RULE 35 (e)

BOTH INTERNATIONAL & INLAND A tug is towing three manned barges in line in fog. The second vessel of the tow should sound _____.

A. one prolonged and two short blasts

⚓ B. no fog signal

C. one short blast

D. one prolonged and three short blasts

040854/RR04271　　　　　　　　　　RULE 35 (e)

BOTH INTERNATIONAL & INLAND A tug is towing three manned barges in line in fog. The third barge of the tow should sound _____.

A. no fog signal

B. one prolonged and two short blasts

⚓ C. one prolonged and three short blasts

D. one prolonged, one short and one prolonged blast

040855/RR04726　　　　　　　　　　RULE 35 (e)

BOTH INTERNATIONAL & INLAND A tug is towing three unmanned barges astern in fog. The third vessel of the tow should sound _____.

A. one prolonged, one short, and one prolonged blast

⚓ B. no fog signal

C. one short blast

D. one prolonged and three short blasts

040856/RR04590   **RULE 35 (e)**
BOTH INTERNATIONAL & INLAND A vessel being towed, if manned, shall sound a fog signal of _____.
A. two short blasts
B. one prolonged and two short blasts
⚓ C. one prolonged and three short blasts
D. three short blasts

040857/RR04633   **RULE 35 (e)**
BOTH INTERNATIONAL & INLAND If practical, when shall a manned vessel being towed sound her fog signal?
A. As close to the mid-cycle of the towing vessel's signals as possible
B. Immediately before the towing vessel sounds hers
C. At any time as long as the interval is correct
⚓ D. Immediately after the towing vessel sounds hers

040858/RR04236   **RULE 35 (e)**
BOTH INTERNATIONAL & INLAND If your vessel is underway in fog and you hear one prolonged and three short blasts, this indicates a _____.
⚓ A. vessel being towed
B. vessel not under command
C. sailing vessel
D. vessel in distress

040859/RR04010   **RULE 35 (e)**
BOTH INTERNATIONAL & INLAND If your vessel is underway in fog and you hear one prolonged and three short blasts, this is a _____.
A. vessel being towed (unmanned)
⚓ B. vessel being towed (manned)
C. sailing vessel
D. vessel not under command

040860/RR04368   **RULE 35 (e)**
BOTH INTERNATIONAL & INLAND In a dense fog you hear a whistle signal ahead of one prolonged blast followed by three short blasts. This signal indicates a _____.
A. fishing vessel underway trawling
B. pilot vessel underway making a special signal
C. vessel not under command
⚓ D. manned vessel being towed

040861/RR04263   **RULE 35 (e)**
BOTH INTERNATIONAL & INLAND In a dense fog, you hear a whistle signal of one prolonged blast followed by three short blasts. This signal is sounded by a _____.
A. vessel not under command
B. fishing vessel underway trawling
C. pilot vessel underway making a special signal
⚓ D. manned vessel being towed

040862/RR04305   **RULE 35 (e)**
BOTH INTERNATIONAL & INLAND In fog, a vessel being towed, if manned, shall sound a fog signal of _____.
A. one prolonged and two short blasts
B. two short blasts
C. three short blasts
⚓ D. one prolonged and three short blasts

040863/RR04736   **RULE 35 (e)**
BOTH INTERNATIONAL & INLAND In restricted visibility a towed vessel must sound a fog signal when it is _____.
A. the last vessel in the tow
B. manned, regardless of its position in the tow
⚓ C. the last vessel in the tow and it is carrying a crew
D. None of the above are correct

040864/RR04875   **RULE 35 (e)**
BOTH INTERNATIONAL & INLAND In restricted visibility, a vessel being towed, if manned, shall sound a signal of _____.
A. one prolonged and two short blasts
⚓ B. one prolonged and three short blasts
C. three short blasts
D. two short blasts

040865/RR04456   **RULE 35 (e)**
BOTH INTERNATIONAL & INLAND What is the required fog signal for a manned vessel being towed at night?
⚓ A. One prolonged followed by three short blasts
B. One prolonged followed by one short blast
C. One prolonged followed by two short blasts
D. Two prolonged blasts

040866/RR04118   **RULE 35 (e)**
BOTH INTERNATIONAL & INLAND When should the fog signal of a manned vessel under tow be sounded?
A. Approximately one minute after the towing vessel's fog signal
B. If the towing vessel is sounding a fog signal, the manned vessel being towed is not required to sound any fog signal
C. Before the towing vessel's fog signal
⚓ D. After the towing vessel's fog signal

040867/RR04073   **RULE 35 (e)**
BOTH INTERNATIONAL & INLAND While underway in fog, you hear a signal of one prolonged blast followed by three short blasts. This is the fog signal for a vessel _____.
A. towing
⚓ B. being towed (manned)
C. under sail
D. at anchor

040868/RR04292   **RULE 35 (e)**
BOTH INTERNATIONAL & INLAND While underway in fog, you hear a signal of one prolonged blast followed by three short blasts. This is the fog signal for a vessel _____.
A. towing
B. at anchor
C. unmanned being towed
⚓ D. manned being towed

040869/RR04392   **RULE 35 (e)**
BOTH INTERNATIONAL & INLAND Which vessel does NOT sound a fog signal of one prolonged followed by two short blasts?
A. A vessel dredging
⚓ B. A vessel being towed
C. A sailing vessel
D. A vessel engaged in fishing

040870/RR04430   **RULE 35 (e)**
BOTH INTERNATIONAL & INLAND Which vessel does NOT sound a fog signal of one prolonged followed by two short blasts?
A. A sailing vessel
B. A vessel engaged in fishing
C. A vessel engaged in dredging
⚓ D. A vessel being towed

040871/RR04321   **RULE 35 (e)**
BOTH INTERNATIONAL & INLAND While underway in a fog, you hear a whistle signal of one prolonged blast followed by two short blasts. This signal could mean all of the following EXCEPT a vessel _____.
A. fishing with trawls
B. not under command
⚓ C. being towed
D. towing astern

040872/RR04277   **RULE 35 (e)**
BOTH INTERNATIONAL & INLAND You are underway in a fog when you hear a whistle signal of one prolonged blast followed by two short blasts. This signal could indicate all of the following EXCEPT a vessel _____.
A. not under command
⚓ B. being towed
C. fishing with trawls
D. towing astern

040873/RR04038   **RULE 35 (g)**
BOTH INTERNATIONAL & INLAND A bell is used to sound a fog signal for a _____.
A. vessel engaged in fishing
B. vessel not under command
⚓ C. sailing vessel at anchor
D. power-driven vessel underway

040874/RR04604   **RULE 35 (g), (k)**
BOTH INTERNATIONAL & INLAND A pilot vessel may continue to sound an identity signal if she is _____.
A. being towed
⚓ B. at anchor
C. aground
D. not under command

040875/RR04469   **RULE 35 (g), (k)**
BOTH INTERNATIONAL & INLAND A pilot vessel may continue to sound an identity signal in fog if she is _____.
⚓ A. at anchor
B. no longer on pilotage duty
C. aground
D. not under command

040876/RR04396   **RULE 35 (g), (k)**
BOTH INTERNATIONAL & INLAND Concerning the identification signal for a pilot vessel, in fog, which statement is TRUE?
A. The pilot vessel may only sound the identity signal when making way.
B. The identification signal must be sounded any time the pilot vessel is underway.
⚓ C. When at anchor, the pilot vessel is only required to sound anchor signals.
D. All of the above

040877/RR04035   **RULE 35 (g)**
BOTH INTERNATIONAL & INLAND When underway in restricted visibility, you might hear, at intervals of 2 minutes, any of the following fog signals EXCEPT _____.
A. two prolonged blasts
B. one prolonged and two short blasts
C. one prolonged blast
⚓ D. ringing of a bell for five seconds

040878/RR04690   **RULE 35 (g)**
BOTH INTERNATIONAL & INLAND Which vessel would sound a fog signal consisting of the ringing of a bell for 5 seconds?
⚓ A. A sailing vessel, at anchor
B. A vessel restricted in its ability to maneuver, at anchor
C. A vessel engaged in fishing, at anchor
D. All of the above

040879/RR04600   **RULE 35 (g)**
BOTH INTERNATIONAL & INLAND Which vessel would sound a fog signal consisting of the ringing of a bell for 5 seconds?
  A. A vessel engaged in fishing, at anchor
  B. A sailing vessel becalmed
⚓ C. A sailing vessel, at anchor
  D. A vessel restricted in its ability to maneuver, at anchor

040880/RR04386   **RULE 35 (g)**
BOTH INTERNATIONAL & INLAND While underway in fog you hear a rapid ringing of a bell ahead. This bell indicates a _____.
  A. vessel backing out of a berth
  B. vessel in distress
  C. sailboat underway
⚓ D. vessel at anchor

040881/RR04350   **RULE 35 (g)**
BOTH INTERNATIONAL & INLAND While underway in fog you hear the rapid ringing of a bell. What does this signal indicate?
⚓ A. A vessel at anchor
  B. A vessel backing down
  C. A sailboat underway
  D. A vessel drifting

040882/RR04481   **RULE 35 (g)**
BOTH INTERNATIONAL & INLAND While underway in fog, you hear the rapid ringing of a bell for about five seconds followed by the sounding of a gong for about five seconds. This signal came from a _____.
  A. vessel engaged in fishing at anchor
  B. sailing vessel at anchor
⚓ C. vessel 150 meters in length at anchor
  D. vessel aground

040883/RR04589   **RULE 35 (g)**
BOTH INTERNATIONAL & INLAND You are operating in restricted visibility and hear a signal of a rapidly ringing bell followed by the rapid sounding of a gong. It could be a _____.
  A. 30-meter sail vessel at anchor
  B. 150-meter power-driven vessel aground
  C. vessel in distress
⚓ D. 300-meter power-driven vessel at anchor

040884/RR04065   **RULE 35 (g)**
BOTH INTERNATIONAL & INLAND You are underway in fog when you hear the rapid ringing of a bell for five seconds followed by the sounding of a gong for five seconds. This signal indicates a vessel _____.
⚓ A. more than 100 meters in length, at anchor
  B. fishing while making no way through the water
  C. fishing in company with another vessel
  D. aground

040885/RR04696   **RULE 35 (g)**
BOTH INTERNATIONAL & INLAND You are underway in fog when you hear the rapid ringing of a bell for five seconds followed by the sounding of a gong for five seconds. This signal indicates a vessel _____.
⚓ A. more than 100 meters in length, at anchor
  B. fishing while making no way through the water
  C. engaged in pair trawling
  D. engaged on pilotage duty

040886/RR04160   **RULE 35 (g)**
                                  Optional Signal (R . _ .)
BOTH INTERNATIONAL & INLAND A fog signal of one short, one prolonged, and one short blast may be sounded by a _____.
⚓ A. vessel at anchor
  B. vessel towing
  C. vessel not under command
  D. All of the above

040887/RR06520   **RULE 35 (g)**
                                  Optional Signal (R . _ .)
BOTH INTERNATIONAL & INLAND A fog signal of one short, one prolonged, and one short blast may be sounded by a _____.
  A. vessel towing
  B. vessel not under command
⚓ C. vessel at anchor
  D. All of the above

040888/RR04587   **RULE 35 (g)**
                                  Optional Signal (R . _ .)
BOTH INTERNATIONAL & INLAND A vessel anchored in fog may warn an approaching vessel by sounding _____.
  A. three distinct strokes on the bell before and after sounding the anchor signal
⚓ B. one short, one prolonged, and one short blast of the whistle
  C. the whistle continuously
  D. five or more short and rapid blasts of the whistle

040889/RR04259   **RULE 35 (g)**
Optional Signal (R . _ .)
BOTH INTERNATIONAL & INLAND What is the optional whistle signal which may be sounded by a vessel at anchor?
A. One short followed by two prolonged blasts
B. Two prolonged followed by one short blast
C. Four short blasts
⚓ D. One short, one prolonged, followed by one short blast

040890/RR04330   **RULE 35 (g)**
Optional Signal (R . _ .)
BOTH INTERNATIONAL & INLAND While underway in fog, you hear a short blast, a prolonged blast, and a short blast of a whistle. This signal indicates a _____.
A. vessel being towed in fog
B. vessel towing in fog
⚓ C. vessel anchored in fog
D. sailboat underway in fog

040891/RR04188   **RULE 35 (g)**
Optional Signal (R . _ .)
BOTH INTERNATIONAL & INLAND You are at anchor in fog on a 120-meter power-driven vessel. You hear the fog signal of a vessel approaching off your port bow. You may sound _____.
A. two short blasts
B. one prolonged, one short and one prolonged
⚓ C. one short, one prolonged, and one short blast
D. one prolonged blast

040892/RR04438   **RULE 35 (g)**
Optional Signal (R . _ .)
BOTH INTERNATIONAL & INLAND You are at anchor in fog. The fog signal of a vessel underway has been steadily growing louder and the danger of collision appears to exist. In addition to your fog signal, what signal may be used to indicate the presence of your vessel?
A. No signal other than your fog signal may be used.
B. Three blasts on the whistle; one prolonged, one short, and one prolonged.
⚓ C. Three blasts on the whistle; one short, one prolonged, and one short.
D. Three blasts on the whistle; one prolonged followed by two short.

040893/RR04145   **RULE 35 (g)**
Optional Signal (R . _ .)
BOTH INTERNATIONAL & INLAND You are in charge of a 120-meter power-driven vessel at anchor in fog, sounding the required anchor signals. You hear the fog signal of a vessel underway off your port bow. You may sound _____.
A. at least five short and rapid blasts
B. two short blasts
⚓ C. one short, one prolonged, and one short blast
D. three short blasts

040894/RR04493   **RULE 35 (g)**
Optional Signal (R . _ .)
BOTH INTERNATIONAL & INLAND You are underway in fog and hear one short, one prolonged, and one short blast in succession. What is the meaning of this signal?
A. A vessel is towing.
⚓ B. A vessel is at anchor, warning of her position.
C. A vessel is in distress and needs assistance.
D. A vessel is fishing, hauling nets.

040895/RR04202   **RULE 35 (g)**
Optional Signal (R . _ .)
BOTH INTERNATIONAL & INLAND You are underway in fog when you hear the following signal: one short blast, one prolonged blast and one short blast in succession. Which of the following would it be?
A. A vessel towing
B. A sailing vessel underway with the wind abaft the beam
⚓ C. A vessel at anchor
D. A power-driven vessel underway and making way through the water

040896/RR04268   **RULE 35 (g)**
Optional Signal (R . _ .)
BOTH INTERNATIONAL & INLAND Your vessel is at anchor in fog. The fog signal of another vessel, apparently underway, has been growing louder and the danger of collision appears to exist. In addition to your fog signal, what signal may be used to indicate your presence?
A. One prolonged, one short, and one prolonged whistle blast
B. No signal other than your fog signal may be used.
C. One prolonged followed by two short whistle blasts
⚓ D. One short, one prolonged, and one short whistle blast

040897/RR04484   **RULE 35 (g)**

BOTH INTERNATIONAL & INLAND A power-driven vessel at anchor, not fishing or otherwise restricted in its ability to maneuver, sounds her fog signal at intervals of not _____.

A. less than two minutes
B. more than three minutes
C. more than two minutes
⚓ D. more than one minute

040898/RR04431   **RULE 35 (g)**
*** *COMMENT* ***
ASSUMES A VESSEL AT ANCHOR, NOT FISHING OR OTHERWISE RESTRICTED IN ITS ABILITY TO MANEUVER.

BOTH INTERNATIONAL & INLAND A vessel 50 meters in length at anchor must sound which fog signal?

⚓ A. 5-second ringing of a bell every minute
B. 5-second sounding of a gong every minute
C. 5-second ringing of a bell every 2 minutes
D. 5-second sounding of both a bell and gong every 2 minutes

040899/RR04329   **RULE 35 (g);**
*** *COMMENT* ***
ASSUMES A VESSEL AT ANCHOR, NOT FISHING OR OTHERWISE RESTRICTED IN ITS ABILITY TO MANEUVER.

BOTH INTERNATIONAL & INLAND Your vessel is 25 meters long and anchored in restricted visibility. You are required to sound the proper fog signal at intervals of not more than _____.

A. 30 seconds
⚓ B. one minute
C. two minutes
D. three minutes

040900/RR04242   **RULE 35 (g), (h)**
*** *COMMENT* ***
ASSUMES A VESSEL AT ANCHOR, NOT FISHING OR OTHERWISE RESTRICTED IN ITS ABILITY TO MANEUVER.

BOTH INTERNATIONAL & INLAND All fog signals shall be sounded every 2 minutes with the exception of a vessel _____.

A. underway or making way
⚓ B. anchored or aground
C. under sail or under tow
D. not under command or restricted in her ability to maneuver

040901/RR04287   **RULE 35 (g), (h)**
*** *COMMENT* ***
ASSUMES A VESSEL AT ANCHOR, NOT FISHING OR OTHERWISE RESTRICTED IN ITS ABILITY TO MANEUVER.

BOTH INTERNATIONAL & INLAND Fog bell signals for vessels at anchor or aground shall be sounded at intervals of not more than _____.

A. 5 minutes
B. 2 minutes
C. 15 minutes
⚓ D. 1 minute

040902/RR04015   **RULE 35 (h)**

BOTH INTERNATIONAL & INLAND A 95-meter vessel aground sounds which fog signal?

A. A rapid ringing of a bell for 5 seconds every 2 minutes
B. A whistle signal of one short, one prolonged, and one short blast
⚓ C. A rapid ringing of a bell for 5 seconds, preceded and followed by three separate and distinct strokes on the bell
D. A prolonged blast of the whistle at intervals not to exceed one minute

040903/RR04290   **RULE 35 (h)**

BOTH INTERNATIONAL & INLAND While underway in a fog you hear a signal of three strokes of a bell, a rapid ringing of the bell, and three more strokes of the bell. This signal is made by a vessel _____.

⚓ A. aground
B. not under command and at anchor
C. at anchor and greater than 100 meters in length
D. at anchor and giving warning

040904/RR04452   **RULE 35 (h)**

BOTH INTERNATIONAL & INLAND You are underway in fog and you hear three distinct bell strokes followed by five seconds of rapid bell ringing followed by three distinct bell strokes. This signal indicates a vessel _____.

A. engaged in underwater construction
B. at anchor
C. in distress
⚓ D. aground

040905/RR04375   **RULE 35 (h)**
BOTH INTERNATIONAL & INLAND You are underway in fog when you hear a signal of three strokes of a bell, a rapid ringing of the bell, and three more strokes of the bell. This signal indicates a vessel _____.

A. at anchor, giving warning
B. not under command at anchor
C. at anchor, greater than 100 meters
⚓ D. aground

040906/RR04561   **RULE 35 (h)**
BOTH INTERNATIONAL & INLAND Your vessel is aground in fog. In addition to the regular anchor signals, you will be sounding _____.

⚓ A. three strokes of the bell before and after the rapid ringing of the bell
B. a blast on the whistle
C. no additional signals
D. three strokes of the gong before and after the rapid ringing of the gong

040907/RR04017   **RULE 35 (h); Optional Signal (U . . _)**
BOTH INTERNATIONAL & INLAND A 200-meter vessel is aground in fog. Which signal is optional?

⚓ A. A whistle signal
B. A bell signal
C. A gong signal
D. All of the above

040908/RR04691   **RULE 35 (h)**
Optional Signal (U . . _)
BOTH INTERNATIONAL & INLAND A 200-meter vessel is aground in fog. Which signal is optional?
A. A bell signal
⚓ B. A whistle signal
C. A gong signal
D. All of the above are mandatory.

040909/RR04693   **RULE 35 (h)**
Optional Signal (U . . _)
BOTH INTERNATIONAL & INLAND A 200-meter vessel is aground in restricted visibility. Which signal is optional?
A. A bell signal
⚓ B. A whistle signal
C. A gong signal
D. All of the above are optional

040910/RR04407   **RULE 35 (h)**
Optional Signal (U . . _)
BOTH INTERNATIONAL & INLAND A 200-meter vessel is aground in restricted visibility. Which signal is optional?
A. A bell signal
B. A gong signal
⚓ C. A whistle signal
D. All of the above

040911/RR04694   **RULE 35 (h)**
Optional Signal (U . . _)
BOTH INTERNATIONAL & INLAND Which statement is TRUE concerning fog signals?
A. All fog signals for sailing vessels are to be given at intervals of not more than one minute.
⚓ B. A vessel aground may sound a whistle signal.
C. A pilot vessel underway and making way sounds the pilot identity signal and another signal.
D. A vessel not under command sounds the same fog signal as a vessel towed.

040912/RR04552   **RULE 35 (h)**
Optional Signal (U . . _)
BOTH INTERNATIONAL & INLAND Which statement is TRUE concerning fog signals?
A. The identity signal of a pilot vessel is the only fog signal sounded by such a vessel.
B. A vessel not under command sounds the same fog signal as a vessel towed.
⚓ C. A vessel aground may sound a whistle signal.
D. All fog signals for sailing vessels are to be given at intervals of not more than one minute.

040913/RR04699   **RULE 35 (k)**
BOTH INTERNATIONAL & INLAND What is the identity signal which may be sounded by a vessel engaged on pilotage duty in fog?
A. 5 short blasts
⚓ B. 4 short blasts
C. 2 short blasts
D. 3 short blasts

040914/RR04382   **RULE 35 (k)**
BOTH INTERNATIONAL & INLAND While underway in fog, you hear a vessel sound four short blasts in succession. What does this signal indicate?
A. A sailboat
B. A vessel being towed
⚓ C. A pilot vessel
D. A vessel fishing

RULE 36 - SIGNALS TO ATTRACT ATTENTION

040915/RR04138   **RULE 36**
BOTH INTERNATIONAL & INLAND A vessel may use any sound or light signals to attract the attention of another vessel as long as _____.
⚓ A. the signal cannot be mistaken for a signal authorized by the Rules
B. red and green lights are not used
C. the vessel signals such intentions over the radiotelephone
D. white lights are not used

040916/RR04735   **RULE 36**
BOTH INTERNATIONAL & INLAND One of the signals, other than a distress signal, that can be used by a vessel to attract attention is a(n) _____.
A. orange smoke signal
B. red star shell
C. burning barrel
⚓ D. searchlight

040917/RR04113   **RULE 36**
BOTH INTERNATIONAL & INLAND Which signal, other than a distress signal, can be used by a vessel to attract attention?
A. Burning barrel
B. Orange smoke signal
⚓ C. Searchlight beam
D. Continuous sounding of a fog signal apparatus

RULE 37 - DISTRESS SIGNALS

040918/RR04733   **RULE 37; ANNEX IV**
BOTH INTERNATIONAL & INLAND Which of the following is TRUE of a distress signal?
A. is used to indicate doubt about another vessel's intentions
⚓ B. may be used separately or with other distress signals
C. consists of the raising and lowering of a large white flag
D. consists of 5 or more short blasts of the fog signal apparatus

040919/RR04182   **RULE 37; ANNEX IV**
BOTH INTERNATIONAL & INLAND Distress signals may be _____.
A. smoke signals
B. red flares
C. sound signals
⚓ D. Any of the above

040920/RR04110   **RULE 37; ANNEX IV**
BOTH INTERNATIONAL & INLAND Continuous sounding of a fog whistle by a vessel is a signal _____.
A. that the vessel is anchored
B. that the vessel is broken down and drifting
⚓ C. of distress
D. to request the draw span of a bridge to be opened

040921/RR04098   **RULE 37; ANNEX IV**
BOTH INTERNATIONAL & INLAND Which of the following indicates that your vessel is in distress?
⚓ A. continuously sounding the fog whistle
B. displaying a large red flag
C. sounding four or more short rapid blasts on the whistle
D. displaying three black balls in a vertical line

040922/RR04070   **RULE 37; ANNEX IV**
BOTH INTERNATIONAL & INLAND You are underway and hear a vessel continuously sounding her fog whistle. What is this vessel indicating?
A. is aground
⚓ B. is in distress
C. desires to communicate by radio
D. desires a pilot

040923/RR04125   **RULE 37; ANNEX IV**
BOTH INTERNATIONAL & INLAND If you saw flames aboard a vessel but could see the vessel was not on fire, you would know that the _____.
A. vessel was attempting to attract the attention of a pilot boat
B. vessel was being illuminated for identification by aircraft
C. crew was trying to get warm
⚓ D. vessel required immediate assistance

040924/RR04026   **RULE 37; ANNEX IV**
BOTH INTERNATIONAL & INLAND Which is a distress signal?
A. Sounding 5 short blasts on the whistle
B. Firing of green star shells
C. Answering a one blast whistle signal with two blasts
⚓ D. A flaming barrel of oil on deck

040925/RR04168   **RULE 37; ANNEX IV**
BOTH INTERNATIONAL & INLAND When a vessel signals her distress by means of a gun or other explosive signal, the firing should be at intervals of approximately _____.
⚓ A. 1 minute
B. 3 minutes
C. 10 minutes
D. 1 hour

040926/RR04203   **RULE 37; ANNEX IV**
BOTH INTERNATIONAL & INLAND If you hear the firing of a gun at one minute intervals from another vessel, this indicates that _____.
A. the gun is being used to sound passing signals
B. all is clear and it is safe to pass
C. all vessels are to clear the area
⚓ D. the vessel is in distress

040927/RR04227   **RULE 37; ANNEX IV**
BOTH INTERNATIONAL & INLAND What does an orange flag showing a black circle and square indicate?
A. signal indicating danger
⚓ B. distress signal
C. signal of asking to communicate with another vessel
D. signal indicating a course change

040928/RR04057   **RULE 37; ANNEX IV**
BOTH INTERNATIONAL & INLAND You see a vessel displaying the code flag "LIMA" below which is a red ball. The vessel is indicating it is in which of the following situations?
A. getting ready to receive aircraft
B. trolling
C. aground
⚓ D. in distress

040929/RR04217   **RULE 37; ANNEX IV**
BOTH INTERNATIONAL & INLAND A man aboard a vessel is signaling by raising and lowering his outstretched arms teach side. What does this indicate?
⚓ A. a distress signal
B. all is clear, it is safe to pass
C. the vessel is anchored
D. danger, stay away

040930/RR04005   **RULE 37; ANNEX IV**
BOTH INTERNATIONAL & INLAND Which signal is recognized as a distress signal?
A. A whistle signal of one prolonged and three short blasts
B. International Code Signal "PAN" spoken over the radiotelephone
⚓ C. A smoke signal giving off orange-colored smoke
D. Directing the beam of a searchlight at another vessel

040931/RR04248   **RULE 37; ANNEX IV**
BOTH INTERNATIONAL & INLAND What is NOT a distress signal?
A. Continuous sounding of fog signaling apparatus
B. International Code Flags "November" over "Charlie"
⚓ C. Basket hanging in the rigging
D. Red flares or red rockets

040932/RR04083   **RULE 37; ANNEX IV; RULE 34 (d)**
BOTH INTERNATIONAL & INLAND All of the following are distress signals EXCEPT _____.
A. a barrel with burning oil in it, on deck
B. the continuous sounding of any fog signal apparatus
C. firing a gun at intervals of about a minute
⚓ D. giving five or more short and rapid blasts of the whistle

040933/RR04446   **RULE 37; ANNEX IV;**
                                      Lifesaving Signals
BOTH INTERNATIONAL & INLAND Which is NOT a distress signal?
A. Dye marker on the water
⚓ B. Vertical motion of a white lantern at night
C. Flames on a vessel
D. Code flags "November" and "Charlie"

040934/RR04318   **RULE 37; ANNEX IV;**
                                      Lifesaving Signals
BOTH INTERNATIONAL & INLAND Which is NOT a distress signal?
⚓ A. The firing of green star rockets or shells
B. A signal sent by radiotelephone consisting of the spoken word "Mayday"
C. A continuous sounding with any fog signal apparatus
D. An International Code Signal of N.C.

040935/RR04269   **RULE 37; ANNEX IV;**
                                      Lifesaving Signals
BOTH INTERNATIONAL & INLAND All of the following are distress signals under the Rules EXCEPT _____.
A. orange-colored smoke
B. red flares
C. the repeated raising and lowering of outstretched arms
⚓ D. International Code Signal "AA"

PART E ANNEXES

ANNEX II - ADDITIONAL SIGNALS FOR FISHING VESSELS FISHING IN CLOSE PROXIMITY

040936/RR04031   **ANNEX II;**
                RULE 26 (d) International; RULE 26 (f) Inland
BOTH INTERNATIONAL & INLAND Additional light signals are provided in the Annexes to the Rules for vessels _____.
A. not under command
B. engaged in towing
⚓ C. engaged in fishing
D. under sail

040937/RR04570   **ANNEX II;**
                RULE 26 (d) International; RULE 26 (f) Inland
BOTH INTERNATIONAL & INLAND Which signal may at some time be exhibited by a vessel trawling?
A. Two red lights in a vertical line
B. A white light over a red light in a vertical line
C. Two white lights in a vertical line
⚓ D. All of the above

PART A GENERAL

RULE 1 - APPLICATION

040938/RR09146   **RULE 1 (a)**
INTERNATIONAL ONLY Where do the International Rules of the Road apply?
A. only to waters outside the territorial waters of the United States
B. only to waters where foreign vessels travel
⚓ C. upon the high seas and connecting waters navigable by seagoing vessels
D. tall waters which are not INLAND waters

040939/RR00198   **RULE 1 (e)**
INTERNATIONAL ONLY You are on a vessel that cannot comply with the spacing requirement for masthead lights. What is required in this situation?
⚓ A. The vessel's lights must comply as closely as possible, as determined by her government.
B. An all-round light should be substituted for the after masthead light and the stern light.
C. The vessel must be altered to permit full compliance with the rules.
D. The vessel must carry only the lights that comply with the rules; the others may be omitted.

RULE 3 - DEFINITIONS

040940/RR00406   **RULE 3 (a)**
BOTH INTERNATIONAL & INLAND For the purpose of the Rules, except where otherwise required, the term _____.
A. "seaplane" includes nondisplacement craft
⚓ B. "vessel" includes wing in ground craft
C. "vessel engaged in fishing" includes a vessel fishing with trolling lines
D. "vessel restricted in her ability to maneuver" includes fishing vessels

040941/RR08071   **RULE 3 (g) (i) - (ii), (g) (vi), (h);**
RULE 28
INTERNATIONAL ONLY Which vessel is NOT regarded as being "restricted in her ability to maneuver"?
A. A vessel engaged in dredging
B. A towing vessel with tow unable to deviate from its course
C. A vessel servicing an aid to navigation
⚓ D. A vessel constrained by her draft

040942/RR08054   **RULE 3 (h)**
INTERNATIONAL ONLY Which statement applies to a vessel "constrained by her draft"?
A. She is designated as a "vessel restricted in her ability to maneuver".
B. The term applies only to vessels in marked channels.
C. The vessel must be over 100 meters in length.
⚓ D. She is severely restricted in her ability to change her course because of her draft in relation to the available depth of water.

040943/RR08002   **RULE 3 (h)**
INTERNATIONAL ONLY Which statement is true concerning a vessel "constrained by her draft"?
A. She is not under command.
B. She may be a vessel being towed.
C. She is hampered because of her work.
⚓ D. She must be a power-driven vessel.

PART B STEERING & SAILING RULES
SECTION SUBPART I
CONDUCT OF VESSELS
IN ANY CONDITION OF VISIBILITY

RULE 9 - NARROW CHANNELS

IF THE STEM OF A QUESTION CONTAINS THE DESCRIPTIVE QUALIFIER "NARROW CHANNEL", THEN THE QUESTION SHOULD BE ANSWERED PURSUANT TO THE PROVISIONS OF RULE 9, INTERNATIONAL AND/OR INLAND AS APPLICABLE.

040944/RR08060   **RULE 9 (d); RULE 34 (d)**
*** COMMENT ***
RULE 9 (D) INTERNATIONAL INDICATES THE USE OF THE DANGER SIGNAL IS OPTIONAL (MAY).

INTERNATIONAL ONLY You are operating a vessel in a narrow channel. Your vessel must stay within the channel to be navigated safely. Another vessel is crossing your course from starboard to port, and you are in doubt as to his intentions. According to RULE 9, you _____.
A. should sound one short blast to indicate that you are holding course and speed
B. are required to back down
⚓ C. may sound the danger signal
D. must sound one prolonged and two short blasts

040945/RR08050   **RULE 9 (e) (i); RULE 34 (c) (i)**
INTERNATIONAL ONLY A sailing vessel is overtaking a power-driven vessel in a narrow channel, so as to pass on the power-driven vessel's port side. The overtaken vessel will have to move to facilitate passage. The sailing vessel is the _____.
A. give-way vessel and would sound no whistle signal
B. stand-on vessel and would sound two short blasts
C. give-way vessel and would sound two prolonged blasts followed by two short blasts
D. stand-on vessel and would sound no whistle signal

040946/RR08012   **RULE 9 (e) (i); RULE 34 (c) (i)**
INTERNATIONAL ONLY In a narrow channel, a signal of intent which must be answered by the other vessel, is sounded during which of the following situations?
A. crossing the course of another
B. overtaking another
C. meeting another head-on
D. All of the above

040947/RR08017   **RULE 9 (e) (i); RULE 34 (c) (i)**
INTERNATIONAL ONLY In a narrow channel, a vessel trying to overtake another on the other vessel's port side, would sound a whistle signal of _____.
A. two short blasts
B. two prolonged blasts followed by two short blasts
C. one short blast
D. two prolonged blasts followed by one short blast

040948/RR08008   **RULE 9 (e) (i); RULE 34 (c) (i)**
INTERNATIONAL ONLY In a narrow channel, an overtaking vessel which intends to pass on the other vessel's port side would sound _____.
A. two short blasts
B. one short blast
C. two prolonged followed by two short blasts
D. one prolonged followed by two short blasts

040949/RR08073   **RULE 9 (e) (i); RULE 34 (c) (i)**
INTERNATIONAL ONLY In a narrow channel, an overtaking vessel which intends to PASS on the other vessel's port side would sound _____.
A. two short blasts
B. one short blast
C. one prolonged followed by two short blasts
D. two prolonged followed by two short blasts

040950/RR08038   **RULE 9 (e) (i); RULE 34 (c) (i)**
INTERNATIONAL ONLY In which case would an overtaking vessel sound a whistle signal of two prolonged followed by one short blast?
A. When another vessels are in the immediate area
B. When overtaking in a narrow channel
C. When overtaking on open waters
D. When overtaking in restricted visibility

040951/RR08027   **RULE 9 (e) (i); RULE 34 (c) (i)**
INTERNATIONAL ONLY Two prolonged blasts followed by one short blast on the whistle is a signal which could be sounded by a _____.
A. vessel anchored
B. vessel overtaking another in a narrow channel
C. fishing vessel
D. mineclearing vessel

040952/RR08005   **RULE 9 (e) (i); RULE 34 (c) (i)**
INTERNATIONAL ONLY You are in charge of a 250-meter freight vessel constrained by her draft proceeding down a narrow channel. There is a vessel engaged in fishing on your starboard bow half a mile away. According to RULE 9, which statement is TRUE?
A. You must sound one prolonged blast to alert the fishing vessel.
B. You are not to impede the fishing vessel.
C. If you are in doubt as to the fishing vessel's intentions you may sound at least five short and rapid blasts on the whistle.
D. You are to slow to bare steerageway until clear of the fishing vessel.

040953/RR08076   **RULE 9 (e) (i); RULE 34 (c) (i)**
INTERNATIONAL ONLY You are underway in a narrow channel, and you are being overtaken by a vessel astern. After the overtaking vessel sounds the proper signal indicating his intention to pass your vessel on your starboard side, you signal your agreement by sounding _____.
A. two prolonged blasts
B. one prolonged, one short, one prolonged, and one short blast
C. two prolonged followed by two short blasts
D. one short blast

040954/RR08048   **RULE 9 (e) (i); RULE 34 (c) (i)**
INTERNATIONAL ONLY You are underway in a narrow channel, and you are being overtaken by a vessel astern. After the overtaking vessel sounds the proper signal indicating his intention to pass your vessel on your starboard side, you signal your agreement by sounding _____.
A. two prolonged blasts
B. two prolonged followed by two short blasts
C. one short blast
D. one prolonged, one short, one prolonged, and one short blast in that order

040955/RR08075   **RULE 9 (e) (i); RULE 34 (c) (i)**
INTERNATIONAL ONLY You intend to overtake a vessel in a narrow channel, and you intend to pass along the vessel's port side. How should you signal your intention?
   A.   Two prolonged followed by two short blasts
     B.   two short blasts only
     C.   Two prolonged blasts only
     D.   two short blasts followed by two prolonged blasts

040956/RR08045   **RULE 9 (e) (i); RULE 34 (c) (i)**
INTERNATIONAL ONLY You intend to overtake a vessel in a narrow channel, and you intend to pass along the vessel's port side. How should you signal your intention?
   A.   Two prolonged followed by two short blasts
     B.   Two prolonged blasts
     C.   No signal is necessary.
     D.   Two short blasts

040957/RR08021   **RULE 9 (e) (i); RULE 34 (c) (i)**
INTERNATIONAL ONLY Your vessel is crossing a narrow channel. A vessel to port is within the channel and crossing your course. She is showing a black cylinder. What is your responsibility?
   A.   Do not cross the channel if you might impede the other vessel.
     B.   Begin an exchange of passing signals.
     C.   Hold your course and speed.
     D.   Sound the danger signal.

PART B STEERING & SAILING RULES
SECTION SUBPART II
CONDUCT OF VESSELS
IN SIGHT OF ONE ANOTHER

RULE 14 - HEAD-ON SITUATION

040958/RR04533   **RULE 14 (a)**
BOTH INTERNATIONAL & INLAND In which situation do the Rules require both vessels to change course?
   A.   Two power-driven vessels meeting head-on
     B.   Two power-driven vessels crossing when it is apparent to the stand-on vessel that the give-way vessel is not taking appropriate action
     C.   Two sailing vessels crossing with the wind on the same side
     D.   All of the above

RULE 15 - CROSSING SITUATION

040959/RR08022   **RULE 15; RULE 34 (a)**
INTERNATIONAL ONLY You are approaching another vessel and will pass starboard to starboard without danger if no course changes are made. What action should you take?
   A.   hold course and sound no whistle signal
     B.   hold course and sound two prolonged and two short blasts
     C.   change course to the right and sound one blast
     D.   hold course and sound a two blast whistle signal

040960/RR00204   **RULE 15; RULE 34 (a)**
INTERNATIONAL ONLY Vessels "A" and "B" are in a crossing situation on the high seas as shown in illustration D014RR below. Vessel "B" sounds one short blast. What is the proper action for vessel "A" to take? See DIAGRAM D014RR
   A.   Hold course and speed
     B.   Answer with one blast and hold course and speed
     C.   sound danger signal
     D.   Answer with one blast and keep clear of vessel "B"

040961/RR08044   **RULE 15; RULE 34 (a)**
INTERNATIONAL ONLY In international waters, you are on Vessel "I" in the situation as shown in illustration D036RR below. Vessel "II" sounds one short blast. Which action should you take? See DIAGRAM D036RR
     A.   Sound one short blast and hold course and speed.
     B.   sound two short blasts, slow down and turn to port
   C.   Hold course and speed
     D.   Sound one short blast and slow down or turn to starboard.

RULE 18 - RESPONSIBILITIES BETWEEN VESSELS

040962/RR08042   **RULE 18 (a) (d) (i) - (ii), (a) (iii)**
INTERNATIONAL ONLY Of the vessels listed, which must keep out of the way of all the others?
   A.   A vessel on pilotage duty
     B.   A vessel constrained by her draft
     C.   A vessel restricted in her ability to maneuver
     D.   A vessel engaged in fishing

040963/RR08115   **RULE 18 (a) (d) (i) - (ii), (a) (iii)**
INTERNATIONAL ONLY Of the vessels listed, which must keep out of the way of all the others?
   A.   A vessel pushing a barge
     B.   A vessel constrained by her draft
     C.   A vessel engaged in fishing
     D.   A vessel restricted in her ability to maneuver

040964/RR00265   **RULE 18 (a) (iii); RULE 34 (a)**
INTERNATIONAL ONLY You are on a power-driven vessel "I" as shown in illustration D036RR below. Vessel "II" is a vessel engaged in fishing. The vessels will pass within 1/2 mile of each other. Which action should you take? See DIAGRAM D036RR
A. sound one short blast, turn to starboard.
B. Hold course and speed without giving a signal.
C. sound one short blast and hold course and speed.
D. sound the danger signal and slow to moderate speed.

040965/RR00263   **RULE 18 (a) (iii); RULE 15**
INTERNATIONAL ONLY You are on a power-driven vessel "I" as shown in illustration D036RR below. Vessel "II" is a vessel engaged in fishing within 1/2 a mile of your vessel. Which action should you take? See DIAGRAM D036RR
A. Hold course and speed without giving a signal.
B. Change course or speed to avoid vessel "II".
C. sound one short blast, and await a response.
D. sound two short blasts, and await a response.

040966/RR08127   **RULE 18 (c) (ii)**
INTERNATIONAL ONLY Which statement is TRUE, according to the Rules?
A. A vessel constrained by her draft shall keep out of the way of a vessel engaged in fishing.
B. A vessel not under command shall keep out of the way of a vessel restricted in her ability to maneuver.
C. A vessel engaged in fishing while underway shall, so far as possible, keep out of the way of a vessel restricted in her ability to maneuver.
D. A vessel not under command shall avoid impeding the safe passage of a vessel constrained by her draft.

040967/RR08058   **RULE 18 (d) (i), (c) (ii), (c) (i)**
INTERNATIONAL ONLY Which vessel is to keep out of the way of the others?
A. A vessel engaged in underwater operations
B. A vessel engaged in trawling
C. A vessel constrained by her draft
D. A vessel not under command

040968/RR08116   **RULE 18 (d) (i) - (ii), (b)**
INTERNATIONAL ONLY Which vessel shall avoid impeding the safe passage of a vessel constrained by her draft?
A. A sailing vessel
B. A vessel restricted in her ability to maneuver
C. A vessel not under command
D. All of the above

040969/RR08067   **RULE 18 (d) (i) - (ii)**
INTERNATIONAL ONLY Which vessel shall avoid impeding the safe passage of a vessel constrained by her draft?
A. A fishing vessel
B. A vessel not under command
C. A vessel restricted in her ability to maneuver
D. All of the above

040970/RR00409   **RULE 18 (f) (i)**
BOTH INTERNATIONAL & INLAND Which vessel should NOT impede the navigation of a power-driven vessel?
A. A sailing vessel
B. A wing in ground craft when taking off or landing
C. A vessel engaged in fishing
D. A vessel not under command

040971/RR00411   **RULE 18 (f) (i)**
INTERNATIONAL ONLY Which statement is TRUE concerning wing in ground (WIG) craft when taking off, landing and in flight?
A. A WIG should show the lights for a vessel restricted in her ability to maneuver.
B. A WIG shall exhibit an all-round flashing yellow light.
C. In situations where a risk of collision exists, a WIG should always give way.
D. A WIG shall keep well clear of all vessels and avoid impeding their navigation.

040972/RR00413   **RULE 18 (f) (ii)**
INTERNATIONAL ONLY You are involved in a crossing situation with a vessel off your port bow. The other vessel is showing a high intensity all-round flashing red light. Which action should you take?
A. Reduce Speed
B. Remain clear of the vessel
C. Alter course to starboard
D. Maintain course and speed

040973/RR00412   **RULE 18 (f) (ii); RULE 23 (c)**
INTERNATIONAL ONLY You are the stand-on vessel in an overtaking situation. The other vessel is showing a flashing red light. What action should you take?
A. Give-way
B. Stand on
C. Heave to
D. Alter course to assist

PART B STEERING & SAILING RULES
SECTION SUBPART III
CONDUCT OF VESSELS
IN RESTRICTED VISIBILITY

RULE 19 - CONDUCT IN RESTRICTED VISIBILITY

040974/RR00408 **RULE 19 (d)**
INTERNATIONAL ONLY What statement is TRUE when operating in fog and other vessels are detected by radar?
⚓ A. You should maneuver in accordance with the steering and sailing rules.
B. You should determine the course and speed of all radar contacts at six minute intervals.
C. You should make a series of small course alterations when maneuvering in order to continually assess the situation.
D. You should make an ample change to port for a vessel crossing on the starboard bow.

PART C LIGHTS AND SHAPES

RULE 23 - POWER-DRIVEN VESSELS UNDERWAY

040975/RR00414 **RULE 23 (c)**
INTERNATIONAL ONLY A vessel displaying a high intensity all-round flashing red light is _____.
A. in distress
B. engaged in dredging
⚓ C. WIG craft
D. restricted in its ability to maneuver

040976/RR00416 **RULE 23 (c)**
INTERNATIONAL ONLY You are on watch and sight a vessel showing a high intensity all-round flashing red light. The light indicates a _____.
⚓ A. WIG craft in flight near the surface
B. seaplane when landing and taking off
C. air-cushion vessel in the nondisplacement mode
D. submarine on the surface

040977/RR00415 **RULE 23 (c)**
INTERNATIONAL ONLY You are on watch and sight a vessel showing a high intensity all-round flashing red light. The light indicates a _____.
A. fishing vessel trolling
B. vessel dredging
C. vessel laying submarine cable
⚓ D. WIG craft when taking off and landing

040978/RR08085 **RULE 23 (d) (ii)**
INTERNATIONAL ONLY At night, a power-driven vessel less than 7 meters in length, with a maximum speed which does not exceed 7 knots, MUST show when underway at least _____.
A. sidelights and a stern light
B. the lights required of a vessel less than 12 meters in length
⚓ C. one white 360° light
D. a white light on the near approach of another vessel

040979/RR08084 **RULE 23 (d) (ii)**
INTERNATIONAL ONLY While underway at night, a power-driven vessel of less than 7 meters in length, whose maximum speed which does not exceed 7 knots, may show which of the following?
⚓ A. one all-round white light, only
B. an all-round flashing yellow light, only
C. a lantern showing a white light exhibited in sufficient time to prevent collision, only
D. sidelights combined in a single lantern, only

RULE 24 - TOWING AND PUSHING

040980/RR08007 **RULE 24 (a) (iv)**
INTERNATIONAL ONLY A towing light is _____.
⚓ A. shown in addition to the stern light
B. shown at the bow
C. an all-round light
D. white in color

040981/RR08053 **RULE 24 (c) (i)**
INTERNATIONAL ONLY A 20-meter power-driven vessel pushing ahead or towing alongside will display _____.
A. a single white light forward
⚓ B. two masthead lights in a vertical line
C. two all-round red lights where they can best be seen
D. two towing lights in a vertical line

040982/RR08088 **RULE 24 (c) (i)**
INTERNATIONAL ONLY A 20-meter power-driven vessel pushing ahead or towing alongside will display _____.
A. two towing lights in a vertical line
⚓ B. two masthead lights in a vertical line
C. a towing light above the stern light
D. two all-round red lights at the masthead

040983/RR08136   **RULE 24 (c) (i)**
INTERNATIONAL ONLY A power-driven vessel pushing ahead or towing alongside will show sidelights, a stern light, and _____.
A. a single white light forward
⚓ B. two masthead lights in a vertical line
C. an all-round red light where it can best be seen
D. two yellow masthead lights in a vertical line

040984/RR08001   **RULE 24 (c) (i)**
INTERNATIONAL ONLY In addition to other required lights, a power-driven vessel pushing ahead or towing alongside displays _____.
A. two all-round red lights in a vertical line
⚓ B. two white masthead lights in a vertical line
C. two lights on the stern, one yellow and one white
D. two yellow towing lights in a vertical line

040985/RR00188   **RULE 24 (c) (i) - (iii)**
INTERNATIONAL ONLY Which of the following does NOT exhibit a yellow light?
A. U.S. submarines
B. air-cushion vessels in a nondisplacement mode
C. purse seiners
⚓ D. towing vessels pushing ahead

040986/RR00256   **RULE 24 (c) (i) - (ii)**
INTERNATIONAL ONLY Vessels "A" and "B" are meeting on a river as shown in illustration D041RR below and will pass 1/4 mile apart. If you are on vessel "A", in addition to the sidelight, which other light(s) will you see on vessel "B"? See DIAGRAM D041RR
⚓ A. two white masthead lights in a vertical line
B. special flashing yellow light
C. two yellow towing lights
D. None of the above

040987/RR00255   **RULE 24 (c) (i) - (ii), (f) (i)**
INTERNATIONAL ONLY Vessels "A" and "B" are meeting on a river as shown in illustration D041RR below, and will pass 1/4 mile apart. Which light on vessel "B" will you see if you are on vessel "A"? See DIAGRAM D041RR
A. two yellow towing lights
B. flashing blue light
C. special flashing yellow light
⚓ D. None of the above

040988/RR00214   **RULE 24 (c) (i) - (iii), (f) (ii)**
INTERNATIONAL ONLY At night, you sight the lights shown in illustration D055RR below. What do the lights indicate? See DIAGRAM D055RR
A. A tug not under command
⚓ B. A tug with a tow alongside
C. A vessel fishing at anchor
D. A pipeline

040989/RR00215   **RULE 24 (c) (i) - (iii), (f) (ii)**
INTERNATIONAL ONLY At night you sight the lights shown in illustration D066RR below. What do the lights indicate? See DIAGRAM D066RR
A. Two vessels pair trawling
B. A vessel engaged in fishing
C. A ship being assisted by a tug
⚓ D. A tug with a tow alongside

040990/RR00213   **RULE 24 (c) (i) - (iii), (f) (ii)**
INTERNATIONAL ONLY You see the lights shown in illustration D066RR below. What do these lights indicate? See DIAGRAM D066RR
A. vessel pushing a barge ahead
B. dredge working at anchor
C. pilot vessel with a launch alongside
⚓ D. vessel towing a barge alongside

040991/RR00208   **RULE 24 (f) (ii)**
INTERNATIONAL ONLY A single vessel being towed alongside shall show _____.
A. a masthead light, sidelights, and a stern light
B. only the outboard sidelight and a stern light
C. one all-round white light
⚓ D. sidelights and a stern light

040992/RR00197   **RULE 24 (g) (iv)**
INTERNATIONAL ONLY A partially submerged object towed by a vessel, during the day, must display which of the following shapes?
A. a black ball only when the length of the tow exceeds 200 meters in length
B. a diamond shape when the length of the tow exceeds 200 meters in length
C. a black ball
⚓ D. a diamond shape when the length of the tow is 200 meters or less

040993/RR00139   **RULE 24 (g) (iv)**
INTERNATIONAL ONLY As seen in illustration D016RR below, which additional day-shape must you show on the forward end of an inconspicuous partially submerged vessel or object being towed more than 200 meters in length? See DIAGRAM D016RR
⚓ A. B
B. D
C. A
D. No day-shape must be shown.

RULE 26 - FISHING VESSELS

040994/RR09147   **RULE 26 (d);**
ANNEX II (1), (2), (3)

INTERNATIONAL ONLY Additional light signals are provided in the Annexes to the Rules for which of the following vessels?

A. engaged in towing
B. not under command
C. under sail
⚓ D. engaged in fishing

RULE 27 - VESSELS NOT UNDER COMMAND AND RESTRICTED IN ABILITY TO MANEUVER

*** COMMENT ***

WHEN OPERATING ON INTERNATIONAL WATERS THE LEGAL TESTS FOR THE USE OF RAM LIGHTS ARE: 1. THE TOWING VESSEL MUST BE POWER-DRIVEN, 2. THE TOWING VESSEL IS SEVERELY RESTRICTED WHEN TOWING ASTERN ONLY. SEE RULE 27 (c) INTERNATIONAL.

040995/RR00371   **RULE 27 (c)**

INTERNATIONAL ONLY If a towing vessel and her tow are severely restricted in their ability to deviate from their course, the towing vessel shall show lights in addition to her towing identification lights. These additional lights shall be shown if the tow is _____.

A. Towed alongside
B. Pushed ahead
⚓ C. Towed astern
D. All of the above

RULE 28 - VESSELS CONSTRAINED BY DRAFT

040996/RR08096   **RULE 28**

INTERNATIONAL ONLY A vessel constrained by her draft may display _____.

⚓ A. three all-round red lights in addition to the lights required for a power-driven vessel of her class
B. the same lights as a vessel restricted in her ability to maneuver
C. the lights for a power-driven vessel which is not under command
D. three all-round red lights instead of the lights required for a power-driven vessel of her class

040997/RR08010   **RULE 28**

INTERNATIONAL ONLY A vessel displaying three red lights in a vertical line is _____.

A. aground
B. not under command
⚓ C. constrained by her draft
D. dredging

040998/RR08062   **RULE 28**

INTERNATIONAL ONLY If you sighted three red lights in a vertical line on another vessel at night, it would be a vessel _____.

A. dredging
⚓ B. constrained by her draft
C. moored over a wreck
D. aground

040999/RR08070   **RULE 28**

INTERNATIONAL ONLY In addition to her running lights, an underway vessel constrained by her draft may carry in a vertical line _____.

A. two red lights
B. a red light, a white light, and a red light
C. two white lights
⚓ D. three red lights

041000/RR08000   **RULE 28**

INTERNATIONAL ONLY To indicate that a vessel is constrained by her draft, a vessel may display, in a vertical line, _____.

A. two 225° blue lights
B. three 360° blue lights
⚓ C. three 360° red lights
D. two 225° red lights

041001/RR08019   **RULE 28**

INTERNATIONAL ONLY If a vessel displays three all-round red lights in a vertical line at night, during the day she may show _____.

A. two diamonds in a vertical line
⚓ B. a cylinder
C. three balls in a vertical line
D. two cones, apexes together

041002/RR08029   **RULE 28**

INTERNATIONAL ONLY What day-shape is prescribed for a vessel constrained by her draft?

A. Two vertical black balls
⚓ B. A cylinder
C. A black cone, apex downward
D. A black cone, apex upward

041003/RR08040   **RULE 28**

INTERNATIONAL ONLY Which vessel may NOT exhibit two red lights in a vertical line?

A. A vessel aground
B. A dredge
C. A trawler fishing in close proximity to other trawlers
⚓ D. A vessel constrained by her draft

RULE 31 - SEAPLANES

041004/RR00417   **RULE 31; RULE 1 (e)**
INTERNATIONAL ONLY A wing in ground (WIG) craft cannot comply with the spacing requirement for masthead lights. What is required in this situation?
- A. The WIG must be altered to permit full compliance with the rules.
- B. The WIG's lights must comply as closely as possible, as determined by her government.
- C. The WIG must carry only the lights that comply with the rules; the others may be omitted.
- D. An all-round light should be substituted for the after masthead light and the stern light.

PART D SOUND AND LIGHT SIGNALS

RULE 33 - EQUIPMENT FOR SOUND SIGNALS

041005/RR00418   **RULE 33 (a)**
INTERNATIONAL ONLY What equipment for fog signals is required for a vessel 13 meters in length?
- A. Whistle, bell, and gong
- B. Bell only
- C. Whistle and bell only
- D. Whistle only

041006/RR00419   **RULE 33 (a)**
INTERNATIONAL ONLY What equipment for fog signals is required for a vessel 15 meters in length?
- A. Whistle only
- B. Bell only
- C. Whistle, bell, and gong
- D. Whistle and bell only

041007/RR00420   **RULE 33 (a); RULE 35 (i)**
INTERNATIONAL ONLY What is the minimum fog signal required aboard a vessel between 12 meters and 20 meters in length at anchor?
- A. rapid ringing of the bell for 10 seconds every minute
- B. three separate and distinct strokes of the bell every 2 minutes
- C. one short, one long, one short stroke of the bell every minute
- D. Any efficient sound signal every 2 minutes

RULE 34 - MANEUVERING AND WARNING SIGNALS

*** COMMENT ***

THE MANEUVERING AND WARNING SIGNALS REQUIRED BY RULE 34 (a) ARE TO BE SOUNDED BY VESSELS INSIGHT OF ONE ANOTHER. THEY ARE ACTION SIGNALS. SEE RULE 34 (a) INTERNATIONAL.

041008/RR08024   **RULE 34 (a) (i)**
INTERNATIONAL ONLY Which signal is required to be sounded by a power-driven vessel ONLY?
- A. A signal meaning, "I intend to overtake you on your starboard side."
- B. A signal meaning that the vessel sounding it is in doubt as to the other vessel's actions.
- C. A signal sounded when approaching a bend.
- D. A signal meaning, "I am altering my course to starboard."

041009/RR08069   **RULE 34 (a)**
INTERNATIONAL ONLY Which signal is sounded ONLY by a vessel in sight of another and NOT in or near an area of restricted visibility?
- A. One prolonged blast on the whistle
- B. Four short blasts on the whistle
- C. One short, one prolonged, and one short blast on the whistle
- D. One short blast on the whistle

041010/RR08080   **RULE 34 (a)**
INTERNATIONAL ONLY Which signal is sounded ONLY by a vessel in sight of another?
- A. One prolonged blast on the whistle
- B. One short, one prolonged, and one short blast on the whistle
- C. Four short blasts on the whistle
- D. One short blast on the whistle

041011/RR00205   **RULE 34 (a)**
INTERNATIONAL ONLY Which whistle signal may be sounded by one of two vessels in sight of each other?
- A. Four short blasts
- B. One prolonged blast
- C. One short, one prolonged, and one short blast
- D. One short blast

041012/RR04315   **RULE 34 (a) (i)**
INTERNATIONAL ONLY While underway and in sight of another vessel you put your engines on astern propulsion. Which statement concerning whistle signals is TRUE?

A. You must sound whistle signals only if the vessels are meeting.

B. You need not sound any whistle signals.

⚓ C. You must sound three short blasts on the whistle.

D. You must sound one blast if backing to starboard.

041013/RR00264   **RULE 34 (a); RULE 14 (a)**
INTERNATIONAL ONLY Two power-driven vessels are meeting in the situation as shown in illustration D037RR below. What does one short blast from either vessel mean? See DIAGRAM D037RR

A. "I intend to hold course and speed."

⚓ B. "I am altering my course to starboard."

C. "I intend to leave you on my port side."

D. "I am altering my course to port."

041014/RR00353   **RULE 34 (a) (i); RULE 15**
INTERNATIONAL ONLY Two power-driven vessels are crossing within one half mile of each other as shown in illustration D042RR below. Vessel "A" sounds one short blast of the whistle. What does this signal mean? See DIAGRAM D042RR

A. "I am altering my course to port"

B. "I intend to intend to overtake you on your port side"

C. "I am intend to leave you on my starboard side"

⚓ D. None of the above

041015/RR00357   **RULE 34 (a) (i); RULE 15**
INTERNATIONAL ONLY Two power-driven vessels are crossing within one half mile of each other as shown in illustration D042RR below. Vessel "A" sounds one short blast of the whistle. What does this signal mean? See DIAGRAM D042RR

A. "I intend to overtake you on your starboard side"

B. "I intend to leave you on my port side"

C. "I am operating astern propulsion"

⚓ D. None of the above

041016/RR00358   **RULE 34 (a) (i); RULE 15**
INTERNATIONAL ONLY Two power-driven vessels are crossing within one half mile of each other as shown in illustration D042RR below. Vessel "A" sounds one short blast of the whistle. What is vessel "B" in this situation? See DIAGRAM D042RR

A. overtaking vessel

B. burdened vessel

C. give-way vessel

⚓ D. None of the above

041017/RR00347   **RULE 34 (a) (i); RULE 15**
INTERNATIONAL ONLY Two power-driven vessels are crossing within one half mile of each other as shown in illustration D042RR below. Vessel "A" sounds one short blast of the whistle. What action should vessel "B" take? See DIAGRAM D042RR

A. sound one short blast and maintain course and speed

B. alter course to the right or slowdown

⚓ C. maintain course and speed

D. sound the danger signal and slow to moderate speed

041018/RR00350   **RULE 34 (a) (i); RULE 15**
INTERNATIONAL ONLY Two power-driven vessels are crossing within one half mile of each other as shown in illustration D042RR below. Vessel "A" sounds one short blast of the whistle. What signal should vessel "B" sound? See DIAGRAM D042RR

A. two short blasts

B. one prolonged, one short, one prolonged and one short blasts

C. one short blast

⚓ D. None of the above

041019/RR00267   **RULE 34 (a)**
INTERNATIONAL ONLY Two power-driven vessels are meeting in the situation as shown in illustration D037RR below. What does two short blasts from either vessel mean? See DIAGRAM D037RR

A. "I intend to leave you on my port side."

B. "I am altering my course to starboard."

⚓ C. "I am altering my course to port."

D. "I am operating astern propulsion."

041020/RR08057   **RULE 34 (a)**
INTERNATIONAL ONLY Your vessel is backing out of a slip in a harbor and you can see that other vessels are approaching. You should sound which of the following signals?

⚓ A. three short blasts when leaving the slip

B. one prolonged blast only

C. the danger signal

D. one prolonged blast followed by three short blasts when the last line is taken aboard

041021/RR08028   **RULE 34 (a)**
INTERNATIONAL ONLY In a crossing situation on international waters, a short blast by the give-way vessel indicates that the vessel _____.

A. is holding course and speed

⚓ B. is turning to starboard

C. intends to pass port to port

D. will keep out of the way of the stand-on vessel

041022/RR08026   **RULE 34 (a)**
INTERNATIONAL ONLY You are in sight of another vessel in a crossing situation, and the other vessel sounds one short blast. You are going to hold course and speed. You should _____.
⚓ A.   sound no whistle signal
B.   answer with one short blast
C.   answer with two short blasts
D.   sound the danger signal

041023/RR08047   **RULE 34 (a)**
INTERNATIONAL ONLY A vessel sounds one short blast. This signal indicates the vessel _____.
A.   intends to pass port to port
B.   intends to pass starboard to starboard
C.   intends to alter course to starboard
⚓ D.   is altering course to starboard

041024/RR08046   **RULE 34 (a)**
INTERNATIONAL ONLY A vessel sounds two short blasts. This signal indicates the vessel _____.
A.   will alter course to port
⚓ B.   is altering course to port
C.   intends to pass starboard to starboard
D.   intends to alter course to port

041025/RR08052   **RULE 34 (a)**
INTERNATIONAL ONLY Two power-driven vessels are meeting. A two blast whistle signal by either vessel means _____.
A.   "I desire to pass starboard to starboard"
B.   "I intend to alter course to port"
⚓ C.   "I am altering course to port"
D.   "I desire to pass port to port"

041026/RR08039   **RULE 34 (a)**
INTERNATIONAL ONLY When vessels are in sight of one another, two short blasts from one of the vessels means _____.
A.   "I intend to change course to port"
B.   "I am altering my course to starboard"
⚓ C.   "I am altering my course to port"
D.   "I intend to change course to starboard"

041027/RR08059   **RULE 34 (a)**
INTERNATIONAL ONLY You are in sight of a power-driven vessel that sounds two short blasts of the whistle. This signal means that the vessel _____.
⚓ A.   is altering course to port
B.   intends to leave you on her starboard side
C.   intends to leave you on her port side
D.   is altering course to starboard

041028/RR09002   **RULE 34 (a)**
INTERNATIONAL ONLY You are on a power-driven vessel, maneuvering as authorized, and are in sight of another vessel. You put your engines full speed astern, which statement concerning whistle signals is TRUE?
⚓ A.   You must sound three short blasts on the whistle.
B.   You need not sound any whistle signals.
C.   You must sound whistle signals only if the vessels are meeting.
D.   You must sound one blast if backing to starboard.

041029/RR08016   **RULE 34 (a)**
INTERNATIONAL ONLY What whistle signal, if any, would be sounded when two vessels are meeting, but will pass clear starboard to starboard?
⚓ A.   No signal is required.
B.   Two short blasts
C.   Five or more short blasts
D.   One short blast

041030/RR08063   **RULE 34 (a)**
INTERNATIONAL ONLY On open water two vessels are in an overtaking situation. The overtaking vessel has just sounded one short blast on the whistle. What is the meaning of this whistle signal?
⚓ A.   "I am changing course to starboard."
B.   "I request permission to pass you on my port side."
C.   "On which side should I pass?"
D.   "I will maintain course and speed and pass you on your starboard side."

041031/RR08018   **RULE 34 (a)**
INTERNATIONAL ONLY On open water, a power-driven vessel coming up dead astern of another vessel and altering her course to starboard so as to pass on the starboard side of the vessel ahead would sound _____.
A.   one long and one short blast
B.   two prolonged blasts followed by one short blast
C.   two short blasts
⚓ D.   one short blast

041032/RR08041   **RULE 34 (a)**
INTERNATIONAL ONLY Vessel "A" is overtaking vessel "B" on open waters and will pass without changing course. Vessel "A" _____.
A.   should sound two short blasts
⚓ B.   will not sound any whistle signals
C.   should sound one long blast
D.   should sound the danger signal

041033/RR08061   **RULE 34 (a)**
INTERNATIONAL ONLY Vessel "A" is overtaking vessel "B" on open waters as shown in illustration D017RR below and will pass without changing course. What action should Vessel "A" take? See DIAGRAM D017RR
A. should sound two short blasts
B. need not sound any whistle signals
C. should sound one long blast
D. should sound the danger signal

041034/RR00237   **RULE 34 (a)**
INTERNATIONAL ONLY Vessel "A" is overtaking vessel "B" on open waters as shown in illustration D017RR below and will pass without changing course. What signal should vessel "A" sound? See DIAGRAM D017RR
A. two prolonged blasts followed by two short blasts
B. no whistle signal
C. two short blasts
D. at least five short and rapid blasts

041035/RR00252   **RULE 34 (a)**
INTERNATIONAL ONLY power-driven vessels "A" and "B" are meeting on a river as shown in illustration D041RR below and will pass 1/4 mile apart. Which action should the vessels take? See DIAGRAM D041RR
A. The vessels should continue on course and pass without sounding any whistle signals.
B. The vessel with the tow should initiate the whistle signals.
C. The vessels should exchange one blast whistle signals and pass starboard to starboard.
D. The vessels should exchange two blast whistle signals and pass starboard to starboard.

041036/RR08092   **RULE 34 (b) (iii)**
INTERNATIONAL ONLY A light used to signal passing intentions must be an _____.
A. all-round white or yellow light
B. alternating red and yellow light
C. all-round white light only
D. alternating white and yellow light

041037/RR08135   **RULE 34 (b) (iii)**
INTERNATIONAL ONLY What characteristic must a light used to indicate passing intentions have?
A. It must be an all-round white light.
B. It can be either an all-round white or yellow light.
C. It must be an all-round yellow light.
D. It must be an all-round red light.

041038/RR08025   **RULE 34 (b) (iii)**
INTERNATIONAL ONLY The light which may be used with a vessel's whistle is to be _____.
A. a white light
B. used prior to sounding the whistle
C. used only at night
D. used when the whistle is broken

041039/RR08081   **RULE 34 (b) (iii)**
INTERNATIONAL ONLY The light which may be used with a vessel's whistle must be _____.
A. a white light
B. used only at night
C. used when the whistle is broken
D. used prior to sounding the whistle

041040/RR08118   **RULE 34 (c) (i); RULE 9 (e) (i)**
INTERNATIONAL ONLY A signal of intent must be sounded in international waters during which of the following situations?
A. the give-way vessel in a crossing situation
B. a vessel meeting another head-on
C. a vessel crossing the course of another
D. a vessel overtaking another in a narrow channel

041041/RR08074   **RULE 34 (c) (i); RULE 9 (e) (i)**
INTERNATIONAL ONLY Two prolonged blasts followed by one short blast on the whistle is a signal which would be sounded by a vessel _____.
A. engaged in mineclearance
B. anchored
C. engaged in fishing
D. overtaking another in a narrow channel

041042/RR00243   **RULE 34 (c) (i); RULE 9 (e) (i)**
INTERNATIONAL ONLY You are on vessel "A" as shown in illustration D032RR below. Vessel "B" sounds two short blasts. What action should you take? See DIAGRAM D032RR
A. not answer the whistle signal from vessel "B"
B. sound two short blasts and maintain course and speed
C. sound one prolonged, one short, one prolonged and one short blasts
D. sound two prolonged blasts followed by two short blasts

041043/RR08068   **RULE 34 (c) (ii); RULE 9 (e) (i)**
INTERNATIONAL ONLY A signal of one prolonged, one short, one prolonged, and one short blast, in that order is given by a vessel _____.
A. being overtaken in a narrow channel
B. engaged on pilotage duty
C. at anchor
D. in distress

041044/RR08056   RULE 34 (c) (ii); RULE 9 (e) (i)
INTERNATIONAL ONLY A whistle signal of one prolonged, one short, one prolonged and one short blast, is sounded by a vessel _____.
A. towing a submerged object
B. at anchor
C. in distress
⚓ D. being overtaken in a narrow channel

041045/RR08072   RULE 34 (d), (c) (ii), (a)
INTERNATIONAL ONLY When two vessels are in sight of one another and NOT in or near an area of restricted visibility, any of the following signals may be given EXCEPT _____.
A. one prolonged, one short, one prolonged, and one short whistle blasts
⚓ B. four short whistle blasts
C. a light signal of at least five short and rapid flashes
D. two short whistle blasts

041046/RR08013   RULE 34 (d), (c) (ii), (a)
INTERNATIONAL ONLY When two vessels are in sight of one another, all of the following signals may be given EXCEPT _____.
A. two short whistle blasts
B. one prolonged, one short, one prolonged and one short whistle blasts
C. a light signal of at least five short and rapid flashes
⚓ D. four short whistle blasts

041047/RR08014   RULE 34 (e)
INTERNATIONAL ONLY A power-driven vessel leaving a quay or wharf must sound what signal?
A. Three short blasts
B. A prolonged blast
⚓ C. No signal is required.
D. A long blast

041048/RR08004   RULE 34 (e)
INTERNATIONAL ONLY When moving from a berth alongside a quay (wharf), a vessel must sound _____.
A. a prolonged blast
B. three short blasts
C. a long blast
⚓ D. no signal is required.

RULE 35 - SOUND SIGNALS IN RESTRICTED VISIBILITY

041049/RR08111   RULE 35 (a)
INTERNATIONAL ONLY Your vessel is backing out of a slip in a harbor. Visibility is restricted. You should sound _____.
A. one prolonged blast followed by three short blasts when the last line is taken aboard
B. one prolonged blast followed by three short blasts when leaving the slip
C. the danger signal
⚓ D. one prolonged blast only

041050/RR08030   RULE 35 (c)
INTERNATIONAL ONLY A vessel not under command sounds the same fog signal as a vessel _____.
A. towing
B. constrained by her draft
C. under sail
⚓ D. All of the above

041051/RR08043   RULE 35 (e)
INTERNATIONAL ONLY Which vessel would NOT sound a fog signal of one prolonged and two short blasts?
A. A vessel sailing
B. A vessel constrained by her draft
C. A vessel not under command
⚓ D. A vessel being towed

041052/RR08064   RULE 35 (e)
INTERNATIONAL ONLY You are underway in fog and hear a fog signal consisting of one prolonged and two short blasts. It could be any of the following EXCEPT a vessel _____.
⚓ A. being towed
B. engaged in mineclearance
C. engaged in fishing
D. constrained by her draft

041053/RR08009   RULE 35 (e)
INTERNATIONAL ONLY You are underway on the high seas in restricted visibility. You hear a fog signal of one prolonged and two short blasts. It could be any of the following EXCEPT a vessel _____.
A. minesweeping
B. engaged in fishing
⚓ C. being towed
D. constrained by her draft

*** COMMENT ***

*MORSE CODE LETTER "H" (. . . .). SIGNAL LETTER
"H" (HOTEL) IS SOUNDED BY VESSELS ENGAGED
IN PILOTAGE DUTIES. SEE RULE 35(K)
INTERNATIONAL.*

041054/RR00397   **RULE 35 (k)**
INTERNATIONAL ONLY Which signal may be
sounded ONLY by vessels in restricted visibility?
A. One prolonged, one short, one prolonged, and one
    short blast, in that order
B. Four short blasts
C. At least five short and rapid blasts
D. Two short blasts

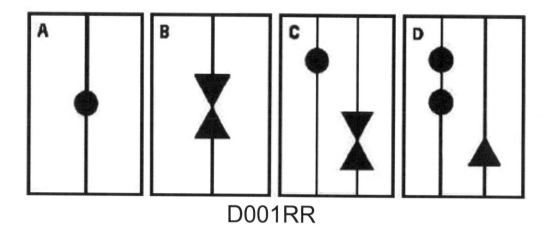

D001RR

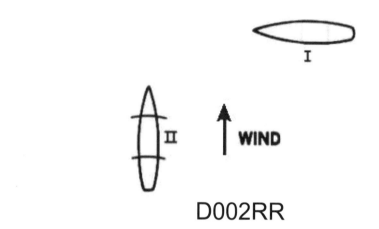

D002RR

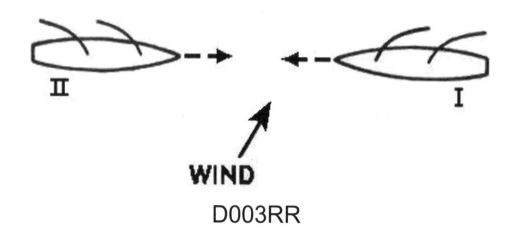

D003RR

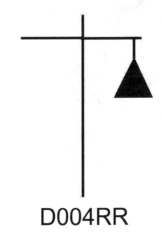

D004RR

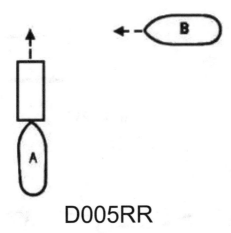

D005RR

D006RR

D007RR

D008RR

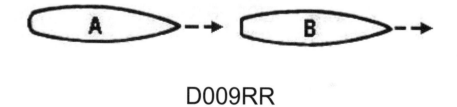

D009RR

D010RR

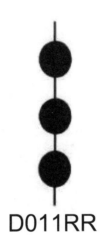

D011RR

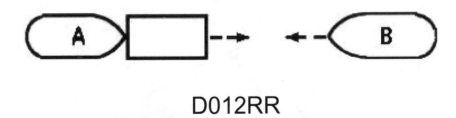

D012RR

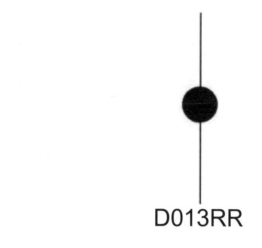

D013RR

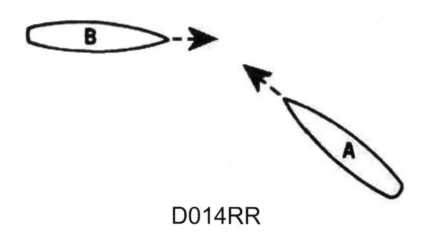

D014RR

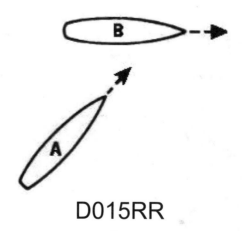

D015RR

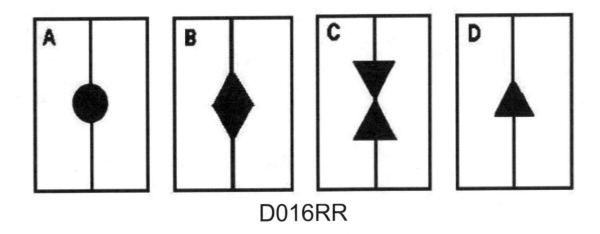

D016RR

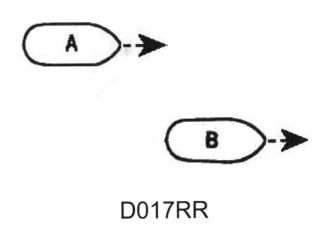

D017RR

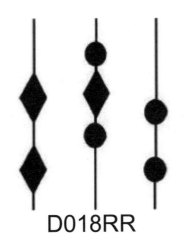

D018RR

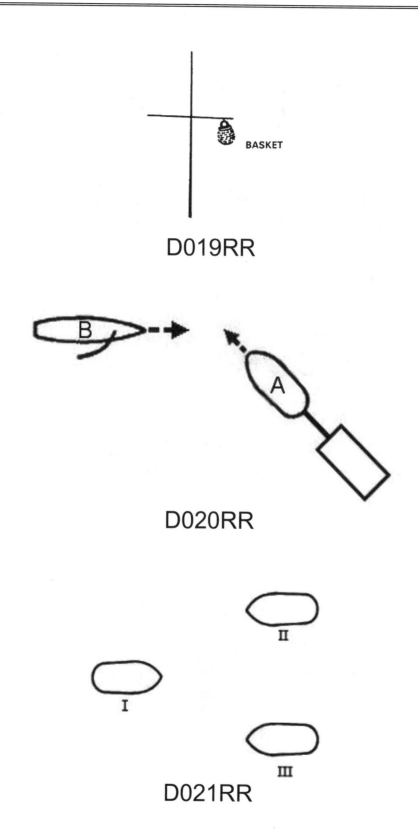

BASKET

D019RR

D020RR

D021RR

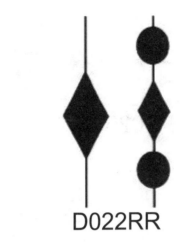

D022RR

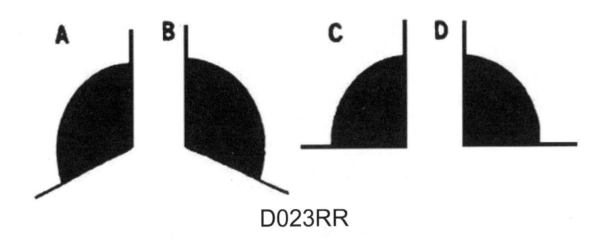

D023RR

D024RR

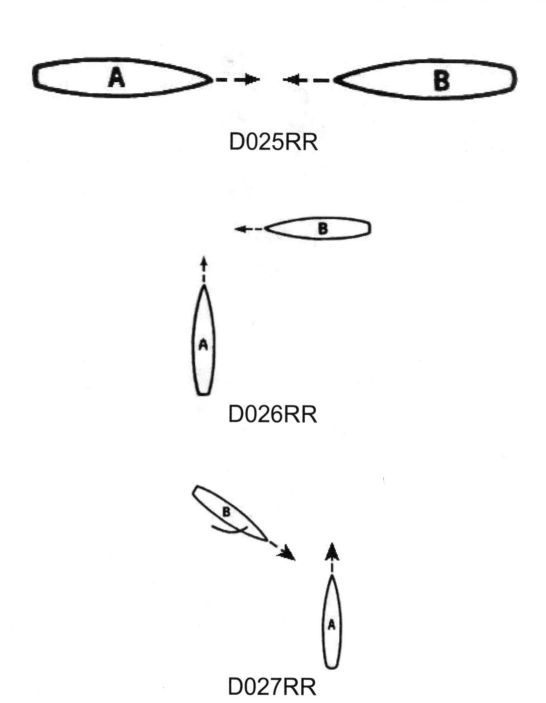

D025RR

D026RR

D027RR

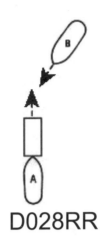

D028RR

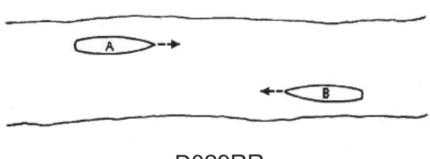

D029RR

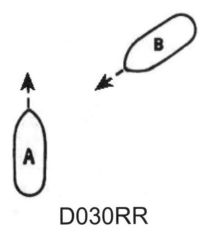

D030RR

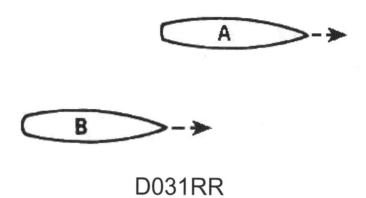

D031RR

D032RR

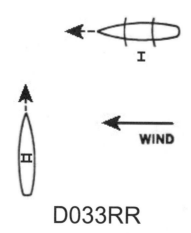

D033RR

D034RR

D035RR

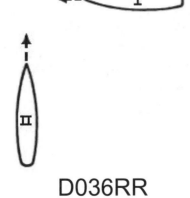

D036RR

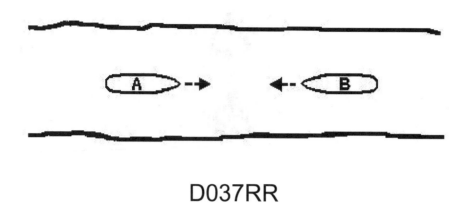

D037RR

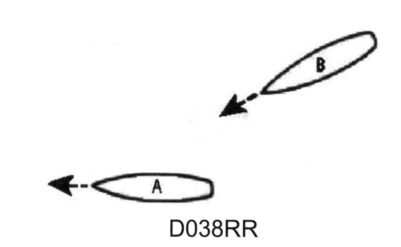

D038RR

D039RR

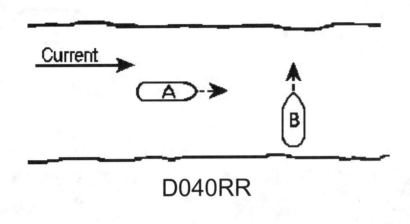

D040RR

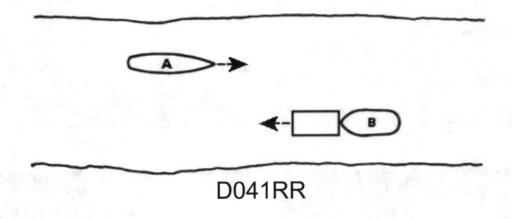

D041RR

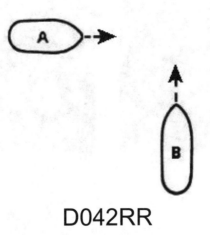

D042RR

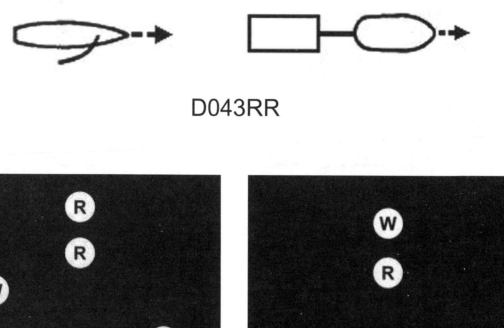

D043RR

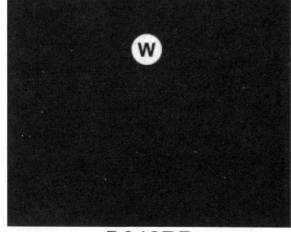

D044RR

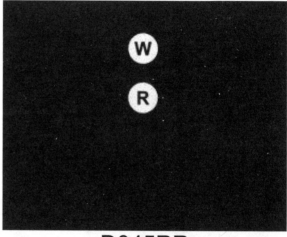

D045RR

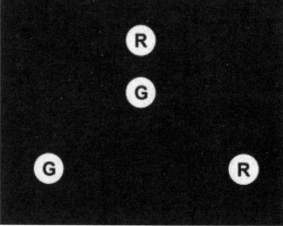

D046RR

D047RR

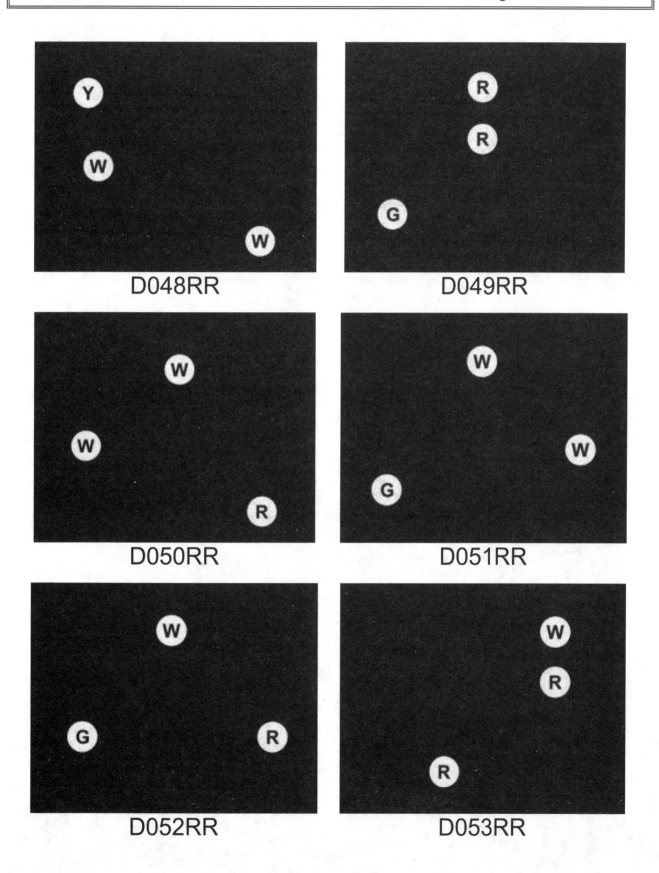

D048RR

D049RR

D050RR

D051RR

D052RR

D053RR

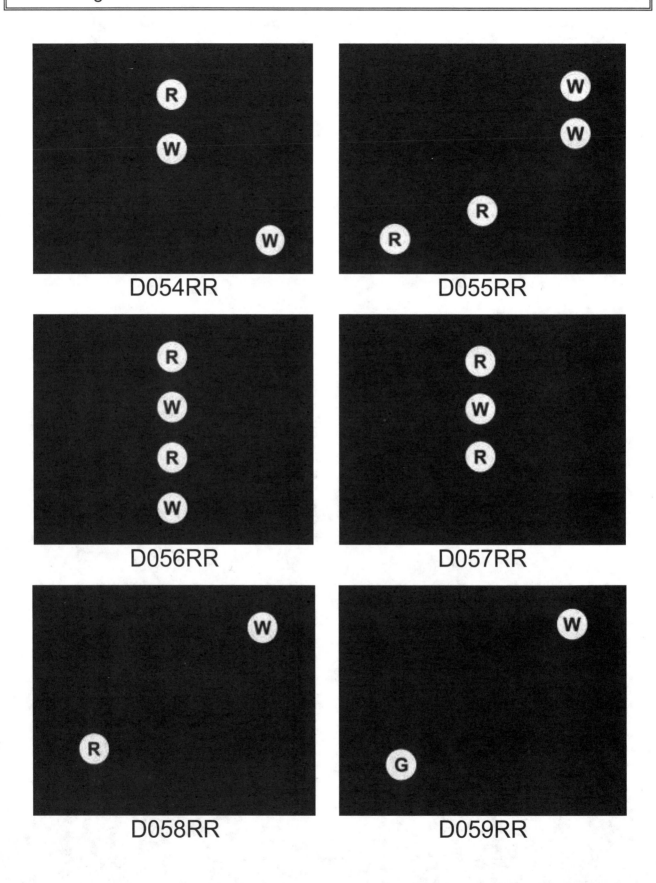

D054RR

D055RR

D056RR

D057RR

D058RR

D059RR

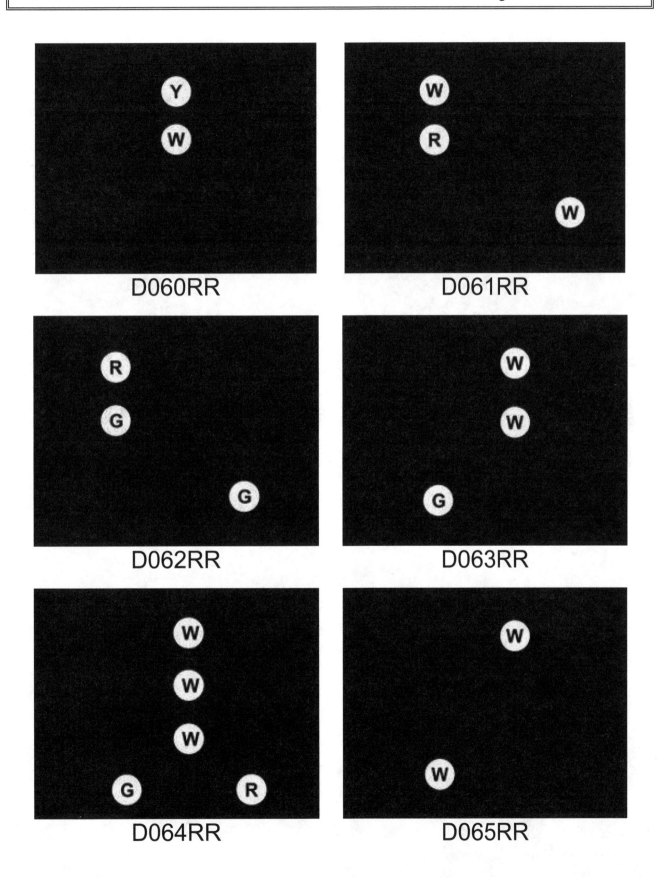

D060RR

D061RR

D062RR

D063RR

D064RR

D065RR

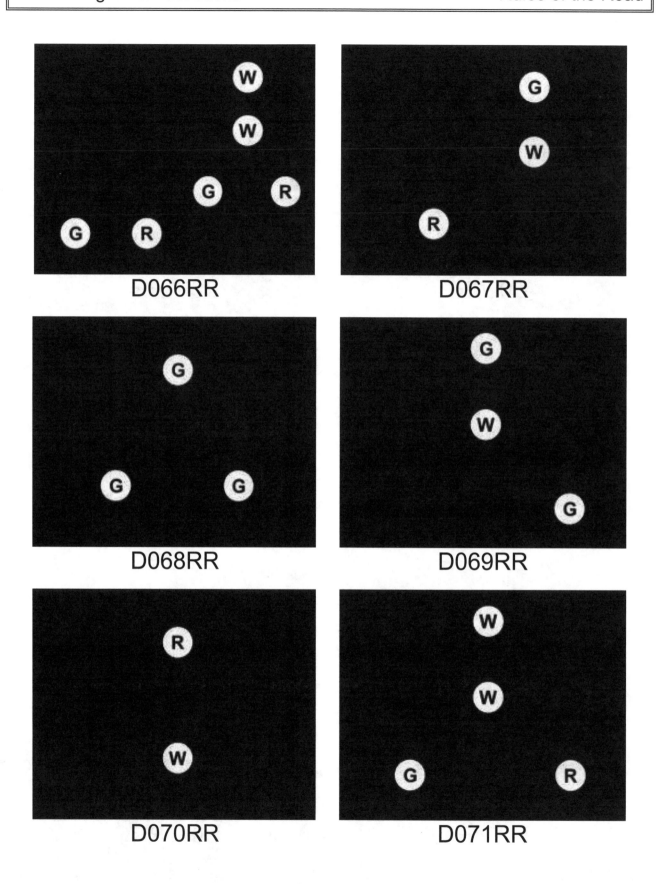

D066RR

D067RR

D068RR

D069RR

D070RR

D071RR

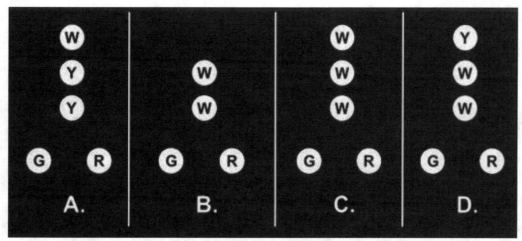

D072RR

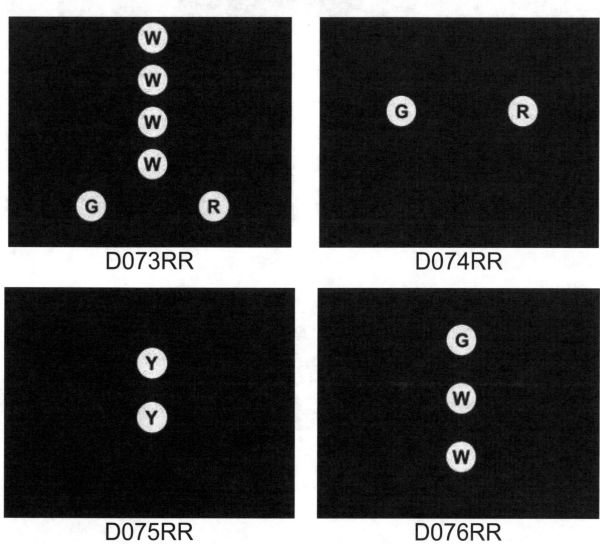

D073RR

D074RR

D075RR

D076RR

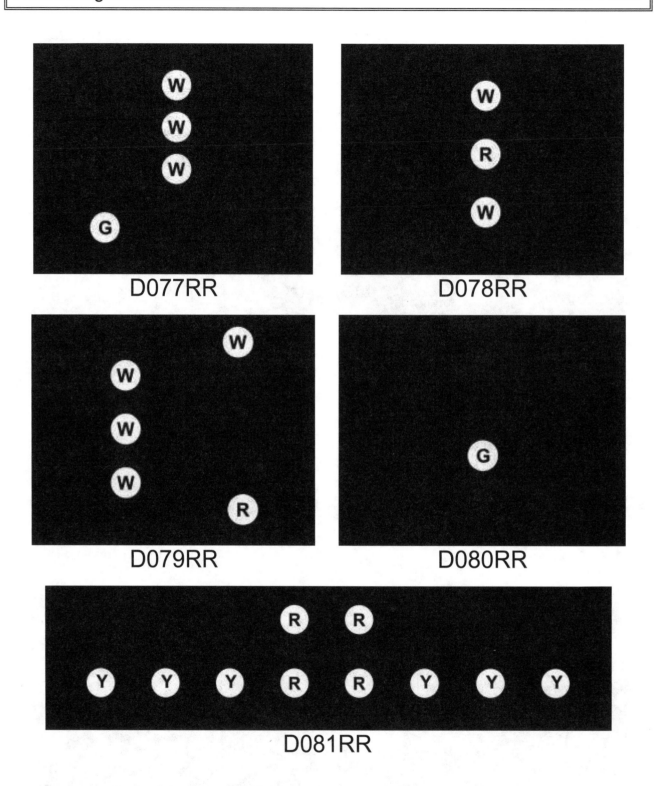

D077RR

D078RR

D079RR

D080RR

D081RR

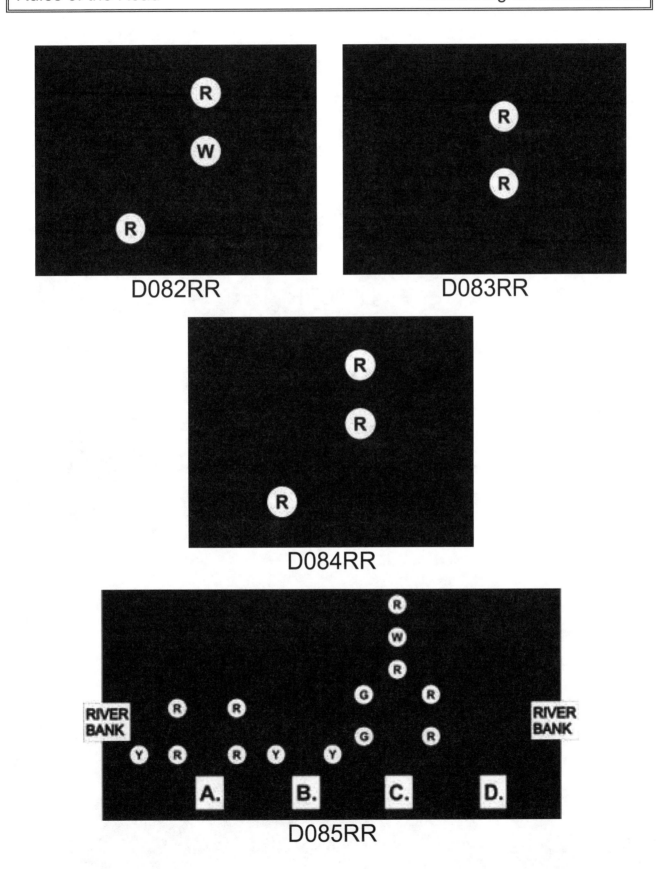

D082RR

D083RR

D084RR

D085RR

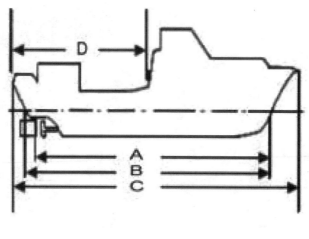

D086RR

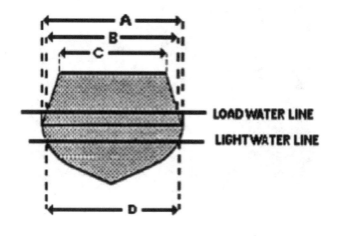

D087RR

040561/RR00168   **RULE 21 (b)**

BOTH INTERNATIONAL & INLAND You are on a vessel heading due north and see the lights shown one point on your port bow. This vessel could be heading _____ . See D051RR

A. NW
B. SW
C. NE
⚓ D. SE

Possible heading is determined in the following manner:

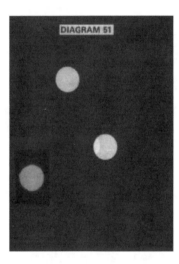

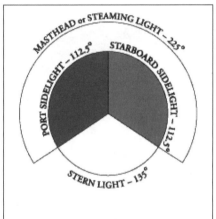

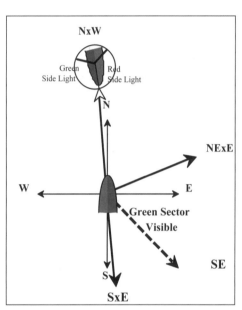

HEADING 000° - 11-1/4° = NxW (348-3/4°)
Green Side Light bearing NxW (348-3/4°)
Compute the reciprocal of the observed bearing then move 10 points (112-1/2°) to the <u>LEFT</u> or in a counter-clockwise direction.

Step No. 1 - Reverse the bearing
NxW (348-3/4°) ± 180° = SxE (168-3/4°)

Step No. 2 - Move 10 points Left
10 points to the left   - 112-1/2°

168-3/4°	SxE
- 112-1/2°	10 points to the left
056-1/4°	NExE

Possible headings are:
NExE (056-1/4°) to SxE (168-3/4°)